MARY FRANCES DRAKE
PROFESSOR, UNIVERSITY OF TENNESSEE, KNOXVILLE

JANICE HARRISON SPOONE
OWNER, RICKIE'S PETITES, KNOXVILLE

HERBERT GREENWALD
PRESIDENT, HERBERT GREENWALD ASSOCIATES, INC., NEW YORK

Retail Fashion Promotion and Advertising

Macmillan Publishing Company

NEW YORK

Maxwell Macmillan Canada

TORONTO

Editor: David Chodoff
Production Supervisor: Publication Services, Inc.
Production Manager: Aliza Greenblatt
Cover Designer: Robert Freese and Herbert Greenwald

This book was set in Baskerville by Publication Services, Inc., and printed and bound by R. R. Donnelley & Sons.
The cover was printed by Lehigh Press.

Cover Credit:

Cover photos courtesy of Les Magasins Taylor, St. Lambert, Quebec (left side), The Better Half, Grand Forks, ND (right corner).

Copyright ©1992 by Macmillan Publishing Company, a division of Macmillan, Inc.

PRINTED IN THE UNITED STATES OF AMERICA

Macmillan Publishing Company
866 Third Avenue, New York, New York 10022

Macmillan Publishing Company is part of the Maxwell Communication Group of Companies.

Maxwell Macmillan Canada, Inc.
1200 Eglinton Avenue East
Suit 200
Don Mills, Ontario. M3C 3N1

LIBRARY OF CONGRESS CATALOGING-IN-PUBLICATION DATA

Drake, Mary Frances.
  Retail fashion promotion and advertising / Mary Frances Drake, Janice Harrison Spoone, Herbert Greenwald
      p. cm.
    Includes index.
    ISBN 0-02-330029-9
    1. Advertising Fashion. 2. Fashion merchandising. 3. Sales promotion. I. Spoone, Janice Harrison. II. Greenwald, Herbert, 1912– . III. Title.
  HF6161.C5D73 1992
  687'.068'8–dc20
                                                                          91-15163
                                                                          CIP

Printing: 1 2 3 4 5 6 7   Year: 2 3 4 5 6 7 8

Preface

Although many textbooks have been published on advertising and sales promotion, few exist on fashion promotion and fashion advertising. This book focuses on the responsibilities of the department store buyer and the specialty store owner and is written primarily for merchandising personnel. Emphasis is placed on the coordination needed between fashion merchandising and sales promotion divisions of the department store. The applications of these methods to specialty stores are also discussed.

This book is intended for retailing students and those entrepreneurs who operate their own promotion and advertising programs. Others, such as display personnel, fashion show coordinators, models, buyers, manufacturers' representatives, and those whose livelihoods depend on retailing may also find the text useful.

It is recommended that the chapters be read in sequence. However, readers with a specific interest may wish to read only some of the chapters or may prefer reading in a different order. In any case, it is recommended that Chapter 1, "Introduction," be read first for an understanding of the nature of fashion. Chapter 2, "Consumer Behavior," occupies an important place because, in the authors' opinion, all good merchandising begins with appreciation of the customer's needs. Chapter 3, "Budget and Planning," is also of fundamental importance because promotional efforts need to be realistic in terms of monetary outlay. Chapters 8 and 9, "Advertising Principles: Print Media," and "Mechanics of Building an Ad: Print Media," are best read consecutively, as are Chapters 10 and 11, "Advertising Principles: Broadcast Media" and "Mechanics of Building an Ad: Broadcast Media."

Acknowledgments

We could never have completed a work of this size without the help of many people. Some of those who helped make it possible are mentioned in the text. In addition, our sincere thanks go to the typists,

Barbara Webber, Pat Shireman, and Donna Sanford, for preparing the manuscript and for encouraging us to persevere, and to Doris Offord for help beyond the call of duty on all types of tasks. Special thanks also are extended to the executives and many employees of Proffitt's Department Store for their valuable assistance with the assembly of material. Without their generous help, we could not have completed this book. They have been our teachers and our friends. We are especially thankful to Jan Penner, formerly of Proffitt's, for lengthy discussions of the fashion show chapter. Robert Taylor, President of Les Magasins Taylor, St. Lambert, Quebec, and Richard Globman, Vice President of Globman's, Martinsville, Virginia, were most helpful in supplying various illustrative materials for the chapters on print advertising. We value the help we received from Howard P. Abrahams in preparing the chapters on broadcast advertising. We are grateful to Laurence Fuersich of Retail Reporting Bureau who furnished a large portion of the illustrations. Lori Eyerly was most generous in providing her publication, "Lori Eyerly's Retail Trends." Our greatest thanks go to The University of Tennessee, Knoxville, for supporting this entire project from beginning to end.

About the Authors

Mary Frances Drake is a Professor in the Department of Textiles, Retailing, and Interior Design at the University of Tennessee, Knoxville. She has also taught at Kansas State University and at the University of Maryland. She was formerly an assistant buyer and manager of the Cain-Sloan Company in Nashville.

Janice Harrison Spoone owns Rickie's Petites in Knoxville, Tennessee. Before starting her own business she was divisional merchandise manager of Proffitt's, Inc., in Alcoa, Tennessee, a buyer for Millers in Knoxville, Tennessee, and a buyer for Titche-Goettinger in Dallas, Texas. She has taught at Oklahoma State University and Western Carolina University.

Herbert Greenwald, as President of Herbert Greenwald Associates, Inc., in New York City, has served as a consultant for specialty and department stores in the United States, Canada, and Mexico. He has been creative advertising manager for Bloomingdale's, Gimbels, and Macy's and has conducted advertising and sales promotion seminars for the National Retail Federation. He has also served on the faculty of New York University's Graduate School of Retailing. He is coauthor of *Independent Retailing—A Money-Making Manual* (Prentice Hall, 1976).

Contents

CHAPTER 3
Planning and Budgeting   39

CHAPTER 4
Dramatizing the Fashion Merchandise:
Using Art Elements and Principles   65

CHAPTER 7
Media Mix   149

CHAPTER 8
Advertising Principles: Print Media   165

CHAPTER 11
Mechanics of Building an Ad: Broadcast Media   261

CHAPTER 12
Publicity and Special Events   277

CHAPTER 13
The Fashion Show   295

CHAPTER 14
Personal Selling   321

CHAPTER 15

Synergism in Promotion 337

CHAPTER 1

Introduction

Promotion is frequently defined as the coordination of all store activities that contribute to sales moving forward or up. The American Marketing Association defines sales promotion as follows: "(1) In a specific sense, those marketing activities, other than personal selling, advertising, and publicity, that stimulate consumer purchasing and dealer effectiveness, such as display, shows and exhibitions, demonstrations, and various non-recurrent selling efforts not in the ordinary routine. (2) In retailing, all methods of stimulating customer purchasing, including personal selling, advertising, and publicity."[1] Although the first definition is encouraged, the second one is more appropriate for fashion retailing. In the broadest sense, sales promotion is any activity used to influence positively the sale of merchandise, services, or ideas. Because this book is about the promotion of fashion goods, promotional activities have been extended to include merchandise presentation, fashion shows, and personal selling. A brief definition of each of these activities follows.

SALES PROMOTION FUNCTIONS
1. *Advertising:* A paid message in a public medium, such as newspaper, magazine, radio, TV, direct mail, or billboards, to influence sales
2. *Publicity:* An unpaid message, usually as a news story in the public media, prompted by newsworthy activities of the store
3. *Special events:* Attractions sponsored by stores, such as celebrity visits, demonstrations, or inducements planned to influence the sale of merchandise
4. *Fashion show:* The presentation of merchandise on a live model to dramatize a fashion story

[1] *Marketing Definitions: A Glossary of Marketing Terms,* compiled by a committee of the American Marketing Association under the direction of Ralph Alexander (Chicago: American Marketing Association, 1963), p. 20.

5. *Visual merchandising:* The display of merchandise in stores and windows to create a timely, three-dimensional impression

6. *Merchandise presentation:* The inviting arrangement of merchandise on fixtures as it is being offered for sale

7. *Personal selling:* A dialogue between a salesperson and the potential customer for the purpose of selling merchandise and meeting the customer's needs

Fashion promotion is an essential element in today's retail environment for the following reasons:

1. Competition in the marketplace continues to grow more intense and more imaginative. Stores that once thought they had a monopoly in the marketplace for certain fashion goods now find this monopoly being challenged by a variety of competitors. For example, a competitor may have access to similar merchandise at lower prices because of overproduction from off-shore resources. The competition may employ highly aggressive tactics, such as offering discount coupons, a practice associated with grocery stores. Another device is the "2 for 1," where the customer buys two items for the price of one.

2. Consumers of retail goods are better educated, often sophisticated, and discriminating in their choices. Fashion customers are devotees of the many fashion magazines as well as fashion programs on television. Along with this type of information, consumer action groups have educated the consumer to such matters as reading labels for fiber content and garment care.

3. Retailers are moving—by choice and by necessity—into a period of more widely varied media selection. Each technological advancement in communication, such as cable television and in-store video demonstrations, soon becomes significant in the development of retail selling strategies.

4. Fashion changes are more complex than the traditional fall, winter, spring, and summer progressions of the past. Increased emphasis on travel, multiple vacations each year, and sports-related fashions all affect modes of retail promotion and provide a challenging variety of choices to the consumer.

Relation of Sales to Fashion Promotion

To understand the changing life choices of the retail customer, it is necessary at the outset to have a clear definition of fashion. Also, it is important to study the cyclic pattern of many fashion trends. A full understanding of retail fashion promotion also requires that young professionals look behind the fashion scene to note that basic business tenets regularly apply to fashion promotional ideas. That is, monetary goals are set and budgets are determined in order to meet objectives. Within a specific store, there is a continuing need for interrelating fashion promotional themes. For example, the advent of the short skirt added focus to fashion in hosiery and shoes. Hosiery fashion offered the consumer variety in patterns and textures. Customer responses that result in effective sales and ultimate departmental success are necessary in the fashion business. How the varied fashion "traffic" moves toward or away from the promoted fashion merchandise is in part a measure of the effectiveness of the fashion promotion.

Definition of Fashion

Fashion is a manner of style of doing something that is accepted by a substantial group of people at a given time and place. Dressing, speaking, eating, working, playing, dating, and teaching are all activities that provide an environment for style. Fashion appears to be a part of almost every element of the modern scene—homes, offices, cars, streets, theaters, offices, and stadiums. No area of fashion is more important or more conspicuous than apparel.

In earlier days, when the selling of styles to customers was a more predictable activity, famous designers sat in their studios and decided on the trends, hired the fashion show models, made the styles, and sold them. But today's fashion consumers often do not follow the dictates of the designers. They decide individually whether or not to accept, buy, and use new styles of a product. Today's consumer accepts newly introduced styles only if something about them calls forth an affirmation of the consumer's lifestyle.

Apparel fashions are three-dimensional expressions of the spirit of the times. Because events change, people change. And, in the modern world, change itself is a positive theme. Customers for today's fashions are eager for new expressions of the period in which they live. In some ways, change is the principal constant. By the time a style has been accepted by a majority of customers, it is already on the way to being obsolete. It is then rejected by the very people who first accepted it. People, tiring of styles, move forward in their attitudes and want something new, something different, or something better.

Every day is another good day to launch a new fashion. Today's best store fashion departments reflect this restless forward attitude of customers. By astute buying and the related promotional effort to distribute merchandise quickly, sales associates and buyers use the "quick-change" temperament of their customers to good advantage.

Fashion Life Cycle

Fashion, like other consumer goods, has a life cycle, as shown in Figure 1.1. A style is introduced by a designer or a fashion maker and, at the time of its initial distribution, has a zero sales volume and a zero fashion impact.

By effective promotional tactics and sales efforts, an appealing fashion begins to move upward in sales. The fashion moves up in accordance with the style's success. A momentum develops and carries the sales of a fashion item up a growth curve. If large numbers of customers are attracted to a style, they are moved to buy it. Other customers, seeing a trend in the making, join with the initially attracted ones and further help the fashion to develop quickly. Sales results can be impressive through the growth period until they hit their peak and plateau out.

Maintaining a long-term peak of sales is possible with a successful style but requires added expenditures of time and effort in fashion promotional activities. The sales promotional activities should be varied to meet differing situations at each stage of the cycle. Advertising and publicity are important for informing potential customers of the new fashions because most style-conscious consumers want to be in the forefront of a fashion, to be leaders in finding new trends in apparel. Advertising continues to be important in the growth stage and can be the element that forces sales to move up the growth curve to a maximal sales peak. At this stage of growth and expansion, additional variations of the style can be promoted to show further depth of merchandise.

As sales decline and finally reach the point of rejection, advertising in any of several media can help dispose of merchandise that has lost its newness, resulting in a sales decline.

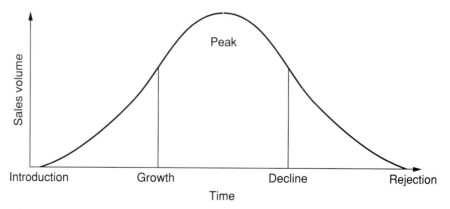

Figure 1.1. Fashion life cycle.

The specific nature of the selling cycle of fashion items has been studied in an effort to predict the length of each stage in the cycle. To date no theory of fashion movement has proven capable of predicting with reliability how long a specific style or style feature will be purchased by consumers. However, it is certain that fashion will continually change in keeping with the way the world changes.

To identify which style is appropriate to the incoming way of life, the retailer must keep up with what is happening in the world, as well as the lifestyles of the consumers. The rate of change in life and fashion continues to accelerate. Technology makes possible new products and faster processing of goods. A booming economy means there is more discretionary income to spend on fashion. The faster a new style is purchased and used, the faster people tire of it and look for a change. Availability of more leisure time allows people greater participation in diversions such as social activities, sports, and vacations. Many of these require special apparel—for example, beach wear, ski outfits, and formal wear. With greater participation in a wider variety of activities, the customer's exposure to different types of clothing is expanded, which increases the acceptance of more style features. This adds to the "smorgasbord" of offerings, which in turn stimulates a larger number of consumers to participation in fashion.

In estimating the life cycle of a fashion, one must also be aware of conditions that retard the movement of fashion. Perhaps the two most negative factors are consumer habits and customs. If customers are traditionally oriented, new styles may not be accepted immediately upon introduction. The established styles will be considered more appropriate. Some religious adherents reject change in clothing style in relation to the group's ideas of modesty and respect. There are sumptuary laws, that is, laws regulating spending for clothing, food, and other needs on moral grounds, designed to prevent the wearing of unacceptable attire. Some schools have dress codes, determined by school administrators. For example, some schools do not allow punk rock styles to be worn to classes. In estimating the rate of fashion change, these retarding factors should be considered.

Focus on the Target Customer

The retailer's task is to glean from the world's markets items that will fit the customer's lifestyle. The retailer is the consumer's purchasing agent and has the responsibility of bringing an appropriate portion of the world's assortment of goods to the consumer's hometown. The retailer tries to have the right item at the right time and at the right price. But no one retailer can have all the right items for everyone. The retailer must select a specific group of people to serve, that is, determine the target customer of the store or shop. By selecting a target customer, the retailer segments the market. The retailer identifies within the mass market the group of customers that appears to be the most promising and directs the promotional effort toward them.

By determining the target customer, the retailer is also identifying the store's merchandise niche. To promote to these customers, the retailer often has to create a distinctive style of promotional communication. An example of a merchandising niche is gourmet cooking. Customers for this merchandising niche will be interested in food products as well as gourmet kitchenware.

Shopper Groups

The target customer fits into one of the eight shopping groups identified in retailing. The National Retail Federation (formerly the National Retail Merchants Association) recommends planning promotional efforts in terms of shopper groups that have clear sets of characteristics, attitudes, and behavior patterns. Following are the descriptive profiles of each group.[2]

Advanced. Representing the most forward position on the fashion attitude spectrum, the Advanced group is composed of the market's *fashion pacesetters*. By anticipating trends, this usually youthful and affluent group has the *confidence and desire to assemble and then introduce new looks*. Advanced shoppers frequent offbeat and small apparel specialty stores. They are impulsive shoppers employing apparel and accessories as a means of expressing their viewpoint, and their prime purchasing consideration is the *ability of merchandising items to make the desired fashion statement*.

Contemporary. The Contemporary shopper group is the tie group within the Contemporary segment, *blending characteristics* of the Young Contemporary, Update and Advanced in a pattern that remains to be defined for this particular market.

Update. Updates have an active lifestyle *requiring apparel which expresses their individuality*, but is also functional and appropriate to their variety of activities. While Updates *gravitate toward new fashion trends, they do not seek to be pacesetters* or to buy for the sake of fashion alone. Being self-assured, they display a willingness to experiment with apparel, and do so by *blending classic styles with more advanced forward fashion*. Price and merchandise quality rank lower than fashion appropriateness. While favoring department stores, Updates also frequent small

[2] National Retail Merchants Association, *Marketing–Sales Promotion–Advertising Planbook* (New York: NRMA, 1986), pp. 6–7.

specialty stores and boutiques. Their *high economic value,* based on generally upscale demographics and high rate of purchase activity, makes the Update group a prime target shopper group for upscale department and specialty stores.

Young Contemporary. The Young Contemporary is distinguished attitudinally from other Contemporary groups by a pattern of *fashion emulation,* rather than leadership. Fashion standards for this group are those associated with high-profile personalities who are accorded recognition by their peers. *Clothes are an important means of self-expression* and of showing others *"I'm with it".* These shoppers are very aware of the latest fashion trends and *wish to be among the first* to be associated with them. Quality is of little importance to a Young Contemporary who becomes bored when apparel is kept too long. They are enthusiastic shoppers, browsers and impulsive buyers. This group has characteristically been an age/size classification.

Transitionalist. The Transitionalist group is the tie group *bridging the gap* between the functionally-oriented Traditional segment and the more fashion-prone Contemporary. These shoppers' attitudes and behavior are in a state of flux as they subscribe equally to both sets of values.

Classic. Classic shoppers view *apparel purchases as an investment rather than a fashion statement. They evidence strong self-awareness and definite viewpoints and are willing to pay more and go to some trouble to find the understated tailored looks* that best represent their self-image. The Classic group tends to be loyal to stores which have *merchandise that embodies their viewpoint* and are the most responsive to *service.* While Classics tend to buy at department stores rather than chains or discount stores, nationally advertised apparel brands are of little interest. Most Classics exercise moderate purchase activity, plan their purchases, and show little interest in sale merchandise.

Moderate. The Moderates have a functional shopping orientation, particularly in regard to apparel, with such purchases being initiated *only after a trend is well established.* Moderates truly represent Middle America in that they acknowledge fashion, but in their context, *fashion means making sure they do not stand out as being different.* Nevertheless, they enjoy shopping and browsing more than any other of the traditional groups. As a group they are budget conscious; hence the name "Moderate" and, as such, they tend to be strong proponents of the national chains.

Traditionalist. The Traditionalist is the tie/blend group within the Traditional segment. Its shopping behavior is best characterized as conventional. While their views are one step removed from the negative orientation of the Conservatives, shopping only generates a moderate level of enthusiasm. Traditionalists are reluctant to adopt fashion changes since they *do not wish to appear different.* Therefore, *apparel is seen as a practical purchase* rather than a mode of self-expression. *Quality, moderate prices, wearability and functionality* are key merchandise features, rather than those concerned with fashion. These attitudes translate into a low rate of purchasing activity which is more replacement oriented and based less on impulse than on advanced planning.

Conservative. Predominantly a downscale group embracing traditional social values, the Conservatives tend to have a sedentary lifestyle. This group is oriented toward *functional, rather than fashion apparel,* due both to economic circumstances and an outlook which discounts apparel as an important means of self-expression. Therefore the Conservatives' purchases are based on *need rather than impulse,* with price, durability and quality being primary considerations. Chains and discounters generate above average interest.

Customer Self-Image and Store Image

As retailers make selections for the target groups they will serve, it is important that they keep in mind those group members' self-images. The store atmosphere as well as the merchandise should be in keeping with the self-images the customers hold. Store buyers need to understand the people to whom they expect to sell goods, whether these prospective customers regard themselves as dignified and elite, friendly and spontaneous, or creative and clever. Assessing customers' self-images can be achieved by sharp, personal observation skills on the part of the sales associates or, on a more formal level, a market evaluation process. Examples of the latter are discussed later in the book; but here at the outset, it is enough to know that a store must have a personality. The closer it is in line with the personality of its customers, the better the selling results. Specialty shops succeed most often when the self-image of the owner/manager matches that of the target customer. L.L. Bean, the outdoor apparel merchant, is an excellent example.

A store's image reflects its personality. It is the total of the stimuli the customer receives about the store and thus forms the expectations that they relate to that store. Image is part of an inducement to buy. A customer, feeling at home in a store whose traits reflect her own, will visit its departments more frequently and make more purchases. One way to attract potential customers into the store is to exhibit reflections of the customers' personalities. When a customer can say, "That's my kind of place," the retailer has achieved a basic goal in merchandising. If customers identify with the store, they will be comfortable and will shop there.

Many factors contribute to a store's image, including the architectural design of the premises, the quality and fashionability of the merchandise, the courtesy of the sales personnel, and the convenience and ease of shopping in the store's various departments. Also to be considered are the store's reputation for making agreeable adjustments on returned merchandise and the customer services offered, including credit charges and accessible parking. In addition, the store's advertising style and special events often determine the customer's first impression of the store.

Objectives of Fashion Promotion

Throughout the planning of the entire retail process, it is important to keep in mind that a continuing promotional program should be established and executed. The best stores, with the best policies and goods, can succeed only if the public knows the store is there and has a good current idea of what merchandise is available. No area of retailing is more dependent on promotion than fashion. Following are some of the specific objectives of fashion merchandisers and sales personnel:

To communicate the store image to its target customers

To establish the store as a distinct fashion authority

To build long-term customer loyalty

To generate interest that will bring a steady flow of regular and new customers to the store

To disseminate timely fashion information and become a source of news of innovations

To remind customers of their desire for new things

To encourage customers to act on the desire for goods from a specific store

To persuade customers to make purchase decisions

To sell the merchandise to customers

To achieve reasonable profit

The first nine objectives are essential if the last is to be realized.

Basically, fashion promotion is a process carried out so that people can learn where to purchase the supporting artifacts of life that will make them into the individuals they want to be. Timeliness is the essential ingredient of fashion promotion, accompanied by good taste and high drama.

Good promotion says, "We know you, we know what you need, and we have it." All promotions should continually make this statement. Fashion promotions should be exciting because they depict the newest, the latest, and the very "now" tangibles. Fashion promotion in its best manner persuades the customer to enthusiastically embrace the new.

Responsibility for Fashion Promotion

The Corporate Connection

The responsibility for sales promotion differs among various types of stores. Some large department stores are chains, such as J.C. Penney or Sears. Others may be members of an organization, such as Federated Department Stores, which includes Bloomingdale's, Lazarus, and others. In either case, individual stores may operate with a degree of autonomy but with certain corporate guidelines. A store, for example, might encourage creative input for promotional ideas or themes and receive actual procedural help from the corporate office.

A buying office may send descriptive explanations and pictorial information about new market trends to affiliates. These packets usually include specific programs for promoting the latest fashion trends for that specific season. In some stores, the corporate office may determine the season's major promotion for all branch stores, including brands, styles, and colors. The store's buyer needs to know the exact nature of the corporate policy on promotion and the degree of involvement with individual stores in order to determine freedom and responsibility for promotion for all participants.

Local Store Responsibilities

At the local store level in most large department store chains, merchandise managers and buyers have the responsibility for sales and, to a lesser degree, responsibility for sales promotion. They share the latter responsibility with the personnel in the sales promotion division. The relationship of the merchandising division to the sales promotion division is shown in Figure 1.2. The largest group of personnel is employed in the merchandising division, which includes all buyers, department managers, and salespersons. The primary function of the merchandising division is the acquisition and selling of inventory. All of the other divisions have the task of supporting sales in various specialized ways. The sales promotion division is primarily responsible for producing and coordinating promotional activity. Because buyers of the goods are usually in a different division from the personnel primarily responsible for promoting those goods, a great deal of communication and coordination are required to produce effective promotions for each season and for the overall management of the store's image.

To work effectively, each division needs to understand the other division's functions. An important objective of this book is to inform those in the merchandising division, especially buyers, of the nature of the

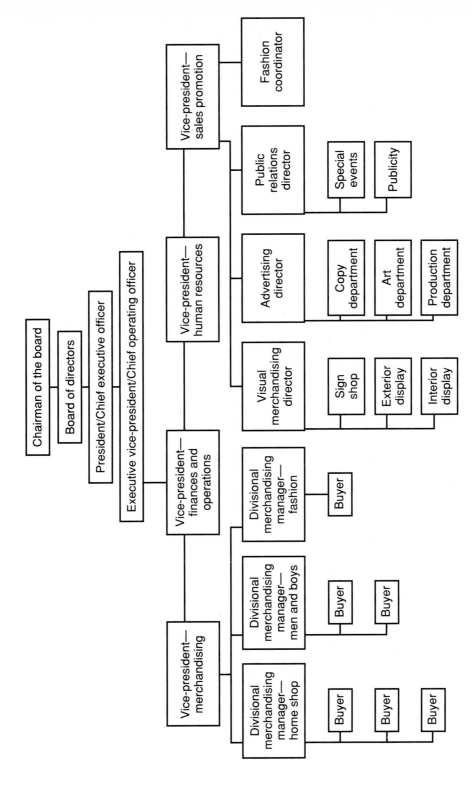

Figure 1.2. Organizational chart for a large department store.

tasks of the sales promotion division, and to teach buyers how they can aid in the effective completion of these tasks.

An important store group is the independent retailer, which is usually smaller than a major chain. In most instances the organizational structure is similar to that of a larger store. The difference is in number of personnel, not in the functions or duties. For example, the function of the vice-president or manager of sales promotion in a big store is assumed by one of the principals, or by the owner in a small store.

Need for a Separate Promotional Division

Coordination

In addition to coordinating the activities of the sales promotion division with those of the merchandising division, the vice-president or manager of sales promotion should coordinate all specific aspects of promotional activities. Radio spots should begin within a few hours of the appearance of newspaper ads, if the newspaper is used also. Signs placed with the advertised items should be ready the day the ad is published. Signs and banners inform customers who respond to the ads and also serve as conspicuous reminders to the sales personnel. In the case of a major promotion, several media may be used—for example, newspaper, radio, television, and direct mail. As in other areas of activity, it is essential that the various media are synergic with one another for maximum impact on target audiences. The various elements of a fashion show must also be coordinated with the media that announce it to the public. These media skills will be discussed later.

An important ingredient of good sales promotion is selecting the proper media mix and using it so that maximum sales results can be achieved. Combining promotional activities produces a synergistic effect that can increase sales markedly. Combining media also greatly increases the need for advance planning.

Specialized Function

Sales promotion has the two-pronged specialized function of persuading the public to think affirmatively of the store and of motivating customers to come in and consider purchasing the merchandise. Skills needed to produce promotional materials and activities are very specialized. One of these is language skills, which are necessary for advertising copy writers to produce interesting ads. Another is a sense of drama, a specialized skill that is necessary for fashion shows.

A major responsibility of sales promotion personnel is to aid in the creation and development of a store image. In doing this, the personnel in the promotional division should understand the importance of interrelated media efforts. For example, signs should reflect the message of the print media. Visual and auditory components of the store image should be consistent with the store personality. For example, a store selling high-fashion merchandise might select classical music for in-store use rather than country music. A consolidated promotional thrust stimulates customer acceptance.

After assessing the out-of-store promotional elements, setting a time schedule, and determining a budget outlay and promotional theme, sales promotion executives delegate assignments related to three major selling support areas in the store: advertising, special events, and visual merchandising (display). These areas should relate closely to the merchandising plan, with all promotional activities showing a unity of theme, emphasis, and timing. For example, tear sheets of newspaper advertisements should be visible in the relevant departments.

Both merchandising and promotion are sophisticated and specialized in today's highly competitive marketplace. Increasingly, it is unrealistic to expect buyers and salespeople to master the promotional skill, so most contemporary merchandising structures include a separate division that takes major responsibility for sales promotion activities.

From the standpoint of store management, a consolidated promotional impact should be conducted. This builds wide customer acceptance of the store in its entirety, not just of the specific promoted items. The store image should be strengthened by each successive promotional event. Dedication to the chosen image should be consistent day in and day out in order to avoid customer confusion.

Continuity of impression is most important. The marketplace is highly sophisticated and increasingly competitive. For this reason alone, a promotion division is essential to identify promotional goals and to serve as a catalyst for accelerating the promotional process.

Summary

Buyers and sales promotional people must function as a team. They must get to know their regular customers and their potential customers well enough that appropriate sales promotional messages can be sent to the public in a manner the target group will find interesting and stimulating. These messages should invite prospective customers to visit the store. When prospects arrive, they should find what they expect— and more. Signs should guide them, prices should please them, and merchandise should be available in the variety and sizes they anticipate.

This ideal situation is achievable when sales promotional activities are maintained as integral parts of the overall marketing plans of a store.

An underlying skill that should be utilized at all stages of a promotional schedule is frequent interpersonnel communication. The development of successful sales campaigns requires a continual flow of information back and forth among all associates of the store. The sales promotional staff is responsible for expediting the communication. In the case of stores that are too small to have a separate promotional department, an administrator of the store may instigate the selection of an advertising agency or may designate the store manager as responsible for promotional efforts. Promotional tasks and advertising responsibilities, both in-store and out-of-store, will be discussed at length later.

CHAPTER 2

Consumer Behavior

Consumer behavior determines the sales of goods and thus the retailer's profit to a great extent. Therefore, retailers need to understand the psychological and sociological forces that guide consumer behavior. Retail strategies must be based on consumer needs and promoted in a manner that will make potential customers aware of their needs (the marketing concept). Accomplishing these tasks requires a knowledge of the determinants of consumer behavior and of consumer purchase decision making. This chapter is concerned with some of the major areas of consumer behavior that are currently very salient in relation to the promotion of fashion goods.

Today's consumer will not be dictated to or manipulated at will by advertisers and promoters. Consumers buy the products and services they perceive to be relevant to their needs and lifestyles. Sales promotion is successful when the consumer is made aware that the product or service offers benefits that will satisfy his or her needs and desires.

Consumer Needs and Motivation

Simply stated, consumers are motivated by their unfulfilled needs to purchase goods and services. By understanding consumer motivation, the retailer can better predict consumer buying behavior. Thus, retailers are eager to identify motives so they can anticipate consumer behavior, particularly buying behavior.

Motivation is the driving force that compels individuals to act. This force is created by a state of discomfort or tension resulting from unsatisfied needs. When the discomfort of the unsatisfied need becomes strong enough, the consumer will take some action to reduce it. The action is prompted by a stimulus that acts as a cue to the consumer's need. For example, the stimulus might be an attractive formal gown in a store display, which reminds the teenager that she needs a dress for the school prom. The retailer can and should provide the external stimuli to arouse the need within the consumer. Advertisements, by providing cues, can direct customers toward the store and the items that can meet their needs. The aroused need becomes the motive that activates the consumer.

Motivation is an internal psychological state that must be inferred from what people say or do. Motives are not visible. Most purchases are directed by several motives, with some having greater importance than others. Further complicating the prediction of consumer behavior is the fact that it is also influenced by other factors, including income, available retail outlets, and time for shopping, to mention only a few.

Unmet needs are the sources that drive an individual to action intended to reduce the accompanying tension and discomfort. Abraham Maslow reasoned that human needs are met in order of their importance to the individual. His theory holds that innate needs, such as food and shelter, must be satisfied before a person will be concerned with less essential needs. Maslow's theorized hierarchy of needs is shown in Figure 2.1. The more basic the need, the stronger it is as a motivator.

The human is born with physiological needs, such as those for food, water, and warmth, which must be met if one is to survive. These needs are generally met in the United States, so they are of little concern to retailers. With the physiological needs satisfied, the consumer begins to be aware of other, higher needs, such as the need for safety and protection

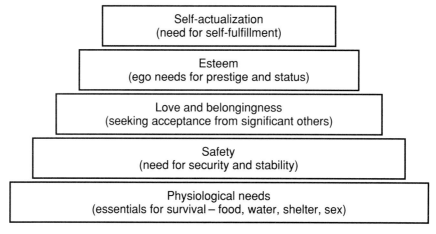

Figure 2.1. Maslow's hierarchy of human needs. (Modified from Abraham H. Maslow, "A Theory of Human Motivation," *Psychological Review* 50 (1943), 370–96. Copyright 1943 by the American Psychological Association.)

from harm. At the third level are love needs, that is, the needs for close relationships with others and for a sense of belonging. Most adolescents evidence a strong desire to belong to their peer groups and actively search out merchandise that will help them fit into their peer groups. By promoting the latest fashion trends to this age group, the retailer lets the teenager know which store has the merchandise that can satisfy this need to belong. Examples of past and present merchandise are Izod shirts, Ralph Lauren polo shirts, denim jackets, Coca-Cola shirts, designer jeans, and a specific fabric look such as washed-out denim.

At a still higher level in Maslow's hierarchy are the esteem needs, including the desire to have the respect and admiration of others. People want to have a position of high status in the eyes of others and to be recognized as special. The consumer with motives functioning at this level wants to stand out from the crowd. The retailer can attract this customer's attention by projecting a store image that reflects the store's capacity to offer goods that will fulfill the consumer's need for distinction, for example, furs, oriental rugs, silverware, crystal, designer-name merchandise, and the latest fashion trend.

Maslow's highest-order need is that of self-actualization, the need to realize one's own potential. At this level, the retailer can appeal to the consumer's desire for self-expression by offering a wide range of selections and services that allow the customer to put together his or her own best look. Wrangler jeans advertisements with the "Live it to the limit" theme are examples of an appeal to the need for self-actualization.

The top three levels of needs (love, esteem, and self-actualization) offer the fashion retailer opportunities for developing appeals to a wide variety of consumers, because these are social needs that cut across most age and income groups. Figure 2.2 shows an advertisement that raises an appeal to the need for love and belongingness, and Figure 2.3 shows an appeal to self-esteem.

Self-Image

The consumer has a mental concept of who he or she is. This self-concept has four parts: (1) the real self, the way one really is; (2) the ideal self, the way one would like to be; (3) the looking-glass self, the way one is seen by others; and (4) the self-image, the way one sees oneself (see Figure 2.4). People try to maintain a positive self-image and, if possible, enhance it. This being the case, consumers will purchase goods that are compatible with their self-images or that enhance their self-images, and they will reject incompatible goods.

One's self-concept can be communicated to others by various means, including activities, speech, and mannerisms. In our society the consumption of goods and services is another means of conveying and

Figure 2.2. Advertisement appealing to the need for love and belongingness. (Courtesy of Guess? Inc.)

enhancing the self-concept. Fashion merchandise, because of its change-ability, is a particularly good vehicle for demonstrating one's alertness and ability to "stay on top of the situation." By requiring frequent up-dating, fashion goods are also a symbol of procession of money. The wise retailer is attentive to the customer by making an effort to discern the image the customer wishes to convey symbolically. For example, if a young woman sees herself as a competent professional, she will respond to promotional efforts consistent with intelligence, dependability, and quality. If a man sees himself as young, he will respond to themes relating to newness, youth, and daring. An example of mismatched images is a store named Smith's Family Clothing that tries to promote designer men's clothing.

Principles of Learning

The concept of learning is very important to the fashion retailer because much of the promotional effort needs to be directed toward educating the customer to essentials of new fashions.

Figure 2.3. An appeal to self-esteem needs. (Courtesy of the Retail Reporting Bureau.)

Cues and visual properties in the environment serve as stimuli giving direction to the consumer's drives. The merchandise itself can be a cue to learning. Even with snow on the ground, a display of early spring suits can signal to customers that it is time to prepare their wardrobes for the forthcoming change of season. An advertisement introducing the new skirt length offers additional cues for learning by exaggerating the length of that garment feature so that it is difficult to overlook.

Even though it may be a cold winter day when a store displays beachwear, if the setting shows a palm tree and a sandy effect, the customer's thoughts will be directed to the benefits of a warm climate. Furthermore, the viewer might well consider the need for a vacation. These visual properties act as cues for purchase decisions.

The behavior a person has learned is more likely to be repeated if the person is rewarded. When a man is told he is handsome in a seafoam-green shirt, he is more likely to buy that color again than a color that was

Figure 2.4. Components of self-concept. Adapted from John Douglas, George A. Field, and Lawrence X. Tarpey, *Human Behavior in Marketing* (Columbus, Ohio: Charles E. Merrill, 1967, p. 65. Reproduced by permission.)

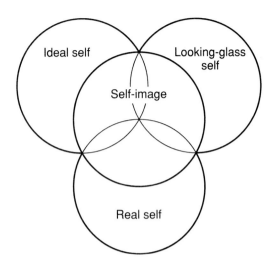

not praised. Customers will soon learn which shop sells them the best merchandise if they receive compliments from other people when wearing merchandise from this shop. Every positive experience customers have, from satisfactory merchandise all the way to helpful salespeople, contributes to their learning that this store is the best place to satisfy their needs.

Repetition is a technique that enhances learning. Few consumers will remember a store or brand name the first time they see or hear it. Most people require repeated exposure to learn a name and then recall it on occasion. Consequently, retailers repeat information often and in similar form; for example, a store logo changes very rarely. Its placement may be in the same position in most advertisements to build up quick recognition and maintain identity.

Repeat exposure is also important in learning a new style. Only innovators are likely to "pick up" on a new style the first time they see it. Most consumers must "educate" their eyes over time to new fashion features such as proportions, print combinations, and colors. The consumer may grasp the most obvious points of the new style on the first viewing, but several exposures to the visual stimulus are needed before all the subtle points are learned. The new fashion look requires promotion very early and often for the consumer to accept it. If the new look is not promoted early and often, learning may be so slow that the consumer is not ready to buy before markdowns are made or the season has expired. The customer will have learned, but too late for the retailer to reap immediate profitable benefit from the promotion.

Perception

Perception is the process of comprehending the world around us through our senses. People receive cues from the environment and translate them so they have meaning. Individuals perceive the environment in unique ways because of differences in expectations, motives, and experiences. What one perceives is affected by the nature of the cues or stimuli one encounters, particularly size, color, and contrast. These are external factors of perception that can be adjusted by the retailer to heighten perception. These factors will be discussed in Chapter 4.

The retailer needs to be cognizant of the fact that consumers act on the basis of their perceptions of reality, not necessarily reality itself. Therefore, the retailer must discern not only reality but the consumer's perception of that reality.

Most consumers in our technologically advanced society are overloaded with stimuli and cannot pay attention to all cues they encounter. The individual chooses from all the stimuli the ones to which she or he will attend. This focusing of attention on certain stimuli and the ignoring of others is known as selective attention. This means that a potential customer may be exposed to the retailer's advertisement but may not "see" the advertisement or process the information in it. Consumers pay more attention to information about products they are planning to purchase, particularly when the advertisement captures an appeal to an unfulfilled need. Retailers work to attract attention through advertising devices varying from originality to boldness, any of which can be effective when the appeal is appropriate. Figure 2.5 illustrates the responses to an advertisement.

Information Processing

In sales promotion, the retailer is trying to communicate information to the consumer. The retailer is sending a message by means of a signal through a channel such as newspaper, mail, or broadcast media to the receiver, the ultimate consumer.

The Source

The sender or the source of the message has an influence on whether or not the communication is accepted. Consumers tend to believe the message that comes from an objective source more than one from a

Figure 2.5. Responses to an advertisement.

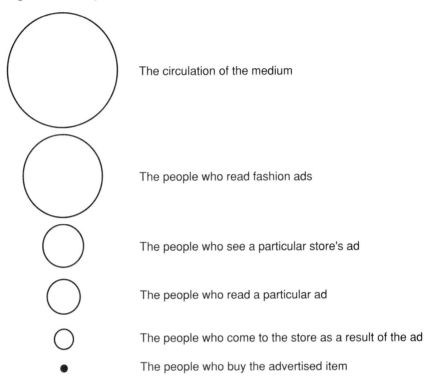

The circulation of the medium

The people who read fashion ads

The people who see a particular store's ad

The people who read a particular ad

The people who come to the store as a result of the ad

The people who buy the advertised item

source with a vested interest. Fashion information in a publicity story is trusted more than the information in an advertisement purchased by a retailer. This is the primary reason retailers strive to get favorable publicity about their stores and merchandise.

When the source of the message obviously stands to profit from the consumer's response to the message, credibility is impacted by additional factors, including reputation, experience, and expertise. Manufacturers' advertisements often contain the statement "sold at better stores everywhere" in the hope of increasing credibility through association with reputable retailers. Salespersons who demonstrate their knowledge of the stock, fashion terminology, and latest methods of coordinating a look increase their believability and authority. The consumer's past experience with the retailer's advertisements and merchandise will influence whether or not the current message is accepted. If the retailer advertises a full selection of skiwear but the consumer finds only two styles in his size, he is not likely to put much trust in that retailer's next advertisement. Credibility can result from an accumulation of experiences with the retailer over time. Advertising credibility is a very valuable asset to the retailer.

Spokepersons used in promotions become part of the source of the message. Their selection needs to be based in part on their credibility with the target customer for the particular product. An attractive, high-status personality who gives the impression of honesty is more persuasive than a spokeperson without these qualities.

The Medium

The receiver must be exposed to the medium through which the message is transmitted. Otherwise, the information has no chance of being interpreted. For teenagers who do not read the newspaper, the advertisement on trendy jackets will not be seen by them; that information does not reach them. With the extensive assortment of media available, individuals select a limited number of media that carry messages relevant to them. The retailer must determine the specialized media habits of the target customer. Because of those specialized habits, determining media mix is a prime requirement for successful advertising. This will be discussed in Chapter 7.

The media offer descriptive data on their audiences to help the advertiser match the target customer profile to a medium's audience profile. Various research specialists have also developed consumer profiles. Shim and Drake[1] identified five profiles by information search pattern of employed women purchasing apparel. The five segments are:

1. Print-oriented information searcher
2. Audiovisual-oriented information searcher
3. Store-intensive information searcher
4. Professional advice information searcher
5. Pal advice information searcher

Each segment has a preferred source of apparel information, which the retailer can use in selecting the medium for conveying information to that target group.

When selecting a medium, the retailer also needs to consider how well the various media categories will serve to promote the specific product being advertised. For example, if the advertisement is introducing a style with new proportions, the media category should have a visual capability, as in newspapers, magazines, or television. If the message is primarily factual information, such as an ad relating to brands or prices

[1]   SoYeon Shim and Mary F. Drake, "Apparel Selection by Employed Women: A Typology of Information Search Patterns," *Clothing and Textiles Research Journal* 6, 2 (Winter 1988), 1–2.

(e.g., Levi's jeans at $22.99), radio is often considered to be the most appropriate and economical media category.

The Message

The message is the information the sender wishes to convey to the audience. The retailer has a variety of messages to send to the target customer, including informing consumers of store services, updating store image, introducing new brands, and persuading consumers to buy specific items. Each message needs to be presented with the appropriate approach and appeal, which will be discussed more in Chapters 8, 9, 10, and 11.

The Receiver

The receiver is anyone who decodes the message. The retailer selects the medium so that the target customer is among the receivers. The retailer's consideration of the messages begins and ends with the receiver/audience. The desired audience is the target customer, and the retailer must not forget the characteristics of the target customer in shaping the message.

Lifestyle

An important influence on the behavior of consumers is their lifestyle—the way they spend time and money. A major lifestyle trend of the 1970s and 1980s was the interest in physical fitness, which includes nutrition as well as exercise.

Consumer lifestyle profiles can be developed by asking individuals about their activities, interests, and opinions. From these psychographic responses, consumers can be segmented by lifestyle, which is very helpful in developing promotional strategies. Plumer's AIO (activities, interest, and opinions) categories for lifestyle determination and demographics are given in Table 2.1. Each category contains eight divisions that include most of the areas involved in the way people spend their lives.

A widely recognized extension of lifestyle research has been carried out by Stanford Research Institute (SRI) using its Values and Lifestyle System (VALS). Through a survey, SRI developed a VALS typology that divides consumers into nine groups, as shown in Table 2.2. Members in each group possess fairly distinct needs, values, activities, opinions, and consumption patterns.

Table 2.1. AIO Categories.

Activities	Interests	Opinions	Demographics
Work	Family	Themselves	Age
Hobbies	Home	Social issues	Education
Social events	Job	Politics	Income
Vacation	Community	Business	Occupation
Entertainment	Recreation	Economics	Family size
Club membership	Fashion	Education	Dwelling
Community	Food	Products	Geography
Shopping	Media	Future	City size
Sports	Achievements	Culture	Stage in life cycle

SOURCE: Joseph T. Plummer, "The Concept and Application of Life Style Segmentation," *Journal of Marketing* 38 (January 1974), 34.

The outer-directed lifestyle groups constituted the largest portion of the adult population in 1980, the time of the survey. Although the retailer may continue to target the same group of consumers, that group will gradually change activities, interests, and opinions. For instance, the "societally conscious" may continue to enjoy healthy outdoor sports but may drop jogging for a different sport, such as bicycling. The retailer needs to be vigilant in observing the target customer's current lifestyle in order to provide appropriate settings for promotions and advertisements.

SRI has recently revised its measure. This new typology, called VALS 2,[2] classifies the U.S. population into eight distinctive subgroups, and it may prove to be more helpful for segmenting consumers in the 1990s. The subgroups are titled Strugglers, Believers, Strivers, Makers, Fulfilled, Achievers, Experiencers, and Actualizers. However, it is too early in the development and use of VALS 2 for SRI to have established the percentages of the population that can be classified in each segment with clearcut descriptions. The alert retailer should watch for the further evolution of VALS 2.

General psychographic segmentation is helpful for large manufacturers; however, it has limited value for the individual retailer of a particular category of products. Studies are needed that include questions about specific categories of products. By coupling lifestyle questions with selection criteria for apparel, Cassill and Drake[3] were able to give more

[2] VALS 2: Your Marketing Edge for the 1990s (Menlo Park, CA: SRI International, Values and Lifestyle [VALS] Program).

[3] Nancy Cassill and Mary F. Drake, "Apparel Selection Criteria Related to Female Consumers' Lifestyles," *Clothing Textile Research Journal* 6, 1 (Fall 1987), 20–28.

Table 2.2. VALS Lifestyle Group.

Type	Percent of Adult Population	Description
Need-driven groups		
Survivors	4	Old, poverty-stricken, poorly educated, fearful
		High purchasers of used cars and meatless meals
Sustainers	7	Resentful, living on the edge of poverty, youngish, fiesty.
Outer-directed groups		
Belongers	35	Aging, conventional, content, patriotic, traditional Middle American
		High purchasers of both large and compact American cars, freezers, cold cereal, and gelatin desserts
Emulators	10	Young, ambitious, flashy, urbanized, average household income, spenders, socially inclined
		Heavy purchasers of high-sugar and high-carbohydrate products, stereo sets, and prerecorded tapes or cassettes
Achievers	22	Middle-aged, prosperous, self-confident, conventional
		Heavy purchasers of luxury and mid-size cars, appliances, photographic equipment, and home electronic products
Inner-directed groups		
I am me	5	Very young, impulsive narcissistic, enjoy recreational activities
		High purchasers of exercise equipment, motorcycles, and racing bicycles
Experimental	7	Youthful, artistic, oriented to inner growth, permissive in personal living, highly educated
		High purchasers of foreign cars, video games, sugar-free soft drinks
Societally conscious	8	Affluent, highly educated, politically liberal, self-confident, high degree of interest in consumer issues, enjoy healthful outdoor sports such as jogging; above-average readers of newspapers, magazines, and books
		Heavy purchasers of subcompact cars, alcoholic beverages, coffee, and fresh, frozen, or canned seafood
Combined inner- and outer-directed groups		
Integrated	2	Psychologically mature, flexible, tolerant
		Have not yet been identified on the basis of demographic and attitudinal items

SOURCE: Adapted with permission of Macmillan Publishing Company from *The Nine American Lifestyles* by Arnold Mitchell, pp. 1–24, 63. Copyright ©1983 by Arnold Mitchell.

specific information to retailers of apparel. For example, they found that the "other directed group" was looking for social apparel that is fashionable, sexy, and conveys an air of prestige. Being physically attractive in fashionable clothing was found to be important to this group, who also favored American goods and valued education. They tended to move less frequently than other groups and may have been established customers of prestige stores. On the basis of these findings, the researchers recommended that promotion of merchandise to this group should be early in the buying season and should stress the brand name, fashionability, and American label while deemphasizing price.

Reference Groups

Consumers can be influenced by other people, such as friends, coworkers, family, and mass media personalities. Some of these individuals and groups serve as points of comparison for the individual in the formation of values, attitudes, and behaviors. Such people are referred to as reference groups and can have a powerful influence on consumer purchase behavior. Figure 2.6 shows the major reference groups that influence an individual's consumption behavior.

Consumers use these groups as frames of reference in guiding their consumer decisions, particularly for highly visible products and brands. Clothing is a public necessity that is visible; therefore, the individual is subject to great influence from other people when purchasing clothing.[4] When the brand is conspicuous, as with Aigner bags and Levi's jeans, reference groups exert considerable influence on the selection of product and brand.[5]

One role groups play is that of information source. Rabolt and Drake found that professional women looked to female reference persons, both at work and outside work, for information about the selection of career clothing.[6] People tend to believe the information supplied by reference groups more than impersonal information sources. Midgley found that for symbolic products such as clothing, individuals search

[4]   William O. Bearden and Michael J. Etzel, "Reference Group Influence on Product and Brand Purchase Decisions," *Journal of Consumer Research* 9 (1982), 183–94.

[5]   Donald W. Hendon, "A New and Empirical Look at the Influence of Reference Groups on Generic Product Category and Brand Choice: Evidence from Two Nations," in *Proceedings of the Academy of International Business: Asia-Pacific Dimensions of International Business* (Honolulu: College of Business Administration, University of Hawaii, 1979), pp. 752–61.

[6]   Nancy Rabolt and M. F. Drake, "Reference Person Influence on Career Women's Dress," *Clothing and Textiles Research Journal* 3, 2 (Spring 1985), 11–19.

Figure 2.6. Major
reference groups for the
consumer.

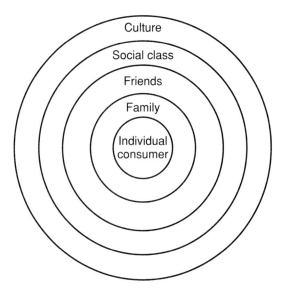

out information from interpersonal sources such as reference groups
rather than impersonal information sources such as newspapers.[7] This
appears to result from the social nature of the symbolic products. Best
friends' opinions are more influential than a full-page color advertisement. Retailers value this word-of-mouth advertising.

Another means by which groups influence consumers is by rewarding conformity to established group norms. Rabolt and Drake found
that although female professionals looked to women for information
on career dressing, they looked to male superiors for approval (norma-
tive guidelines) in an effort to dress in a manner acceptable to upper
management who were predominantly male.[8]

All reference groups affect consumer purchase behavior to some degree, but small cohesive groups such as family and friends have the
greatest influence. These groups offer frequent interaction, and the
consumer's behavior is very visible to the group members.

Retailers can benefit from understanding group influence and identifying reference groups of the target customer. Group appeals can be
incorporated in promotions and advertisements. When the product or
brand is conspicuous, the retailer should consider emphasizing the social acceptability of the item.

The three primary types of reference group appeals in promotions
involve celebrities, experts, and the "common man." Celebrities often

[7] David F. Midgley, "Patterns of Interpersonal Information Seeking for the
    Purchase of a Symbolic Product," *Journal of Marketing Research* 20 (February
    1983), 74–83.
[8] Rabolt and Drake, op. cit.

represent the "good life" that the consumer desires. L'eggs pantyhose has used Juliet Prowse, a well-known dancer with beautiful legs, in reference group appeals in advertisements. The "common man" appeal allows the prospective customer to see someone like himself/herself who is satisfied with the advertised product. This is useful when one is trying to reach the majority adopter group with a moderate-price, high-volume fashion item.

Opinion Leadership

Consumers can be and often are influenced in their selection and purchase of goods by other people. In informal conversations with family members, friends, neighbors, and coworkers, consumers share product-related information in what is referred to as word-of-mouth communication. Opinions are exchanged in this manner, with the dominant communicator known as the opinion exchanger or leader. The opinion leader informally influences others who are opinion receivers or opinion seekers. Opinion leaders give both information and advice about products. This type of advertisement is frequently seen in television commercials.

The roles in communication can shift so that the opinion leader in one product category becomes an opinion receiver in another product category. Opinion leaders tend to specialize in the product categories in which they have great interest and experience. They participate in product-related conversations for a variety of reasons that probably meet some basic needs. Opinion leaders may be motivated to give information and advice to gain attention, appear in-the-know, gain status, or achieve a feeling of superiority. Opinion receivers benefit from product information exchange by gaining the actual product information, by reducing the time needed to search for the information, and by reducing the perceived risk in purchasing through a personal endorsement of a new product or brand.

Retailers are interested in identifying opinion leaders in order to capitalize on their influence on other consumers. Consumer researchers have attempted to develop profiles of opinion leaders only to find that opinion leaders do not differ from nonleaders in terms of demographics. However, a few general statements can be made about opinion leaders as compared to nonleaders. Opinion leaders have a greater interest in the product category[9] and are better informed about this product

[9] Lawrence G. Corey, "People Who Claim to Be Opinion Leaders: Identifying Their Characteristics by Self Report," *Journal of Marketing* 35 (October 1971), 48–53.

category of leadership.[10] They also are more likely to try a new product[11] and are willing to talk about it.[12] This willingness to talk may stem from having the personality characteristics of self-confidence and gregariousness.[13] Also, opinion leaders read more on consumer issues, participate more often in consumer-related activities, and derive greater satisfaction from them. Opinion leaders have greater exposure to media.[14]

A retailer's promotional strategy can capitalize on opinion leadership by depicting it in advertisements. A store's selection of a "teen board" of advisors from various schools in the town or city can aid in establishing the teenagers as fashion opinion leaders in their respective schools (see Figure 2.7). The firm can then benefit from activities designed to stimulate word-of-mouth communication in which the teen board provides information and advice favorable to the firm's products, such as junior and young men's clothes. Information from this type of personal communication with a reference person will be more readily believed than information provided in store advertising or by salespeople.

Diffusion of Innovation

Because opinion leaders help accelerate the diffusion of innovation and are often innovators themselves, they are essential to the spread of new fashion ideas. "Diffusion is the process by which an innovation is communicated through certain channels over time among the members of a social system."[15] Diffusion is a special type of communication in which the information concerns something new, thus entailing some degree of uncertainty. "An innovation is an idea, practice, or object that is perceived as new by an individual or other unit of adoption." [16] New styling details are fashion innovations when the consumer perceives them as being new and different from those of the previous season. The retailer is anxious to spread the new fashion innovations early in the season and is therefore eager to know who will be the first to accept innovation.

[10] James H. Meyers and Thomas S. Robertson, "Dimensions of Opinion Leadership," *Journal of Marketing Research* 9 (February 1972), 41–46.

[11] Ibid.

[12] Corey, op. cit.

[13] Ibid.

[14] Charles W. King and John O. Summers, "Overlap of Opinion Leadership across Consumer Product Categories," *Journal of Marketing Research* 7 (February 1970), 43–50.

[15] Everett M. Rogers, *Diffusion of Innovations*, 3rd ed. (New York: The Free Press, 1983), p. 5.

[16] Ibid, p. 11.

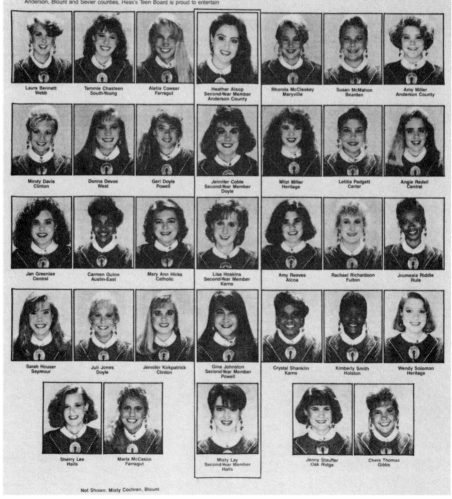

Figure 2.7. Establishment of fashion opinion leadership in an advertisement. (Courtesy of Hess's, Allentown, Pa.)

Rogers used the mean and standard deviation to divide a normal adopter distribution into five categories, as shown in Figure 2.8. The adoption curve indicates different categories of adopters: innovators, early adopters, early majority, late majority, and laggards, according to the stage in the fashion cycle when they adopt the style. The retailer needs to understand the categories in relation to adopters' receptivity to promotions.

Innovator Categories

Rogers has described each adopter category as follows:

Innovators are venturesome people eager to try new products. They usually receive their information on new styles from the mass media. Publicity is of particular importance in reaching innovators.

Early adopters want respect and are usually asked for information and advice by members of their social group. They are opinion leaders and serve as role models for their peers. Personal selling is valuable in contacting early adopters, if they can be identified. Publicity and advertising are important sources of information for these opinion leaders.

Early majority members try to adopt new ideas before others in their social group. They rarely hold leadership positions and usually deliberate for some time before adopting the new style. The early

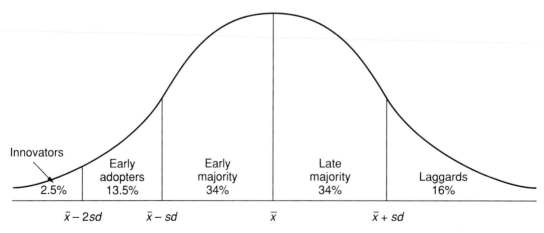

Figure 2.8. Adopter categories, based on relative time of adoption of innovation. (Reprinted with permission of The Free Press, a division of Macmillan, Inc. from *Diffusion of Innovations,* Third Edition, by Everett M. Rogers. Copyright © 1962, 1971, 1983 by The Free Press.)

majority group has considerable contact with salespeople, mass media, and early adopters.

Late majority members do not adopt an innovation until a majority of others in their social system have done so. They are skeptical about new products and adopt them cautiously. Peer group pressure is necessary before adoption will take place. Most of the information that counts for this group comes from other late adopters rather than from outside information sources. Advertising, personal selling, and publicity are of little value in influencing this group.

Laggards are the last social group to adopt an innovation. They are tradition-bound, suspicious of the new, and extremely cost-conscious. Laggards are poor targets for most promotional tools, and many retailers prefer not to promote to this group at all. However, discounters often target the late majority and laggards as their customers. When a trend is dying, goods can be purchased below average cost from the manufacturer; thus, the retail price will be low and will appeal to laggards. Fashion leaders most often do not care what is on sale or what is in a discount store.

Innovators are the first consumers to adopt an innovation. In terms of communication behavior, the innovator is the greatest user of impersonal sources, such as mass media, to gain information about the new. However, they do interact with other innovators, and some are opinion leaders who share information and advice with others in their social system. The next consumers to purchase the innovation are the early adopters, who are particularly important in providing word-of-mouth communication of the innovation. They are more numerous than the innovators and have more opinion leaders than any other category of adopters, making them vital to the spread of an innovation. Retailers are primarily interested in influencing innovators and opinion leaders through promotions of new styles because these groups are essential to the success of new fashions. Retailers should be alert to the adopter categories of their target customers and depict that type in their advertisements. Fashions can be sold to all categories but the promotional strategies must differ to suit the characteristics of the targeted category of adopters. For example, a sweater promotion at $39.99 will not appeal to the innovators and early adopters. They are looking for newness and expect to pay over $100.00 for a new sweater.

Attributes of Innovation

The rate of adoption of an innovation is affected by the perceived attributes of the innovation, which are relative advantage, compatibility, complexity, trialability, and observability.

"*Relative advantage* is the degree to which an innovation is perceived as being better than the idea it supersedes."[17] The nature of the innovation determines, to a large extent, the specific nature of the relative advantage, such as economic, physical, or social. In apparel fashions, the advantage of wearing the new is the gain of social status. The new may not have the advantage of being more functional or aesthetic, but simply of being newer. The innovation's ability to look different from the old and familiar can confer on it a freshness and excitement that carries higher social status.

"*Compatibility* is the degree to which an innovation is perceived as consistent with existing values, past experiences, and needs of potential adopters."[18] The briefness of swimwear has been increasingly adopted as society's values have moved away from a great concern for modesty in clothing to more interest in the health and beauty of the body. The briefer swimsuits are viewed as functional and honest and are compatible with the current values of physical fitness and health. First society's values evolve, then the consumer accepts the new products that reflect society's new values.

"*Complexity* is the degree to which an innovation is perceived as relatively difficult to understand and use."[19] Learning to combine multiple patterns into one fashion ensemble is more difficult to master than simply adding a scarf. The more difficult an innovation is to learn or use, the less likely it is to be adopted. New style ideas can be evaluated on this basis as they are presented in the market. The higher the quality and price, the more this concept is accepted and admired, as seen in designer clothing.

"*Trialability* is the degree to which an innovation may be experimented with on a limited basis."[20] The smaller the effort and investment required to try the innovation, the greater the chance for adoption, and vice versa. The trialability of the midi fashion in the early 1970s was low, because the consumer who wanted to try the midi dress for winter needed to buy knee-high boots and a midi-length coat. She had to adjust not only to a new skirt length, but also to a different and more expensive type of footwear. The older short coat was unthinkable over a midi dress, so a large expenditure was required for a midi coat. These conditions, along with women's positive attitudes toward youthful appearance, activity, and freedom, worked against the adoption of the midi during its introduction into the market. It was too drastic a change. A slower lengthening of hemlines is accepted as it gives the eye time to adjust.

[17]   Ibid, p. 213.
[18]   Ibid, pp. 230–31.
[19]   Ibid, p. 231.
[20]   Ibid, p. 231.

"*Observability* is the degree to which the results of an innovation are visible to others."[21] Fashion goods, by definition, are social in nature and have high visibility. Clothing is not just visible, but is seen *on* the wearer, which can result in immediate feedback to the wearer. Thus, clothing is the example par excellence of visible social merchandise. Therefore, the adoption rate of clothing innovations is at the highest level. Because newness is so desirable in a fashion context and clothing is so "socially" visible, innovations in clothing styles have greater potential for adoption than those in other product categories.

Stages of Innovation

The decision to adopt a new style idea is reached in five stages: knowledge, persuasion, decision, implementation, and confirmation, as depicted in Figure 2.9.

Stage 1, *knowledge,* occurs when one is first aware of the innovation and begins to gain some understanding of it. This is the stage for large, prestige advertisements early in the season to penetrate the consumer's awareness. More than one advertisement prominently presenting the new style feature will be necessary to reach a large portion of the target group before they enter the store. Key displays should further define the new fashion look and give more information about how to wear it.

Stage 2, *persuasion,* occurs when the individual forms an attitude, either positive or negative, toward the innovation. During this stage, the consumer becomes actively involved with the innovation and seeks out information. The individual is assessing the attributes of the innovation, so promotions should address these when possible. The individual is seeking to reduce feelings of uncertainty about accepting the innovation. Fashion promotions that show trial levels of acceptance, such as a casual jacket in sportswear as opposed to a more expensive business suit or coat, may convince skeptics they are not risking much with the purchase of the jacket. If the innovation is complex or difficult to master, promotion techniques that teach the consumer will be helpful. For instance, having a manufacturer's representative demonstrate new methods of arranging scarves with handout drawings and directions can educate the prospective customer. If the innovation is a complex total look, such as the Oriental look, workshops can be held with hair stylists, makeup artists, and others to explain the key features and skills needed to bring the look off.

During Stage 2, individuals often seek information from peers, whose personal opinions are more convincing than impersonal information given by the media. This means that a sizable group of consumers must

[21] Ibid, p. 232.

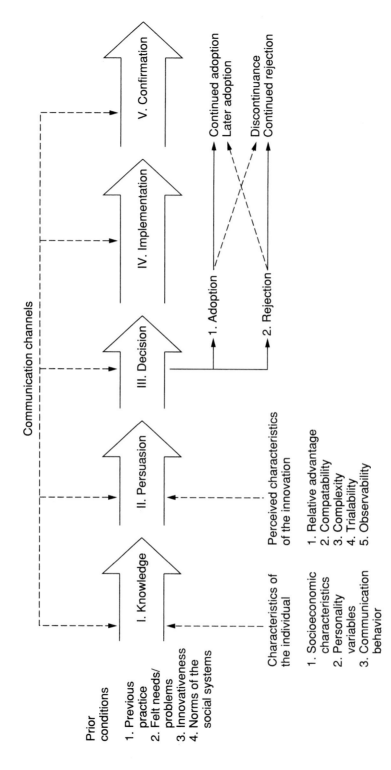

Figure 2.9. A model of stages in the innovation decision process. (Reprinted with permission of The Free Press, a division of Macmillan, Inc. from *Diffusion of Innovations*, Third Edition, by Everett M. Rogers. Copyright © 1962, 1971, 1983 by The Free Press.)

have been reached by retail promotion in Stage 1 and early in Stage 2. These promotions need to not only reach the consumers, but excite them to the point of discussing the innovation. In this way, when consumers ask their friends, "Have you seen the new short skirts? What do you think about them?" they will receive some affirmative answers that will reduce their feelings of uncertainty. If others are aware of the fashion, then the consumer will begin to think maybe it isn't a flash in the pan. "Maybe I should look into this, even try it."

Stage 3, *decision,* occurs when the consumer participates in activities that lead to a decision to adopt or reject the innovation. This is the stage in which consumers will try the innovative item to determine its appropriateness for them. Most people who actually try the innovation will eventually adopt it to some degree. Obviously, personal selling is important to the trial of the innovation. Also, having an assortment of versions of the innovation is helpful. If one version is not appropriate, another can be tried. Having necessary components of the look readily available can be crucial. In the case of the midi, for example, the customer could not visualize the look without boots. Fashion shows can serve as a partial trial for some customers if a model similar to them in appearance wears the new style. Magazine pictures, mannequins, and employees wearing the look will help the eye adjust to the new fashion.

Stage 4, *implementation,* occurs when the person moves from the decision to accept the innovation to actually using it. The retailer wants the consumer not only to accept the new fashion but to buy it in several items. The process of educating the consumer to the new look is too expensive not to lead to multiple sales. At this stage, advertisements depicting the innovation in a variety of categories and in a wide assortment encourage the customer to purchase the look several times. For example, the oversized look could be promoted in shirts, jackets, suits, and coats.

Stage 5, *confirmation,* occurs when the consumer seeks reinforcement for the decision he or she has made to accept or reject the innovation. The individual is seeking to avoid dissonance, a feeling of disequilibrium, in this stage. The individual may change the earlier decision, depending on the messages received at this stage. If the consumer rejects the innovation in this decision stage only to learn that most other people have accepted it, that individual may reverse the decision and adopt the innovation. The reverse might also occur. The consumer may buy one product with the innovative feature and get negative reactions to it. For instance, if the customer takes the new fashion item home and the spouse is especially critical of the innovation, the customer may return it.

Ordinarily, the retailer has little direct input to the consumer at the confirmation stage. Most of the retailer information should have been given to the customer at an earlier stage. If it has been correct and adequate, it will foster positive feedback during this stage. Most of the feedback for the customer during the confirmation stage comes from his or her own experience using the innovation, such as trying a complicated arrangement of the new scarf, or from other people's reaction to the consumer's use of the innovation ("Susan, you look so dramatic in that outfit"). If the innovation is compatible with the consumer's values and needs, and the retailer has promoted correctly in the earlier stages, this last stage will take care of itself. If not, there is little the retailer can do to encourage acceptance at this stage.

Summary

All the phenomena discussed in this chapter and others, including age, ethnic background, and geographic location, influence consumers in their decisions to buy or not to buy. The wise retailer is aware of them and uses them skillfully in promoting goods to the potential customer. A store can appeal to more than one fashion adopter group but not to all groups. The buying staff and management of the store must decide which groups are their customer base. When customers walk into the store, it should be obvious whether the store is appealing to their fashion needs. Innovators and laggards will never be customers of the same store. *Know your customer!*

CHAPTER 3

Planning and Budgeting

Retailers have very few areas in which they can reduce expenses. They must pay the utility bill and the rent. However, the sales promotion budget is one area where retailers can minimize expenses. They can cut down on the size of an advertisement, eliminate a fashion show, or decrease the amount of time spent on visual presentation. However, retailers prefer making realistic sales promotion plans they can live with from the start so that drastic cuts will not be necessary later during the season. For them to achieve such a plan, the budget process must be approached systematically.

Planning Methods

There are basically two different approaches to determining the total amount of money to be allocated by the store for sales promotion. A combination of these can be considered a third approach.

1. Percentage-of-sales method
2. Cost-of-goals method
3. Combination of methods 1 and 2

Percentage-of-Sales Method

Top store management usually reviews the preceding year's sales, sets a sales plan, and decides how much they think the firm should spend in the coming year for sales promotion. Each year the store needs to increase sales from the previous year. Planning this increase can justify an increase in the sales promotion budget. A firm that has been in business several years and has a history of its sales volume and its sales promotion expenditures may calculate the percentage of sales that the preceding year's promotional effort represents. This percentage is applied to planned or anticipated sales for the coming year.

Because planned future sales usually represent an increase over the preceding year's sales, the resulting budget for sales promotion is usually increased annually. Stores vary in the percentage they designate for total promotion, which includes all media advertising, visual presentations, and in-store promotions such as fashion shows. These figures may range from as low as 2% to as high as 8%, with 4% being about average.[1] (See Table 3.1 for department stores' averages.) Generally, as store volume increases, the percent spent on promotion decreases. This figure relates principally to media expenditures but includes some salaries and display expense as well.

An example of the percentage-of-sales method is as follows:

Store's anticipated annual sales ($50,000,000) $\times$ Store's fixed percentage for sales promotion (4%) $=$ Sales promotion appropriation ($2,000,000)

[1] Retailers can find the industrywide percentage spent on promotion from various sources, including National Retail Federation, National Cash Register Company, and trade journals. The U.S. Small Business Administration has numerous free publications one can receive by contacting the local office.

Table 3.1. Typical Sales Promotion Expenses for Department Stores with Sales of $20–$50 Million, as a Percent of Total Company Sales.

	1967	1973	1974	1978	1980	1982	1986	1987
Total sales promotion	3.93	3.95	4.09	4.13	4.35	4.54	4.46	4.29
Sales promotion management	*	*	*	0.26	0.22	0.21	0.28	0.12
Advertising other than media	*	*	*	0.24	0.26	0.22	0.21	0.38
Media total	2.88	2.94	3.10	3.10	3.15	3.33	3.32	3.22
Newspaper	2.29	2.43	2.50	2.28	2.20	2.29	2.11	2.12
Radio	0.12	0.28	0.30	0.23	0.15	0.19	0.27	0.15
TV	*	*	*	0.19	0.28	0.38	0.16	0.15
Direct mail	0.14	0.12	0.17	0.23	0.20	0.41	0.56	0.51
Other	0.08	0.11	0.09	0.14	0.32	0.05	0.22	0.29
Shows, special events, and exhibits	*	*	*	0.09	0.12	0.21	0.16	0.11
Display	*	*	*	0.56	0.60	0.58	0.48	0.46

*Data unavailable for this year.

SOURCE: Figures are from the National Retail Merchants Association, *Financial and Operating Results of Department and Specialty Stores.* Percentages for media were calculated. Abstracted by permission of NRMA (now the National Retail Federation).

In this example the planned or anticipated sales are $50,000,000 for the year, and the fixed percentage the store has been spending on promotion is 4%. When these figures are multiplied, they produce a figure of $2,000,000 for the sales promotion budget for the coming 12-month period. Regardless of the final dollar amount, the percentage of sales spent on promotion should be within an accepted range. Maintaining control of dollar expenditures for promotion helps ensure a final profit. The percentage-of-sales method is the most commonly used method for determining the total promotion budget.

Sales promotion is a controllable expense. That is, management associates of a store can decide not to spend money on advertising. Many small stores choose to locate in high-traffic areas, which require high rent, instead of spending dollars for sales promotion. They are exchanging one expense for another. This kind of decision varies in effectiveness depending on the kind of merchandise to be sold. For example, a store for farm supplies would not need to locate in an enclosed, high-rent mall. Most shop owners have a choice of where to locate. Proprietors of clothing stores, ice cream shops, or gift shops could choose to locate in an expensive mall because of the high traffic in such an area. A tall men's shop owner might choose a less expensive place because his merchandise fills a clothing need not usually filled by other stores and will draw customers on its own. In this case management must determine where other shops are located that offer service to such a customer. An excellent idea might be to locate *near* a mall rather than *in* a mall, thus enabling convenient shopping, lower rent, and parking near the entrance. This decision would permit funds for advertising.

A store with $50 million gross sales would generally plan to spend from $125,000 to $175,000 annually on newspaper, radio, and television ads, excluding in-house expenses. In contrast, a small store with $500,000 gross sales would have only about $12,000 to $17,500 to spend. Small stores commonly do not hire someone to help with promotion, so their total 4% to 5% could be planned for media advertising. Thus, this small store could plan on spending $20,000 to $25,000 for the year. This amount could be spent on promotion in newspaper, radio, direct mail, and special events.

For a new store opening, a dollar amount can be set aside for advertising this event only. For example, a company with a $40 million sales plan, including existing stores and the new store, could set aside $15,000 for media expenditures for launching the new store. The amount could vary greatly among stores with similar sales volume because of differences in situations and operations. Factors to consider are: Is this market a new one for the company? Is the store name well known? What amount of money will be spent by the mall association, if the store is not a free-standing one? Does this market require advertising in an additional newspaper, or do the newspapers currently used cover this new location? How large is the current mailing list or charge-account customer base in this location? Should radio or television be part of the advertising package? What are media rates in this market?

Except for unusual situations, such as a new branch store opening, the percentage that promotion expenditures represent remains fairly constant from year to year. The percentage results from store policy, which is fairly stable except in case of a major change, as in ownership or management. A change of one-half of a percentage point in promotion allocations is considered significant.

The advantages of the percentage-of-sales method are:

1. It is simple. Advertising managers can simply plug the numbers derived from past experience into the formula and generate next year's planned figures.
2. It is safe. The method tends to keep the store's sales promotion appropriation similar to the amounts it has been able to afford in the past; therefore, yearly budget discussions can be simplified and shortened.

The disadvantages of the percentage-of-sales method are:

1. It tends to produce repetition in promotional effort because the plans start with last year's experience and build into the next year.
2. The system engenders less creativity and imagination than a more open method.
3. It limits aggressive buyers by setting the budget at a level lower than actual sales may justify. The thinking is that if the good aggressive buyers were given more promotion money, they might increase sales still more. Thus, this method of allocation can result in a frustrating situation for the good buyer.

Cost-of-Goals Method

When the cost-of-goals method is used, top store executives define the long-range sales and profit objectives. They brainstorm about major promotional programs that will generate these planned sales. Then they determine how many dollars it will take to carry out the selected promotional program.

A variation of this method allows divisional merchandising managers or buyers to determine how much they need to spend for promotion in order to meet the planned sales figures. Each division prepares a "wish list," writing down all desired plans along with expected expenditures. Costs are discussed and evaluated so that the best ideas are used. Winning ideas form the major promotional thrust of that season.

Advantages of the cost-of-goals method are:

1. Plans are tied less firmly to last year's performance, making it possible to use newly conceived ideas.
2. It challenges buyers to be more aggressive in their planning.
3. Buyers and divisional managers are closer to the merchandise and customers, so there is a heightened understanding of sales potential. Also, a department occasionally varies in sales volume and its subsequent need for sales promotion. For example, accessories are more important in some seasons than others. The cost-of-goals method could take this into account, unlike the percentage-of-sales method, which produces a blanket percentage from year to year regardless of the sales momentum of individual departments.
4. When major changes such as remodeling or expansion occur, this method is especially useful, because past figures cannot accurately predict future potential when changes take place.

Disadvantages of the cost-of-goals method are:

1. A buyer can become overly expansive and generate unrealistic goals.
2. If the buyers are allowed to set figures, they will produce a disparity among the departments in the store's overall promotional effort. In the end, the total store image must be protected; departmental goals should not blur or distort it.
3. Top executives lose a degree of control when buyers and divisional managers are allowed to set their own allocations.

Combination Method

To maximize the advantages, some stores employ a combination of the two previously described methods. The allocation process begins with members of management setting planned figures based on what is thought to be reasonable sales potential for the coming year. Judgment based on experience guides management in estimating the amount of money needed for sales promotion to achieve the planned sales. At this point, management can check how realistic this sales promotion figure is by employing the percentage-of-sales method.

The combination method maximizes the advantages and minimizes the disadvantages of both the percentage-of-sales and cost-of-goals methods. However, this method takes more time than either of the other methods. Also, someone still has to make a judgment when the comparison of percentages reveals a significant difference. If management maintains that the percentage spent last year is the only realistic percentage, other associates involved in planning might just as well use the percentage-of-sales method only and save time. If management is open to other definitions of "realistic," then the combined method gives new ideas an opportunity to be heard and gives the creator of the promotion ideas a specified time to convince management of their merits.

CHECKING BUDGET FEASIBILITY   For example, management may have set anticipated sales for the coming year at $20,000,000 and estimated it will cost $2,000,000 to execute the sales promotion program that tops their wish list. They can calculate the percentage of anticipated sales the promotional allocation represents by dividing the proposed sales promotion allocation by the anticipated sales as follows:

$$\begin{matrix} \$2,000,000 \\ \text{(sales promotion} \\ \text{allocation)} \end{matrix} \div \begin{matrix} \$20,000,000 \\ \text{(anticipated sales)} \end{matrix} = 0.10 = 10\%$$

In this example the proposed sales promotion allocation is 10% of the anticipated sales. The figure is unrealistic in terms of the goal of showing a profit at the end of the year.

Another check on the feasibility of a proposed budget is a comparison with the preceding year's promotion figures. Suppose that records of the same store used in the preceding example show a former sales volume of $18,000,000 and an expenditure of $720,000 for sales promotion, which was 4% of the sales volume. The proposed 10% sales promotion allocation seems excessive compared with the 4% of last year. However, some change in operation or a super sales promotion opportunity might justify allocating a larger percentage. A move from 4% to $4^1/_2\%$ seems more realistic in this case.

Cooperative Advertising

The retailer can extend the promotion budget by acquiring financial assistance from vendors of products the store purchases. Many manufacturers and some fiber bureaus are ready to help retailers promote their products through some type of cooperative advertising, usually referred to as *co-op*. Cooperative advertising arrangements are joint promotions, typically by the manufacturer and the retailer, to advertise the manufacturer's products usually in a local medium. Each party pays a portion of the advertisement costs. Agreements vary from company to company, and from time to time in the same company; therefore, there are no across-the-board typical agreements.

There are some commonalities, however. Manufacturers usually have a budget for co-op advertising, and the buyer should initiate the request for money at the time he/she is shopping the line. However, prior to the buying trip the buyer should have considered the general planning for promotion for the season and determined a feasible amount to request in co-op dollars, as well as have a rough idea of the type of goods and timing of the ad. In this way, the buyer can be specific about the advertisement and the shipment of goods when talking with the manufacturer's sales representative about the order.

Typically, the amount of dollars allowed for co-op advertising is based on the volume of goods purchased. The allocation may be based on the amount of goods bought of one style (the one to be advertised) or the total amount of goods bought from the manufacturer that season. Typically the money is calculated as a percentage of the volume of goods purchased. Most manufacturers pay only up to 50 percent of the cost of the ad space or time, exclusive of production cost. However, the manufacturer may go as high as 100 percent, for instance, for a new store opening.

The agreement inevitably includes rules regarding the advertisement. The manufacturer's name must appear prominently in the ad. Typically the agreement specifies the size of the manufacturer's logo in relation to the size of the retailer's logo. For example, the manufacturer may specify that his logo appear at least in the subheading of the ad. Sometimes the rules are so restrictive that the retailer is well advised to reject the co-op money rather than lose control of the ad. See Figure 3.1 for a typical co-op advertisement.

After the advertisement has been printed or broadcast, the retailer submits a claim to the manufacturer, accompanied by invoice copies from the medium and tear sheets or videotapes of the actual ad as it ran. Usually the vendor will pay fairly promptly when the requirements of the contract are met and the claim includes the proper evidence that the advertisement did occur.

Co-op advertising obviously can be a financial aid to the retailer, but it is also beneficial to the manufacturer as it gets the brand name in a local medium with a retailer. Some stores count heavily on the additional advertising money gained through co-op arrangements. The cosmetic industry has built its success in large part on co-op advertising with leading retailers.

Figure 3.1. An example of a cooperative advertisement between a garment manufacturer and a retail store. (Rickie's Petites, Knoxville, Tenn.)

Developing a Six-Month Sales Promotion Budget

Once the total dollar figure for sales promotion for the coming year has been arrived at, the next stage in budgeting is to make a specific six-month plan. This requires the allocation of dollars by month and department. Department stores have a more detailed planning process than small independent stores because of the many departments involved. Therefore, a typical department store's budgeting process requires precise details for the allocation of promotion funds. Many stores base their budget on the fiscal year, so that the six-month periods are from February through July and from August through January.

Executive Brainstorming

Department stores begin the six-month budget process with executives participating in brainstorming sessions about 6–12 months before specific promotions occur. The department store's promotion calendar is divided into two six-month periods, with spring being February through July and fall being August through January. The 6–12-month lead time is necessary if associates in all areas of the store are to effectively execute their plans on major promotions, such as back-to-school, catalog, and storewide promotions. For example, ladies' sportswear buyers must know a year in advance if they are to purchase imports for a newspaper advertisement, a catalog, or other promotion media. The quantities purchased are determined by the promotional means selected. Some ladies' fashion goods from American manufacturers are purchased five months before an advertisement is seen by a retail customer. If management at some level does not make plans for an advertisement, opportunities for promotion will practically disappear. When timing is a problem for a buyer, preliminary plans may be made informally in discussions between a general merchandise manager and divisional manager.

Top executives, including the president, general manager, and vice-president of sales promotion, assess very early the situation of the store in terms of (1) national, regional, and local economy; (2) the specific store's expected share of the market; (3) competition; and (4) planned changes such as new highway exits, new branch stores, or closing of industries in the area. The executives will come to some agreement about the store's situation and outlook. For example, they may acknowledge that the economy looks stable but not robust, that the store is holding its own with competition, or that a new branch is opening in the fall that should provide excitement and stimulation to business.

After some top-level debate on store-related situations, management then sets the tone of sales promotion for the six-month period. For example, a community store might opt to sell only "quality merchandise" or "fashion at a price." Sometimes a decision about the media will result from these brainstorming sessions. For example, it might be decided that specific fashion items could be shown advantageously on television. Others might benefit from less expensive in-store videotape showings.

Executive brainstorming sometimes includes discussions on reruns of ideas from previous years, such as a ladies' spring fashion catalog sent to all charge accounts, a fashion catalog with a new fashion appeal, or a decreased or increased amount of radio promotion for the young junior customers. These executives should communicate with divisional merchandise managers and buyers wherever possible before making final decisions.

There are two theories on creative ideas about promoting a store. One is that creative ideas come from the bottom up (e.g., from buyers to divisional merchandise managers to general merchandise managers to the president). The other theory is that creativity is handed down from the top level. The consensus among the writers of this text, however, is that both systems should be in effect to produce the best ideas and have them executed well.

Through a variety of discussions, top management members establish the dominant sales promotion goals. For instance, they could decide that the goal is to launch a new branch and establish it as a fashion store in a shopping mall while maintaining sales volume in existing stores. Through one of the three budgeting methods (usually the percentage-of-sales method), top management can determine a six-month budget for the total number of store outlets for all promotional efforts. This strategic program is then divided so that each area of promotion— visual merchandising, advertising, and public relations—has an allotted amount to be spent in the six-month period. At the same time, executives divide the budget among merchandise divisions of the store—women's fashions, men's and boys', infants' and children's, home store, budget store, and others.

The amounts given to each division vary according to the type of merchandise, volume of sales, and contribution to the store's image. For example, women's fashion departments typically receive more than children's or housewares because of their greater contribution to a fashion image.

Middle Management Notification

Twice a year top and middle management personnel come together to "kick off" the upcoming season and to inform and motivate store personnel. The agenda and style of the meeting varies from store to store but usually includes the executives' opinions on business potential and their major goals for the period. It is each executive's opportunity and responsibility to motivate middle management. At the end of the meeting or in private individual meetings later, heads of promotional areas and individual divisional merchandise managers are given their shares of the promotion budget, which have been decided upon earlier by top executives.

Allocations for Various Promotional Activities

Stores vary in their allocations for different promotional activities, depending on past success. From the National Retail Merchants Association's (now the National Retail Federation) report of average expenditures on sales promotion, percentages have been calculated for 1987 (see Figure 3.2).[1] The largest single expenditure was for advertising media,

[1] Member stores of NRMA voluntarily report this information so that non-member stores and those member stores not submitting figures are not included, meaning these data may not represent the averages for all retail stores in 1987.

Figure 3.2. Typical 1987 sales promotion allocations for department stores with sales of $50 million. (Based on figures for 1987 shown in Table 3.1.)

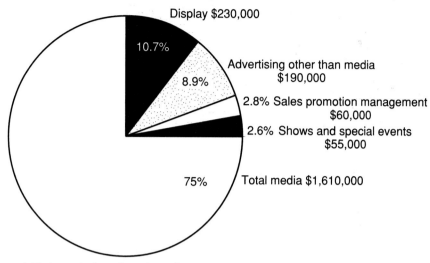

Display $230,000

10.7%

Advertising other than media $190,000

8.9%

2.8% Sales promotion management $60,000

2.6% Shows and special events $55,000

75% / Total media $1,610,000

4.29% promotion allocation = $2,145,000

amounting to almost 75% of total promotional expenses. Visual merchandising (display) was allotted about 10.7% in the NRMA report and fashion shows and special events only about 2.6%. Newspapers continue to be the major retail advertising medium.

MEDIA ADVERTISING ALLOTMENT Media advertising, on the average, accounted for about 75% of the total promotional allotment (using NRMA figures); it can be divided in various ways. A sizable amount usually goes to media publicizing store-wide events, such as anniversary sale circulars, Christmas kick-off promotions, store catalogs, Christmas catalogs, and fashion (image) advertisements. Remaining advertising funds are divided among divisional merchandise managers, who promote their individual areas using the combination method of budgeting. Three major elements are considered in determing these allocations: sales volume of separate areas, need of the store at large, and the preceding year's success record.

Buyers are then allocated budgets by their divisional merchandise managers. These allocations are based on such factors as:

1. The preceding year's successes
2. Promotional ideas from buyers
3. Management requests for development of new areas
4. Expanded promotions for large-volume areas

5. Initial promotions for new resources

6. Continuing image-maker resources

7. Resources that provide large cooperative advertising allocations

Many people at various levels provide input to the processes of budget planning. In most stores where there is open communication among executives, buyers, and sales personnel, ideas about expenditures are exchanged frequently. Requests are made, suggestions are considered, and tentative budgets are communicated both up and down the organizational ladder. When an allocation appears to be in its final form, a budget chart is developed showing categories of expenditures in actual amounts, expected co-op dollars coming in from manufacturers, dates of promotions and events, selected media and tentative tone, and size and length of commercial messages. These projections are sent to the general merchandise manager for final approval.

In traditional times, a 12-month budget was commonly accepted and adhered to. In the current, fast-moving merchandising scene, a six-month budget schedule is used by most stores. Even the six-month projection sometimes must be altered as unforeseen marketing opportunities arrive and related promotions must be developed on shorter notice. In many stores there is a supplemental budget allowance, often called the "kitty" or contingency fund, which is usually set up to handle projects that require more money than originally intended or to accommodate new, creative promotional ideas that emerge after the initial budget plan has been accepted and approved. With this supplemental allowance, a great deal of buyer ingenuity is encouraged. Many times an increased market share is the result.

VISUAL MERCHANDISING ALLOCATION   The visual merchandising director's budget, which was about 10.7% of the sales promotion budget in 1987, usually covers the many tangible props, signs, racks, mannequins, pennants, and flyers used to enhance the effectiveness of all promotions in the store. These visual tools are of prime importance for fashion shows, special sales events, Christmas and other seasonal events, anniversary sales, and a myriad of other regular selling events that bring requests from buyers and merchandise associates. A supplement to a regular budget usually covers special signs and unitemized expenditures for display units.

Initial outlay of money for new props and other visual display items consumes a major portion of yearly visual merchandising budgets. Sizable amounts are often allocated for the care and maintenance of these vulnerable articles, which receive rough treatment since they are on the floor, where traffic flows by them. Salespeople as well as display personnel may be required to move or dress the mannequins and put merchandise on the various display props. Therefore, upkeep of all visuals is a budget item, and optimistic display associates often underestimate the possible dangers.

SPECIAL EVENTS ALLOCATION   The budget for a special events director may be one of the more flexible ones in the entire promotional structure. NRMA (NRF) figures show that special events, shows, and exhibits together received only about 2.6% of the promotion budget in 1987. Occasionally a special event department arranges a publicity-gaining activity in response to a call from management (in-store request). At other times, this department may embark on a large-scale plan for a special event in response to a local civic event or an appeal from a city or community-based organization (out-of-store request). Due to these "extras," which add responsibility and create unforeseen expenditures, the special events director usually breaks down a budget request into three broad categories:

1. Sales promotional events based on specific departmental needs, which are predictable and have a six-month lead time
2. Sales promotional events in response to management suggestions relating to building the entire store image, which sometimes can be predicted based on a six-month planning period and at other times can be arranged within greatly reduced time frames
3. Special events in response to community requests, which include tie-ins with a wide spectrum of activities such as opera seasons, community theater openings, public school campaigns, and fund drives by civic groups

The budget for special events is more likely than other budgets to be planned by the build up method because creativity is so important.

FASHION SHOW ALLOCATION   In large department stores fashion shows are the responsibility of the fashion director or coordinator, although the recent trend has been to group them as part of special events and assign the responsibility to the special events director. The fashion director establishes a schedule based on requests from management, from evaluating last year's events, and from the season's new ideas. Her goal is to help set the image of the store in a glamorous tone and to entice customers into the fashion areas. In-store fashion shows are the best use of her time and money, because the customer is brought into the store, where merchandise is for sale immediately.

The fashion director's budget includes models' fees, special lighting, music for shows, special props, fees for certain community events, and extra help during busy times. Table 3.2 illustrates a fashion director's sample budget for six months.

Table 3.2. An Example of a Fashion Director's Six-Month Budget in a
Department Store with a Volume of $25–$45 Million.

		Total budget: $51,570
Month	Item	Cost ($)
August	Salaries	3,500
	Travel to market	1,000
	Models for newspaper photography	250
	Magazine photo	100
	Fashion workshop for employees	800
	Seventeen shows (four store locations)	13,000
	Models for cosmetic promotions	350
September	Salaries	2,500
	Benefit show for abused children*	3,500
	Models for cosmetics promotions	350
	Models for designer room trunk show	175
October	Salaries	3,000
	Benefit show for business and professional women (using earlier show)*	1,500
	Show for cancer society (using earlier show)*	1,700
	Fur salon showing—informal modeling	175
	Lingerie department—informal modeling	250
	Seventeen magazine spring slides (purchased from magazine)	125
	Seventeen fall cast book	45
November	Salaries	2,500
	Travel to market	1,000
	Models for cosmetic promotions	375
	Models for designer room trunk show	200
December	Salaries	2,500
	Models for cosmetic promotion	375
	In-store fashion shows	800
January	Salaries	2,500
	Models for cosmetic promotion	1,000
	Show for symphony guild	3,500
	Added expenses:	
	Miscellaneous	1,000
	Additional show, to be determined	3,500

*Planning two or three shows within a few days will cut expenses greatly and free the
fashion coordinator for other projects. Plan this only if the shows can be repeated with
minor changes.

Finalizing the Budget

Eventually all areas are pulled together for a final plan to be presented to all involved. Store managers could be included at this stage as well as the buying staff. All areas of the store must be supporting the same image. For example, the linen department should not advertise $100 sheets if the dress department never buys a dress to retail over $100. The entire store must appeal to the same class of customers. Management will set these guidelines in each store, and the divisional merchandise managers will help guide the buyers.

Distributing Six-Month Allocations to Departments

In addition to its use in determining the annual budget, the concept of percent-of-sales can be employed in dividing the six-month budget by month. Management may find it convenient to base the percent of promotion expenditures per month on the percent of sales that each month represents in terms of anticipated sales. For instance, if April is projected to produce 7.5% of the year's sales, then 7.5% of the sales promotion budget would be allocated to April. Management can consult preceding years' figures. Table 3.3 shows the average percentage of sales by region and month for department stores.

Sales are usually lowest in January, with upswings in May/June and August. The peak occurs at the end of the year, at Christmas. Many stores follow this movement in their distribution of sales promotion dollars. An exception to the blanket application of the percent-of-sales method is the Christmas season. December sales can be as much as 16 to 20% of the year's anticipated sales, depending on the type of business, and the retailer probably would not want to spend in December as much as 20% of the promotional dollars. It would be wiser to allocate some of this amount to October and November, thereby building a preliminary customer response to the Christmas season. The reverse is true in January. Sales are typically low after Christmas. Even so, a store should not allow its image to fade from the customer's mind. Therefore, a retailer may find it wise to spend more on sales promotion in January than the sales volume would indicate.

Many retailers believe more dollars should be planned for higher-volume months. For example, the months with high volume for swimwear will be the hot summer months—May, June, and July—so the bulk of swimwear promotion dollars should be scheduled for April, May, June and July. The swimwear sales peak should be preceded by an advertising program, usually a month in advance of the peak sales. In this way, customers already know where to shop. A retailer well known

Table 3.3. Department Store Sales by Region and Month as a Percent of Total Annual Sales.

Region	Jan.	Feb.	Mar.	Apr.	May	June	July	Aug.	Sept.	Oct.	Nov.	Dec.	Total
East north central	5.6	5.5	7.4	7.5	8.1	7.8	7.2	8.1	7.7	8.9	10.4	15.8	100%
East south central	5.3	5.5	7.8	7.8	8.0	7.7	7.5	8.0	7.5	8.6	10.3	16.0	100
Middle Atlantic	5.2	5.6	7.2	7.4	8.1	8.1	6.8	7.8	7.9	8.6	10.7	16.6	100
Midwest	5.6	5.6	7.4	7.5	8.1	7.9	7.3	8.1	7.7	8.8	10.3	15.7	100
Mountain	5.7	6.0	7.3	7.4	7.9	7.7	7.4	8.4	7.6	8.1	10.2	16.3	100
New England	5.6	5.5	7.2	7.5	8.1	8.1	7.0	7.8	7.8	8.4	10.4	16.6	100
Northeast	5.2	5.6	7.2	7.4	8.1	8.1	6.9	7.8	7.9	8.6	10.6	16.6	100
Pacific	6.0	6.0	7.3	7.3	7.7	7.7	7.4	8.2	7.8	8.0	10.0	16.6	100
South	5.6	5.8	7.8	7.7	8.0	7.7	7.4	8.1	7.5	8.3	10.0	16.1	100
South Atlantic	5.6	5.9	7.8	7.8	7.9	7.6	7.2	7.9	7.5	8.3	10.2	16.3	100
West	5.9	6.0	7.3	7.3	7.7	7.7	7.4	8.3	7.7	8.1	10.1	16.5	100
West north central	5.7	5.7	7.4	7.5	8.2	7.9	7.3	8.2	7.7	8.7	10.2	15.5	100
West south central	5.8	5.9	7.8	7.6	8.1	7.8	7.7	8.5	7.4	8.1	9.5	15.8	100

SOURCE: U.S. Department of Commerce, 1988.

for its swimwear will frequently begin fashion advertising for swimwear as early as January. July dollars will be spent on off-price promotional ideas.

An aid in planning and budgeting is a list of important dates for the year. One source of such a list is the Newspaper Advertising Bureau, which supplied the list in Table 3.4. Easter does not occur on the same date each year and therefore requires an annual date adjustment.

For establishing a more detailed tentative departmental plan by month, a form such as Table 3.5 may prove helpful. There is space for a description of the planned promotion and a column to indicate the type of promotion—fashion, clearance, or store sale. The cost column has not been completed since this figure depends on the area of the country in which the store is located. The buyer for the individual department is responsible for planning its advertisement by the month within the total store plan. This involves deciding on dates the ads will run, the type of medium to use, and the specific items to be advertised. Final proofing of the ad is done by the advertising department. For these tasks the Newspaper Advertising Bureau makes a planbook available each year. A sample worksheet is shown in Figure 3.3.

Budgeting for Specialty Stores

Sales promotion expenditures of specialty stores with more than $5 million volume averaged about 4.06% of sales volume in 1986 (see Table 3.6). This amount includes advertising, display, fashion shows, and the salaries of in-store personnel in these areas of responsibility. In stores with sales volume less than $5 million, the store manager, owner, or other employee may be in charge of store promotions. Some stores hire freelance talent to write copy, set up displays, or organize fashion shows. In some ways, this practice is more economical because a store pays only for services needed. Radio stations write the ad copy for stores, and newspaper reps assist with the preparation of ads. Often a store associate sets up displays or helps with signs.

Specialty Store Budget Form

The chart in Table 3.7 is an example of how a specialty store owner should plan advertising dollars. This chart is a combination media plan and budget plan. It also leaves a space to record actual expenditures, which can help the owner stay within the budget, and it requires a limited amount of time to complete. The form should include material helpful to the owner or buyer. The manager or owner can design a form suitable to her own store's unique needs.

Table 3.4. Important Dates, 1989–1993.

	1989	1990	1991	1992	1993
New Year's Day	Sun. Jan. 1	Mon. Jan. 1	Tues. Jan. 1	Wed. Jan. 1	Fri. Jan. 1
M. L. King, Jr. Day	Mon. Jan. 16	Mon. Jan. 15	Mon. Jan. 21	Mon. Jan. 20	Mon. Jan. 18
Lincoln's Birthday	Sun. Feb. 12	Mon. Feb. 12	Tues. Feb. 12	Wed. Feb. 12	Fri. Feb. 12
Valentine's Day	Tues. Feb. 14	Wed. Feb. 14	Thurs. Feb. 14	Fri. Feb. 14	Sun. Feb. 14
President's Day	Mon. Feb. 20	Mon. Feb. 19	Mon. Feb. 18	Mon. Feb. 17	Mon. Feb. 15
St. Patrick's Day	Fri. Mar. 17	Sat. Mar. 17	Sun. Mar. 17	Tues. Mar. 17	Wed. Mar. 17
Passover**	Thurs. Apr. 20–Apr. 27	Tues. Apr. 10–Apr. 17	Sat. Mar. 30–Apr. 6	Sat. Apr. 18–Apr. 25	Tues. Apr. 6–Apr. 13
Easter Sunday	Sun. Mar. 26	Sun. Apr. 15	Sun. Mar. 31	Sun. Apr. 19	Sun. Apr. 11
Easter Monday*	Mon. Mar. 27	Mon. Apr. 16	Mon. Apr. 1	Mon. Apr. 20	Mon. Apr. 12
Secretaries Day	Wed. Apr. 26	Wed. Apr. 25	Wed. Apr. 24	Wed. Apr. 22	Wed. Apr. 21
Mother's Day	Sun. May 14	Sun. May 13	Sun. May 12	Sun. May 10	Sun. May 9
Armed Forces Day	Sat. May 20	Sat. May 19	Sat. May 18	Sat. May 16	Sat. May 15
Victoria Day*	Mon. May 22	Mon. May 21	Mon. May 20	Mon. May 18	Mon. May 24
Memorial Day	Mon. May 29	Mon. May 28	Mon. May 27	Mon. May 25	Mon. May 31
Flag Day	Wed. June 14	Thurs. June 14	Fri. June 14	Sun. June 14	Mon. June 14
Father's Day	Sun. June 18	Sun. June 17	Sun. June 16	Sun. June 21	Sun. June 20
Canada Day*	Sat. July 1	Sun. July 1	Mon. July 1	Wed. July 1	Thurs. July 1
Independence Day	Tues. July 4	Wed. July 4	Thurs. July 4	Sat. July 4	Sun. July 4
Civic Holiday*	Mon. Aug. 7	Mon. Aug. 6	Mon. Aug. 5	Mon. Aug. 3	Mon. Aug. 2
Labor Day	Mon. Sept. 4	Mon. Sept. 3	Mon. Sept. 2	Mon. Sept. 7	Mon. Sept. 6
Grandparents' Day	Sun. Sept. 10	Sun. Sept. 9	Sun. Sept. 8	Sun. Sept. 13	Sun. Sept. 12
Jewish New Year**	Sat. Sept. 30	Thurs. Sept. 20	Mon. Sept. 9	Mon. Sept. 28	Thurs. Sept. 16
Columbus Day	Mon. Oct. 9	Mon. Oct. 8	Mon. Oct. 14	Mon. Oct. 12	Mon. Oct. 11
Thanksgiving Day*	Mon. Oct. 9	Mon. Oct. 8	Mon. Oct. 14	Mon. Oct. 12	Mon. Oct. 11
Mother-in-Law's Day	Sun. Oct. 22	Sun. Oct. 28	Sun. Oct. 27	Sun. Oct. 25	Sun. Oct. 24
Halloween	Tues. Oct. 31	Wed. Oct. 31	Thurs. Oct. 31	Sat. Oct. 31	Sun. Oct. 31
Election Day	Tues. Nov. 7	Tues. Nov. 6	Tues. Nov. 5	Tues. Nov. 3	Tues. Nov. 2
Veterans Day	Sat. Nov. 11	Sun. Nov. 11	Mon. Nov. 11	Wed. Nov. 11	Thurs. Nov. 11
Remembrance Day*	Sat. Nov. 11	Sun. Nov. 11	Mon. Nov. 11	Wed. Nov. 11	Thurs. Nov. 11
Thanksgiving Day	Thurs. Nov. 23	Thurs. Nov. 22	Thurs. Nov. 28	Thurs. Nov. 26	Thurs. Nov. 25
Hanukkah**	Sat. Dec. 23–Dec. 30	Wed. Dec. 12–Dec. 9	Mon. Dec. 2–Dec. 19	Sun. Dec. 20–Dec. 27	Thurs. Dec. 9–Dec. 16
Christmas Day	Mon. Dec. 25	Tues. Dec. 25	Wed. Dec. 25	Fri. Dec. 25	Sat. Dec. 25
Boxing Day*	Tues. Dec. 26	Wed. Dec. 26	Thurs. Dec. 26	Sat. Dec. 26	Mon. Dec. 27

*Denotes Canadian holiday

**Denotes Jewish holiday (begins at sunset the night before)

SOURCE: Courtesy of the Newspaper Advertising Bureau, Inc.

Table 3.5. Department Plan.

Sportswear Departmental Plan

Budget $ _____
Plan $ _____

Month	Description	Medium	Size	Cost	Fashion (F), clearance (C), or store sale (S)
Feb.	Fashion ad—new trend	Newspaper	¾ page	(Varies by each store, with information on local media costs provided by the store's advertising department)	F
	Valentine gift ad	Newspaper	½ page		F
Mar.	Value book	Catalog	16 pages		F
	Sale	Newspaper	1 page		S
	Fashion ad	Newspaper	¾ page		F
	Fashion ad	Newspaper	¾ page		F
	Fashion ad	Newspaper	¾ page		F
Apr.	Swimwear fashion campaign (total store involvement, with fitting seminars, fashion shows, giveaways)	Television	3 weeks coverage		F
	Playwear ad	Newspaper	¾ page		F
May	Swimwear fashion ad	Newspaper	¾ page		F
	Playwear fashion ad	Newspaper	¾ page		F
	Fashion ad	Newspaper	½ page		F
June	Playwear sale	Catalog	16 pages		S
	Fashion transitional ad	Newspaper	½ page		F
July	Swimwear preview	Newspaper	½ page		F
	Fall fashion ad	Newspaper	¾ page		

SAMPLE	SUNDAY	MONDAY	TUESDAY

THE 4-STEP AD PLAN

1. Select goal

Division	Sales Goal $	% of Goal
A	$7,500	25%
B	2,400	8
C	3,900	13
D	4,800	16
E	5,100	17
F	6,300	21
TOTAL	30,000	100%

2. Decide budget

% of sales	5
Dollars	1,500
Co-op	600
Total	2,100
Rate	$4/COL. IN.
Inches	525

3. Select promotion

List each division's monthly sales percentage of total sales. Then allot percentages of the month's total advertising. Calculate the linage for each division.

Division	% of Sales	% of Adv.	Linage
A	25%	25%	130"
B	8	6	32
(PLUS CO-OP)			
C	13	15	79
(EXPANDED)			
D	16	19	100
(OVERSTOCKED)			
E	17	17	89
F	21	18	95
TOTAL	100%	100%	525

4. Schedule ads day by day

22

SUNDAY 1

Depts. C = 20"
F = 25"
45 col. in. ad
Lead Item...price
Item...price
Item...price
Item...price

MONDAY 2 — night opening

TUESDAY 3

SUNDAY 8

Depts. E = 25"
D = 15"
40 col. in. ad
Lead Item...price
Item...price
Item...price
Item...price

MONDAY 9 — night opening

TUESDAY 10

SUNDAY 15

Depts. A = 35"
F = 20"
55 col. in. ad
Lead Item...price
Item...price
Item...price

MONDAY 16 — night opening

TUESDAY 17

SUNDAY 22

Depts. C = 4"
F = 10"
B = 10"
+Co-op = 12"
D = 5"
41 col. in. ad
Lead Item...price
Item...price
Item...price

MONDAY 23 — night opening

TUESDAY 24

SUNDAY 29

End of Mo. Sale ad
Depts A = 25"
F = 30"
E = 29"
84 col. in. ad
Sale Item...price
Sale Item...price
Sale Item...price

MONDAY 30 — night opening

2-Day "End of Month Sale"

TUESDAY 31

Figure 3.3. A sample worksheet for planning advertising. (Courtesy of the Newspaper Advertising Bureau, Inc.)

WEDNESDAY	THURSDAY	FRIDAY	SATURDAY
4 "Holiday Sale" ad all Departments 10 col. inches <u>60 col.in·ad</u> Lead Item... price Item... price Item... price Item... price Item... price	**5** Holiday Store Open	**6** night Opening	**7**
11	**12** "Dollar Days Sale" Ad Depts: A=35" C=25" D=20" <u>80 col.in. ad</u> Sale Item... price Sale Item... price Item... price	**13** Payroll Day night Opening	**SAMPLE WORK SHEET** **Important points:** • The local automobile assembly plant pays its employees every other Friday. • Retail traffic is traditionally heaviest on Monday, Friday and Saturday. • Local night openings are on Monday and Friday. • Department B has a tie-in event with co-op support in the fourth week of the month. • Department C has just expanded. • Department D is overstocked.
18	**19** Depts: A=25" D=15" <u>40 col.in·ad</u> Sale Item... price Item... price Item... price	**20** night Opening	**Follow the 4-step ad plan:** 1. Set a sales goal for each department. 2. Apply the advertising budget figure to the sales goal to ascertain your linage for the month.
25	**26** Depts: C=20" E=25" Sale→D=35" <u>80 col. in. ad</u> Sale Item... price Item... price Item... price Item... price	**27** Payroll Day night Opening	3. Decide how much of the month's advertising to give each department. Figure in additonal co-op funds as recorded on your co-op advertising control sheet. 4. Keep in mind the six important points listed above and schedule your ads to anticipate each opportunity.
			23

Figure 3.3. *(continued)*

Table 3.6. Typical Sales Promotion Expenses for Specialty Stores with Sales over $5 Million, as a Percent of Total Company Sales.

	1967	1973	1974	1978	1980	1982	1986
Total sales promotion	4.14	3.51	4.03	3.70	3.84	4.22	4.06
Sales promotion management	*	*	*	0.40	0.24	0.17	0.08
Advertising other than media	*	*	*	0.29	0.47	0.29	0.59
Media total	2.93	2.56	2.94	2.35	2.50	3.12	3.11
Newspaper	2.57	2.16	1.99	1.52	1.61	1.78	2.07
Radio	0.02	0.04	0.25	0.19	0.10	0.11	0.26
TV	0.19	0.30	0.63	0.25	0.30	0.51	0.04
Direct mail	0.15	0.12	0.09	0.27	0.34	0.57	0.44
Other	*	*	*	0.13	0.15	0.16	0.31
Shows, special events, and exhibits	*	*	*	0.10	0.19	0.12	0.01
Display	*	*	*	0.59	0.53	0.53	0.26

*Data unavailable for this year.

SOURCE: Figures are from the National Retail Merchants Association, *Financial and Operating Results of Department and Specialty Stores.* Percentages for media were calculated. Abstracted by permission of NRMA (now the National Retail Federation).

Specialty stores spend very little money on fashion shows and special events. Some special events take the owner or manager away from the store, and this can prove costly. Also, managers may not feel comfortable engaging in these activities. It may be advantageous to hire out-of-store talent unless the cost is prohibitive. If a clothing store receives a request from a club or civic group to produce a fashion show or exhibit, members of the group or club often can help in many ways to keep the cost low. Their members may be models, which can also result in sales.

Comparison of Specialty Store with Department Store Planning

In comparison to specialty shops (see Table 3.6), many department stores (see Table 3.1) spend large amounts of money on shows and special events. Such expenditures of the specialty shop depend on the owner, the community, and the type of merchandise. Benefits of spending money on shows may not be immediately evident, since few or no direct sales may result. The most important reason for fashion shows is the image-strenghtening impressions created by casting customers in the roles of sophisticated models.

Whereas a department store functions with a large number of people providing creative ideas and varying levels of entrepreneurship, a specialty shop forces a small number—often as small as one person—to

Table 3.7. Specialty Store Advertising Budget

Season ____ Spring
Year ____

| | | | MONTHLY BUDGET | | | YEAR TO DATE | | |
| | | | | This Year | | | This Year | |
Month	Medium	Description	Last Year	Budget	Actual	Last Year	Budget	Actual
Jan.	Postcard	Direct mail for clearance of merchandise	$478	$500	$469	$478	$500	$469
Totals								

61

develop an entire strategy for the organization. Although this situation puts stress on the person "in the driver's seat," many specialty shop owners thrive on this kind of responsibility. There are pitfalls, however. Faulty planning can be more than an unfortunate choice. A department store, with a built-in strength born of its size, can survive numerous individual miscalculations. Such a safety margin does not exist in a small specialty shop. For these reasons, it is important that the individual in charge move into the budgeting and planning periods with forethought and caution.

Guidelines for Specialty Stores

Some of the problem spots in specialty shop planning can be avoided by following guidelines such as these:

1. Keep fairly detailed records of promotional ideas. Set up an alphabetized file, arranging the ideas by key word. For example, if a shop proprietor believes that suppliers might provide some new co-op dollars, a folder could be inserted under *C*. In the file could go probable dates and events for which a manufacturer would be likely to offer the extra funds.

2. If a shop has counterparts in other cities that sell similar goods in similar circumstances, a file should be set up to hold that shop's ads. For example, if the owner of Rickie's Petites observes that a similar store named Sal's Small Shop located 500 miles away uses radio to good advantage, it would be wise for the owner of Rickie's to take note of it. Listening to a good commercial and writing down the copy is easy—and at a later time could be very helpful. (The transcription should go under *S* for Sal's. This system would keep Sal's ads separate from those of other competitors.) It is always more efficient to keep written records—even hastily written notes—than it is to say, "I'll remember that." A busy shop owner may not be able to call to mind the various names of specialty stores that use their purchased ad space well. Another idea is to tape newspaper ads, direct mail pieces, and other ideas in a large scrapbook. A scrapbook is much easier to use than folded pieces of paper unorganized in a folder. A separate book should be used for the retailer's own ads.

3. Also important for written records is a running schedule of future advertising and promotional plans. By putting expected purchases down on paper, a shop owner can readily note the expected spread of media purchases. For instance, if the owner is buying newspaper space in January, he may want to alternate this medium with radio for February and direct mail for March, leaving an extra amount

for spring purchases in April. Only by keeping records—beyond the simple retention of check stubs—can a proprietor have a graphic reminder of where the money is being spent.

4. Specialty shop owners—many of whom buy their stores after a career in department stores—should use a six-month lead time, just as they did in the larger retail ambience. When on a buying trip to check new lines and make selections for the upcoming season, a shop owner often will find available suggested advertisements in the showroom.

5. One caution to a new entrepreneur is that sales representatives from radio stations, television stations, and newspapers may feel free to walk into the store at any time. They should not be allowed to take up business time when associates are busy with more important details.

6. Another caution is never to see a media representative without setting up an appointment. Otherwise, one will not be mentally prepared to make wise budget decisions and may be persuaded to spend extravagantly. Decisions to spend money should not be made while media representatives are present. Keeping a checklist can help maintain orderly media purchases.

Evaluating the Success of the Plan

To determine the success of the plan for sales promotion, some method of evaluation is necessary. The most common methods are based on sales and are shortsighted. Some retailers count the number of promoted items sold. A high number of units sold equals success. However, the promotion may have generated store traffic resulting in sales of other items not promoted. Therefore, some retailers will use total sales for several days after promotion. Certainly, the retailer expects some sales improvement from a promotion; however, other benefits may accrue. A good promotion gets the word out on the store and builds the store's positive image. This benefit is not readily apparent from sales figures but will build up slowly over time. A store can ill afford to overlook the long-range benefit of staying in the public eye and building a strong image for fashion.

Summary

Sales promotion budgeting and planning are complicated and can be confusing. Store executives usually initiate the plans, providing a framework for expenditures in various categories. The budget takes on other dimensions as divisional managers, merchandising managers, buyers, and promotional area heads seek to provide funds for widely varied sales promotional specifics.

When budgeting, one should have a realistic expenditure plan for the future. Good notes and records of the amount of money spent and results need to be maintained for future planning. If budget problems arise, discuss them honestly with management. Freedom to change ideas is desirable so that a better plan can be developed if situations or merchandise warrant it.

CHAPTER 4

Dramatizing the Fashion Merchandise: Using Art Elements and Principles

Most people do not associate window or interior displays, advertisements, or retail stores with art; however, these use the art of design, which has a visual impact on the viewer. The retailer wants the shopper's perception of the store's visual environment to be positive, which will promote the sale of merchandise. To this end the merchant needs a system for organizing the store's visual images. Creating effective visual images involves the use of design elements and creative principles. The design elements discussed in this chapter are color, texture, line, form, and space. The creative principles are the guidelines for organizing these elements to achieve the desired results. The principles to be discussed are unity, variety, emphasis, rhythm, balance, and proportion. These all apply to the store itself, merchandise presentation, display, and advertisements.

The retailer must develop visual images that will heighten the customer's perception of the store's merchandise as desirable, that is, create the feeling that the goods will make a positive difference in the customer's life. It is even better if the customer can be led to feel that the merchandise is so desirable that it should be purchased now.

Light

Light makes vision possible. Without light, none of the design elements or principles used with the merchandise would be perceivable. Beyond making objects visible, light has a sense of mystery about it. It cannot be touched or felt, yet it is real. It can move, even pulsate as if alive. It can vitalize and dramatize a scene.

In retail promotional efforts, light has several purposes:

1. To attract the customer's attention
2. To create an appropriate mood for the merchandise
3. To contribute to a positive visual image of the merchandise
4. To allow careful inspection of the merchandise

Light is a major factor in creating an appropriate store or department ambience that promotes the qualities of the merchandise and contributes to a pleasant shopping experience. The lighting and coloring in Color Plate 1 conveys a calm, sophisticated feeling appropriate for evening wear. Contrast this in your mind with a display window of swimwear in sunny yellow light. Good lighting minimizes the time needed to examine the merchandise and reduces eye strain.

Light is radiant energy that acts on the retina of the eye to make objects visible. The visible spectrum of energy encompasses wavelengths corresponding to violet, on the short end, to red, the longest visible wavelength. A light source that contains energy spanning the visible spectrum is known as white light. When white light is passed through a prism, it is refracted and produces the spectrum shown in Figure 4.1.

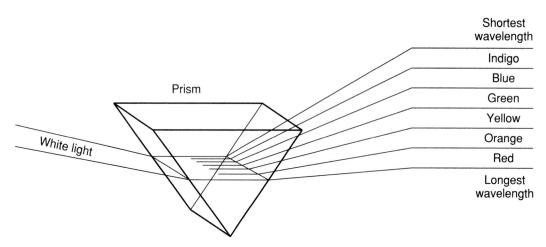

Figure 4.1.   The color spectrum produced by passing white light through a prism.

Illuminance Levels

The Illuminating Engineering Society of North America (IES) recommends different lighting levels for various merchandising areas, as shown in Table 4.1. The lighting for displays should be brighter than that of the other areas in order to attract the customer's attention. IES advises that the ratio between illuminance of displayed merchandise and illuminance in the area where the customer appraises the merchandise should be 3 to 1. A greater difference in the lighting of the two areas makes it difficult for the customer's eyes to adjust quickly and easily.

Relationship to Color

Light and color are interrelated. Light sources radiate different wavelengths, influencing the appearance of colored objects and producing warm or cool color renditions. This is referred to as "color temperature" and ranges from 9,000 kelvins (K), which appears blue (cool), down to 1,500 K, which appears orange-red (warm). Figure 4.2 shows color temperature by light source regardless of the pigments in objects being lighted. Cool lights (more kelvins) are good for general lighting to guide the customer through the store's aisles. Warm lights (fewer kelvins) are more energizing near the merchandise as well as more flattering to customers' skin tones.

The light source controls the appearance of colors in merchandise and other objects. This phenomenon is referred to as color rendition. To enhance a color in the merchandise, the light must have the wavelength of the color within it. If a light source does not contain the wavelength of the color being viewed, the color will appear grayed or dulled. Table 4.2 indicates the color rendition factors for various light sources.

To help the customer in selecting fashion goods, it is desirable to use lighting that shows the merchandise under the same type of light as that in which the merchandise will be used. For instance, swimsuits will be used primarily in sunlight, whereas evening wear will be worn with lighting closer to candlelight. By using a light source that approximates the light of the occasion of merchandise use, the retailer can avoid the color appearing different to the customer when it is used and thus avoid a dissatisfied customer.

The buyer/manager needs to understand lighting well enough to evaluate its effectiveness in presenting the merchandise. If major changes in lighting are needed, a lighting engineer can be consulted. Representatives for lighting fixtures often provide assistance in lighting selection. Also, manufacturers such as Sylvania and General Electric provide brochures with useful lighting information and suggestions.

Table 4.1. Recommended Illuminance for Lighting Design in Merchandising Areas.

Area of Tasks	Description	Type of Activity Area*	Illuminance**	
			Lux	Footcandle
Circulation	Area not used for display or appraisal of merchandise for sales transactions	High	300	30
		Medium	400	20
		Low	100	10
Merchandise[†] (including showcases and wall displays)	That plane area, horizontal to vertical, where merchandise is displayed and readily accessible for customer examination	High	1,000	100
		Medium	750	75
		Low	300	30
Feature displays[†]	Single item or items requiring special highlighting to visually attract and set apart from the surroundings	High	5,000	500
		Medium	3,000	300
		Low	1,500	150
Show windows				
Daytime lighting				
General			2,000	200
Feature			10,000	1,000
Nighttime lighting				
Main business districts— highly competitive				
General			2,000	200
Feature			10,000	1,000
Secondary business districts or small towns				
General			1,000	100
Feature			5,000	500

*One store may encompass all three types within the building:

High activity: Where merchandise displayed has readily recognizable usage. Evaluation and viewing are shown to attract and stimulate the impulse buying decision.

Medium activity: Where merchandise is familiar in type or usage, but the customer may require time and/or help in evaluation of quality, usage for the decision to buy.

Low activity: Where merchandise is displayed that is purchased less frequently by the customer, who may be unfamiliar with quality, design, value, or usage. Where assistance and time is necessary to reach a buying decision.

**Maintained on the task or in the area at any time.

[†]Lighting levels to be maintained in the plane of merchandise.

SOURCE: Illuminating Engineering Society of North America, *Lighting Merchandising Areas.* (New York: IES, 1986), p. 17.

Figure 4.2. A traditional color wheel of 12 colors, beginning with the primary colors of red, yellow, and blue.

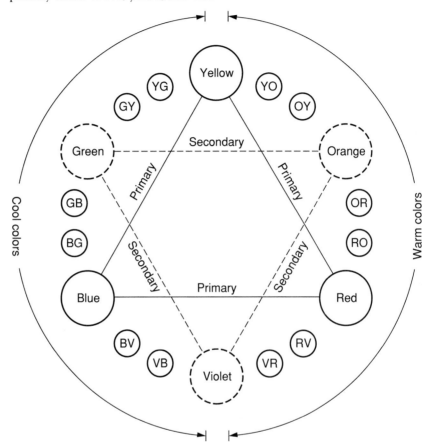

Design Elements

Color

Typically, color is the first element we see when looking at an object or scene. It affects us physically and psychologically and is one of the most important elements in creating response, especially to display. Being in a space painted red can speed up the rate of the heartbeat, whereas blue space can lower the rate of the heartbeat. A dull, drab color has a depressing effect on people, and a bright color such as orange seems to

Table 4.2. Color Rendition Factors of Lamps.

Lamp Type	General Rendition and Effect	Colors Emphasized	Colors Grayed
CWX—Cool white deluxe	Very good rendition (cool)	All	None
Fluorescent CW—Cool white	Good rendition (cool)	Orange Yellow Blue	Red
Color-improved mercury	Fairly good rendition (cool)	Red Yellow Blue	Green
WWX—Warm white	Good rendition (warm)	Red Orange Yellow Green	Blue
WW—White	Fair rendition (warm)	Orange Yellow	Red
Incandescent	Very good rendition (warm)	Red Orange Yellow	Blue
Sodium vapor	Fair rendition (yellowish)	Orange Green Yellow	Red Blue

SOURCE: Modified from Illuminating Engineering Society of North America, *Lighting Merchandising Areas* (New York: IES, 1986), p. 47.

elevate one's mood. Color is the single most important design element in the fashion field because of its tremendous impact on the viewer.

Color is an inexpensive, versatile means of creating mood and drama in the presentation of fashion merchandise. Much of the color comes from the merchandise itself, which requires no additional expense. Research shows that the proper choice of color in store windows and store interiors has significant drawing power. Warm colors (reds, oranges, and yellows) physically attract customers to shop. On the other hand, cool colors (blues, greens, and violets) are more appropriate for areas where customers will be deliberating over a big-ticket purchase such as a fur coat. Color used properly can attract the eye of the potential customer, create the desired mood, and stimulate the viewer to make a purchase decision.

Skillful use of color begins with an understanding of its three dimensions—hue, value, and intensity.

Hue is the color family name, such as red, blue, or yellow. Hue indicates the color's position in the spectrum, that is, its arrangement in the order of wavelengths. The spectrum is produced by the refraction of white light passing through a prism, as seen in Figure 4.1. A rainbow is a familiar example of a spectrum. A *color wheel* or palette of color can be made by bending the spectrum into a circle. Color Plate 3 shows a Munsell color wheel.

Hues have generally recognized psychological qualities depending on their value and intensity as follows: red, aggressive; yellow, sunny and cheerful; green, restful and frank; blue, quiet and peaceful; and purple, somber and serious.

Value indicates the lightness or darkness of a color. Value can be viewed in terms of a scale of grays ranging from white to black. Color Plate 3 shows Munsell's value scale from light to dark. For example, the hue blue can vary from baby blue to midnight navy. Light values are referred to as *tints,* and dark values are referred to as *shades.* Value as well as hue contributes to mood. Light values have airy, fresh, feminine qualities, whereas dark values impart serious, sophisticated qualities. If a color scheme is composed of contrasting values such as light and dark, it can create a mood of drama and excitement.

Intensity or *chroma* refers to the brightness, purity, or saturation of color. (See Color Plate 3.) High- or full-intensity colors are clear and bright. Scarlet is typical. These intense colors catch the eye and stop the customer long enough for her to notice the merchandise. High-intensity colors are active and stimulating. Low-intensity colors are grayed or dull in appearance, for example, maroon. Dull or low-intensity colors tend to create a calm and restful mood.

COLOR SCHEMES   Colors often occur in various combinations, referred to as color schemes. Combining colors attractively is an art marked by individual style and preference. Although there are no laws for combining colors, there are some formalized methods for producing harmonious color schemes that students may find helpful. These methods are illustrated on a wheel of 12 colors in Figure 4.2.

The two major categories of color scheme in terms of hue are *related* and *contrasting*. The first category is referred to as *related* because this type of color scheme utilizes one or more hues in common, that is, colors that are adjacent on the color wheel. Related color schemes tend to produce a stable feeling and allow the mood of the hue of the color scheme to be expressed clearly. The second category is referred to as *contrasting* because there are no common hues in these color schemes. Contrasting color schemes are often bold and dramatic.

Related Color Schemes;   The principal types of related color schemes are *monochromatic* and *analogous*. A monochromatic harmony uses only one hue in various values from almost black to almost white and intensities from brilliantly saturated to very gray. (See Figure 4.3*a*.) This mixing of black, white, and grays can be used in all schemes because it includes neutrals, which are not considered colors. If texture is a selling point, a monochromatic color scheme may be a good choice for highlighting textures, which would be more apparent when the colors are all the same or similar.

Analogous color schemes comprise three colors that are adjacent on the wheel, which means they contain a common hue, as shown in Figure 4.3*b*. An example is yellow-orange, yellow, and yellow-green. Another example, from the cooler side of the color wheel, is blue, blue-violet, and violet. An analogous color scheme offers more variety in colors than a monochromatic scheme and avoids the possibility of clashing colors since there is a common hue to provide harmony.

Contrasting Color Schemes; Contrasting color schemes are subdivided as follows:

1. Complementary
2. Double-complementary
3. Split-complementary
4. Triad
5. Tetrad

Complementary schemes are formed by two hues that are directly opposite each other in the color wheel, such as red and green, orange and blue, or yellow-orange and blue-violet. (See Figure 4.3*c*.) Complementary color schemes can be exciting because opposites are combined. However, they are more difficult to handle than analogous schemes because their colors can clash. One of the two colors should be present in a larger amount than the other and thereby become the dominant hue for the scheme.

Double-complementary schemes are based on two adjacent colors combined with their complementary or opposite colors, such as yellow-orange and yellow with violet and blue-violet, or red-orange and orange with blue and blue-green. (See Figure 4.3*d*.) This scheme incorporates both contrast by means of opposite hues and similarity by means of related hues. The related hues give a sense of unity, making this scheme slightly easier to produce than a simple complementary scheme.

A *split-complementary* color scheme is composed of any hue plus the two hues on either side of its complement, such as yellow with red-violet and blue violet, or blue-green with red and orange. (See Figure 4.3*e*.)

Triad schemes are built on three hues equidistant from each other, such as red, yellow, and blue; or orange, green, and violet. (See Figure

Figure 4.3.   Color schemes.

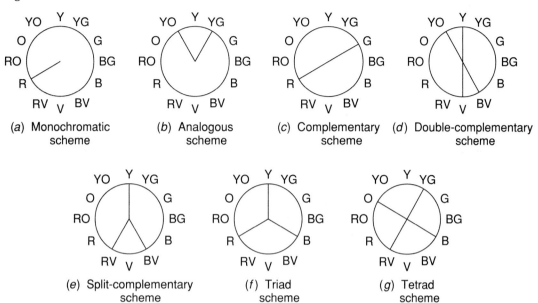

(a) Monochromatic   (b) Analogous   (c) Complementary   (d) Double-complementary
     scheme   scheme   scheme   scheme

(e) Split-complementary   (f) Triad   (g) Tetrad
     scheme   scheme   scheme

4.3*f.*) The combination of unrelated hues is lively, but harmony may be difficult to create because of the variety generated.

A *tetrad* scheme combines four hues equidistant from each other on the color wheel, such as orange, yellow-green, blue, and red-violet. (See Figure 4.3*g.*) When three or more hues are combined, the color scheme works better if the value or intensities are similar so as to create some unity. The various hues provide the contrast and interest.

The merchandise itself can provide the color schemes for the display. In a merchandising grouping, a multicolor item such as a figured blouse can establish the color scheme. When an item comes in several colors, that range of hues can become the color scheme. The question then is how to arrange them harmoniously. Frequently the colors will work well if arranged in an order similar to the color wheel or rainbow.

The colors within the merchandising area also contribute to the color scheme. The hues in the flooring, carpet, walls, and partitions may be very apparent or rather inconspicuous. Orange, red, and yellow in the walls and ceiling demand attention and must be considered as an important part of the presentation of the merchandise. Clear, bright greens, yellows, and red-oranges would be good items to place on the forward stands on the aisle. They would harmonize with the clear, bright colors on the walls to carry out the active mood for a sportswear or junior department. Colors on the fixtures that are deep in a department are less important than the colors on forward fixtures, because the aisle provides space for the shopper to see the total picture of the front merchandise against the backdrop of the wall. There is less space farther into the department, so the colors are seen close up, eliminating the background wall from view.

More neutral colors for walls, flooring, and carpeting provide an inconspicuous background for many color schemes. For example, in a blouse department the range of colors that the blouse is stocked in provides the color scheme.

If the merchandise itself does not suggest a color scheme, ideas for timely color harmonies can be found in current fashion magazines that have good color reproduction. A leading source of display ideas is the Retail Reporting Bureau, which publishes several books showing color photos of the best work in window interior display. They also issue a monthly collection of color photographs that demonstrate the best in current display creativity.

Texture

Whereas color catches the eye, texture draws the customer to the merchandise for close examination. Texture is more subtle than color but is nevertheless important in gaining a positive response from the customer.

Texture is the quality of the surface of an object or material. It has visual and tactile aspects. As a visual element, texture is the result of light being reflected or absorbed by the surface of the object or material. Satin reflects light, and velveteen absorbs light. As a tactile element, texture is essentially the "feel" of material as a person touches it.

The texture of the merchandise helps determine the particular mood in a display or presentation. One texture or type of texture could dominate a display so that there is a sense of harmony without confusion; however, contrasting textures help to achieve excitement. The display shown in Color Plate 2 plays up the smooth, shiny surface of the picture frame and the skirt by placing them near the more textured beaded blouse and jacket. Sometimes an unexpected combination of texture is most effective in capturing shoppers' attention, for example, satin with denim or linen with tweeds.

Line

Line directs the eye. Lines are of two basic types: straight and curved. Curved lines convey a feeling of grace, leisure, and softness and are often associated with feminity, as in Figure 4.4. Straight lines usually communicate strength and stability and are often associated with masculinity. Because of these associations, the dominant lines in women's advertisements are often curved, and the dominant lines in men's advertisements are usually straight.

The direction of the line is also expressive. A diagonal line conveys action and excitement. Sportswear and children's advertising and departmental interiors often use diagonals to generate the feeling of dynamic activity, as seen in Figure 4.5.

Vertical lines create an impression of dignity and stability and can be used well in prestige advertisements of higher-priced goods. Classic styles in men's and women's merchandise often can be featured to advantage when vertical lines are employed.

Horizontal lines create a mood of tranquility and repose and are effective in ads as well as displays for loungewear and lingerie, as shown in Figure 4.6.

Figure 4.4. The curved lines of the draped fabric as well as the curved lines in the garments create a relaxed, feminine mood. (Giusti, San Juan. Reproduced by permission of the Retail Reporting Bureau.)

Figure 4.5.   These diagonal lines convey a spirit of action. (Courtesy of the Retail Reporting Bureau.)

Although one type of line should dominate in a display or advertisement, other lines are needed to complete the composition and to add subtlety and interest. Figure 4.7 shows a display of men's wear. The dominant straight, vertical lines convey a sense of dignity, stability, and masculinity appropriate to this type of merchandise. The diagonal lines of the lapels and the curved lines of the shoulders and neck provide some interest while retaining the mood.

Figure 4.6. The horizontal line of the model gives a feeling of relaxation to this sleepwear window. (Saks Fifth Avenue, New York. Reproduced by permission of the Retail Reporting Bureau.)

Figure 4.7. Straight, vertical lines of the suit dominate this masculine display while the diagonal lines of the lapels provide a secondary direction. (Bergdorf Goodman, New York. Reproduced by permission of the Retail Reporting Bureau.)

Form

When lines connect they create form, which is the shape of the object. Straight lines produce angular forms, and curved lines create circular forms. Forms express moods similar to the lines that define them. In advertisements and displays the merchandise and props are the forms and should be chosen for the appropriateness of their shape for the particular promotion. Display forms come in different sizes and can be arranged in a variety of positions. The mannequins in Figure 4.8 are accented because of their contrast in shapes and lines.

Figure 4.8. Contrasting shapes and forms focus the eye on the mannequins in this display. (Lord & Taylor, New York City. Reproduced by permission of the Retail Reporting Bureau.)

Space

Space is the distance between forms. It is the expanse between objects, that is, the background upon which a figure is placed. The amount of space given to background helps to create mood and emphasis. Blank background in an advertisement is termed *white space*. Figure 4.9 has generous white space, which lends a feeling of authority to the advertisement. Figure 4.10 has little white space and many figures, which tends to create a sense of activity and excitement to move sales merchandise.

In terms of a store, space is the expanse between fixtures and in aisles. The size of the forms or fixtures has an impact on the customer, but so does the space in between. Open space has a calming effect because there is little visual stimulation from objects. This calmness is highly desirable in an area that contains high-priced merchandise that requires careful deliberation before a purchase is made. Furs and designer clothes are two such fashion departments.

Empty space allows the eye to be attracted to the few forms that do appear in the space, giving them important focus, as in Figure 4.11.

Figure 4.9. The white space in this advertisement emphasizes the figure in a commanding manner. (Courtesy of the Retail Reporting Bureau.)

Abundant space can be an exclamation point to a fashion statement. Using space extravagantly adds to a store's prestige image. This is true of space in a department layout as well as in advertising design.

When fixtures are very close together or merchandise is very crowded on the fixture, the customer becomes overloaded with negative visual stimulation. The result can be customer confusion, disgust, and fatigue. Many customers become uncertain about how to approach the shopping process and simply leave the scene. Little open space also crowds the customer and salesperson together, violating the customer's personal space. Edward T. Hall[1] observed that people prefer to maintain a personal distance of $1\frac{1}{2}$ to 4 feet. Friends may come close to this zone but do not penetrate it often. If customers are pressed into closer proximity than this while shopping, they will not find it pleasurable and will cease to shop.

[1] Edward T. Hall, *The Hidden Dimension* (New York: Doubleday, 1966).

Figure 4.10.   The lack of white space in this advertisement helps to move the eye from figure to figure and creates a sense of excitement and action. (Courtesy of the Retail Reporting Bureau.)

Crowded arrangements of merchandise usually project a bargain-store impression. Successful discount retailers use crowded merchandise arrangements skillfully to create a bargain-packed atmosphere. Even their advertising contains such visual clutter. Thus, the controlled use of empty space or crowded space is a valuable tool in projecting the character of a prestige store or a bargain discounter.

Design Principles

The principles of design guide the organization of the design elements for an effective visual impression. These principles help the display person decide where to place the merchandise in the display area. The five principles to be considered are unity, variety, emphasis, rhythm, balance, and proportion.

Figure 4.11. Empty space adds importance to the suit in this window. (Woodward & Lothrop, Washington, D.C. Reproduced by permission of the Retail Reporting Bureau.)

Unity

Unity is the arrangement of parts to produce a single, harmonious whole. In this sense, unity is the overriding master design principle. Unity is the compatibility of elements with each other and with the composition as a whole; thus, it is sometimes referred to as harmony. The first essential in achieving unity is to have a central idea or theme. The elements are then combined so that they reinforce this idea/theme.

Unity is achieved through the repetition of elements. This repetition ensures some commonality, as in related color schemes (discussed earlier in this chapter) or in use of a similar value of intensity of colors. Unity in light produces harmony in mood, for example, soft lights for tender moments. Unity in textures can reinforce the central theme, such as using leather and tweed for Derby Day. Repetition of diagonal lines in the face-out fixture and the mannequins in Color Plate 4 are very effective in holding the young men's department together in a harmonious whole. The obvious repetition of several mannequins dressed in the same garment practically guarantees unity as well as heightens the customer's awareness of the item. The impact and success of this method has contributed to its wide use.

Unity in an advertisement can be produced in a number of ways. First, the artwork should illustrate the same theme the words are conveying. Using the same style of lettering or typeface in different sizes will produce a unifying repetition of lines and shapes.

Appropriate use of the principles of unity is extremely effective in projecting the store's character. Attractive advertising and interior presentation are the best vehicles for heightening the customer's perception of the character of the store.

Variety

Variety means introducing a different aspect of an element for the purpose of creating interest. Unity limits novelty while variety produces contrast and interest. The two principles are linked, but unity must prevail if the composition is to work as a whole. However, unity must be balanced by some variety, or the visual image will be too dull to move the customer to action. Contrast in elements creates a tension that can make the composition lively. Contrast, especially if it is novel, is often the attention getter.

In Figure 4.12 the repetition of the jackets acts as a unifying element to this designer department for men. The small size and different shapes of the shirts, sweaters, and pants add interest. The contrasting sizes and shapes help prevent boredom. The designer's name and a partial form focus the passing shopper's eyes on the center of the department.

The skillful use of contrast in shape and size in a newspaper advertisement can draw the reader's attention to the headline, text, and illustration. Variety in voice and delivery style in a radio advertisement can spark the interest of the listener.

Emphasis

The design principle of emphasis involves the dominance and subordination of elements to create a center of attention. It arrests the eye at the most important part of the design and holds it there for a longer period of time than at any other part of the design. The eye looks for a place to rest. If it does not find a center of attention, it tires from the search and looks away. At that point the retailer has lost the opportunity to communicate the message.

Emphasis can be achieved in a number of ways. A frequently used method is the repetition of an element. A display created totally in

Figure 4.12.   Unity and variety in shapes and sizes make this an interesting and pleasing arrangement of merchandise. (Abraham and Strauss. Reproduced by permission of the Retail Reporting Bureau.)

purple would be difficult to ignore. The shopper's eye is attracted by the sheer amount of the color. Size is an obvious means of creating a focal point. The largest figure in an advertisement will draw attention and hold it longer than small figures. The advertisement in Figure 4.13 captures the readers' attention by means of an oversized model.

Contrast of any type can create emphasis, intensifying visual perception. Great embellishment prolongs the visual involvement and thus provides a point of focus. For example, the patterned jackets in Figure 4.14 command greater attention than do the solid accessories.

By contrast, an area devoid of pattern directs the eye to the object. This is the reason an advertisement with a large amount of white space captures the eye and focuses it on the figure, as in Figure 4.9. This concept of space providing emphasis works equally well in a display. Less merchandise in a window means more emphasis on the few items that are there.

Generally, a composition needs one major point of emphasis that holds the viewer's visual attention longer than any other point. This is achieved in part by subordinating all other elements (color, texture, line, form, space, etc.) to the major one.

Figure 4.13. Emphasis is achieved in this advertisement through the use of an oversized figure. (Courtesy of the Retail Reporting Bureau.)

All suburban stores open today 12-5 (closed Downtown). Order by phone 24 hours a day, 7 days a week. Dial toll-free 1-800-742-5397.

Rhythm

Rhythm is the regular organization of movement that carries the eye through the design. Emphasis focuses the eye on a point from which it begins its movement throughout the design. Rhythm provides continuity in a design by smoothly leading the eye from one piece of merchandise

Figure 4.14. In this display, emphasis is created by the pattern and the oversize photograph of the jacket. (Loewe, New York. Reproduced by permission of the Retail Reporting Bureau.)

to another until all are seen. Visual rhythm is achieved by means of repetition, progression, and radiation.

Repetition gives a regularity to the movement of the eye, as if it knows what is coming next. This produces an impression of constancy and stability. These impressions are helpful in promoting classic styles of clothing, especially for professional wear.

Progression is a more dynamic means of achieving eye movement than is repetition. It employs the sequential evolution of an element— for example, using light, medium, and dark colors sequentially in a design. Figure 4.15 shows an example of progression in size of objects similar in shape.

Another way to create rhythm is by radiation, that is, use of a circular arrangement that guides the eye from a central point around the parts of the design. Figure 4.16 illustrates an advertisement utilizing radiation to direct eye movement. Designs that employ radial rhythm or movement are often dramatic. However, this method of creative rhythm offers less variety than the other two methods.

Figure 4.15. Progression in size of the figures creates movement in this advertisement. (Courtesy of the Retail Reporting Bureau.)

In advertising, rhythm or movement is referred to as "gaze motion" and is often created by less formal means than those mentioned here. Advertisements are created to be read. Since English is read from left to right and from top to bottom, most English-speaking consumers are accustomed to making these types of eye movements when reading.

The simplest method for directing the eye is a continuous line, either straight or curved. In an advertisement, the reader's eye enters the ad in the upper left corner. It may proceed from left to right in a straight line, as shown in Figure 4.17.

In many ads (especially prestige ads) the eye starts at the top left quarter of the arrangement and proceeds downward to the lower right corner, as in Figure 4.18*a* and Figure 4.19. In more complex ads the eye path of the reader may proceed in a Z direction, as shown in Figure 4.18*b* or in a circular direction, as shown in Figure 4.18*c* and in Figure 4.16. Much of

Figure 4.16. Radial movement creates rhythm in this advertisement. (Courtesy of the Retail Reporting Bureau.)

the movement will be determined through the layout of the advertisement, which will be discussed more later.

Balance

Balance is a sense of equilibrium that provides a feeling of stability. When things are unbalanced, people have an uneasy feeling. Balance has to do with the relationship of the elements within the composition (advertising, display, etc.). Balance results when the parts of the design have equal visual weight. This is easily illustrated with a seesaw. When children of the same weight are on each end, the seesaw balances on the fulcrum at center point, as shown in Figure 4.20.

SYMMETRICAL BALANCE   Visual weight works like physical weight to produce a sense of balance. Balance achieved through the use of identical objects or very similar objects on either side of the center is known as symmetrical or formal balance and produces a sense of dignity, calm, and repose. Symmetrical balance is effective in promoting classic goods for important occasions, such as confirmation dresses or business suits for a job interview. Figure 4.21 shows a formally balanced advertisement that

Figure 4.17. This advertisement shows one method of directing the eye movement through an advertisement. (Courtesy of the Retail Reporting Bureau.)

has a bit of drama added through the use of diagonal lines in the garments and the legs.

ASYMMETRICAL BALANCE   Balance can also be achieved using unlike objects. This type of balance is referred to as asymmetrical or informal balance. Again using the seesaw as an example, asymmetrical balance can be illustrated using objects that are visually equal in weight but not equal in style or shape, as in Figure 4.20b and c. The display in

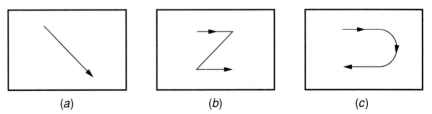

Figure 4.18. Three typical gaze motions used in newspaper and magazine advertisements.

Figure 4.19. The gaze motion in this advertisement begins at the top left and proceeds downward to the lower right corner of the page. (Courtesy of the Retail Reporting Bureau.)

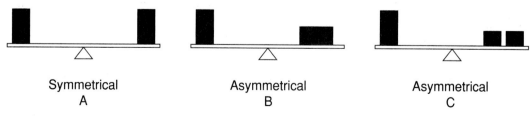

Figure 4.20. Types of balance.

Figure 4.21. Formal or symmetrical balance used in an advertisement. The diagonal lines of the legs make the ad more interesting than vertical legs would have. (Courtesy of the Retail Reporting Bureau.)

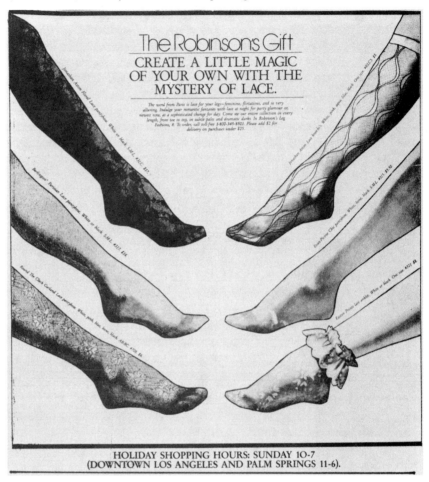

Figure 4.22 achieves balance even though the objects in the display are of different sizes. Balance is achieved in part by the extra visual weight created by the open drawer at the lower right. In the case of objects of different weight, the heavier one could be moved closer to the center to achieve balance, as illustrated in Figure 4-20*b*.

Asymmetrical balance generates a sense of active informality. This type of balance is preferred in advertising and display over formal balance because it is more stimulating to the eye. Furthermore, it offers more variety in the arrangement of merchandise. The sense of action

Figure 4.22.   This Father's Day display is balanced asymmetrically for interest. (Macy's, San Francisco. Reproduced by permission of the Retail Reporting Bureau.)

can carry over to customers and move them to purchase decisions more quickly than the formality of symmetrical arrangements of merchandise.

The preceding examples showed balance in terms of size; however, balance needs to occur in other elements as well. For example, dark values of colors appear heavier than light values. Dull textures appear heavier than smooth textures and should be placed closer to the center to balance the design.

Proportion

The design principle of proportion involves ratios, the quantitative comparisons of parts of a design to each other and to the whole. These ratios apply to sizes (length to width to height), to amounts of color used (the amount of red, for instance, in a design in relation to the amount of white), to spaces (the quantity of open spaces in relation to closed ones, and the intervals between these), to forms (the size of small forms in relation to large, or the number of round forms versus square), and to texture (the amount of smooth surface compared with rough)."[2]

Incorporating objects that are disproportional to the merchandise can attract attention. Props that are out of scale with the merchandise bring a fresh approach to otherwise routine displays. This technique is especially effective with small accessory items. Using a giant shoe or handbag can draw the eye to an otherwise diffuse array of small items.

There is more to visual presentation than meets the eye. Although sound and fragrance are not actually a part of the visual image of the store, they can be considered along with the visual because they also contribute greatly to the store ambience. Most retail stores have music playing in the background. Obviously, it should be in keeping with the store image and target customer—for example, rock music for a trendy shop appealing to young people and classical music for the expensive fur department. Many upscale stores are using expensive fragrances to engage another sense in order to heighten the pleasure of each shopping experience and to lend more prestige to the store image.

Summary

The skilled practitioner can create effective displays, advertisements, and other promotional designs while bending or breaking some of the principles that have been discussed in this chapter; however, the prudent individual would be wise to heed them for best results. The intent is to manipulate the elements of design in promotion to bring about a perception of the merchandise that is favorable and that will move the potential consumer to positive action immediately. A class in the use of art principles would be an invaluable course for anyone in the merchandising and promotion areas.

[2] Helen Marie Evans and Carla Davis Dumesnil, *An Invitation to Design* (New York: Macmillan, 1982), p. 51.

CHAPTER 5

Visual Merchandising

To display is to show, to exhibit, to make visible. A display must show merchandise in order to sell the customer. *Visual merchandising* is the accepted broad term used for the function of showing goods. The older and more limited term *display* is often used to refer to an individual visual presentation of goods. Visual merchandising can encompass all aspects of the total visual impact of the store and its merchandise. This includes store design, fixtures, and merchandise presentation. Definitions of the terms *visual merchandising* and *merchandise presentation* may vary somewhat from store to store. Generally, visual merchandising is the more expansive term and can encompass window displays and interior displays. It can also include the visual merchandise presentation of the goods for sale on the floor of the store (see Chapter 6). As shopping malls proliferate, the store itself becomes the vehicle for visual presentation.

The purpose of visual merchandising is to promote the sale of merchandise while reflecting the store image. It also informs the public of the type of merchandise in the store—whether it is clothing, housewares, or flowers. The price range of the goods, the fashion character, and the quality of the merchandise should also be presented in the visual merchandising of the store.

The purpose of a display is to sell specific merchandise. A display can also be the follow-through of an ad. It should attract attention and stimulate the customer sufficiently to lead to a purchase decision. The image the shopper can acquire through using the merchandise should be presented in the display.

Displays can be used to introduce a new product, a fashion trend, or a new "look" or idea. Effective displays educate the consumer as to how the new item can be used or worn and how it can be accessorized. Such a display results from the combination of art, design, and merchandising.

A well-planned display should say something special to the shopper about the merchandise, the store, and the management, thus reinforcing and enhancing the store's image.

Plans and Schedules

Seasons

The four seasons of the year—spring, summer, fall and winter—determine the promotional calendar for developing themes for visual presentation. The weather patterns of the region where the store is located also help to determine the type of displays. For example, winter in Florida is not the same as winter in New York. The major themes of the store revolve around these regional seasons. The exception is Christmas, a definite display period that lasts four to eight weeks. The greatest dollar outlay is spent for Christmas presentation because of the volume of retail sales and the excitement created by this holiday.

SPRING AND SUMMER   Spring merchandise, often combined with spring flowers, creates a refreshing feeling in a store. Because the meaning of spring is new growth and rebirth of nature, the trims are often flowers—either real or artificial. The flowers commonly reflect a current color trend to blend with the apparel and to create a joyous impact. Multicolor flowers can be used to create a feeling of the season without limiting the displays to specific color themes. Large green plants can be used to give a sense of growth as well as quality. Select plants that require a low amount of light unless there is easy access to light and time to work with the plants. The personnel at a greenhouse can supply appropriate purchase ideas. Many large stores, rather than purchasing and caring for the plants, arrange to have plant maintenance provided by companies from which they rent the plants. If imitation plants are used, they look best from a distance, where an illusion can be created. However, anything false can have a negative impression on many people. A quality fashion store selling natural fibers of cotton, wool, linen, and silk would create mixed messages by using obviously false flowers and plants.

FALL AND WINTER   Fall also exemplifies a beginning—new school year, new jobs, new clothes. This is a time of high sales volume in fashion stores, and the display budget is larger than for spring. Fall trim relies on the perception of the changing colors of nature. The colors of orange and brown with deep reds and yellows are associated with leaves and the fall fruits of apples, pumpkins, gourds, and nuts and influence the trims used. Fabrics such as plaids, corduroy, and flannel as well as skeins of yarn can be used for an artistic display.

Holiday Promotions

Promotions for regular-price and sale-price merchandise evolve from holidays. The most popular holidays for display opportunities are:

Valentine's Day (February 14). Displays are usually set up two weeks prior, with red as the principal theme.

Easter (date varies). Stores feature dressier apparel along with spring flowers. Children's stores or departments can use eggs, bunnies, and chickens for props. These areas should have displays three weeks prior to Easter.

Mother's Day (second Sunday in May). A single-color or floral theme can be a simple way to pull the idea together in Mother's Day gift areas. Banners and signs are often used to remind customers of the approaching holiday. These displays need to be set up two weeks prior to Mother's Day.

Memorial Day (usually the last Monday in May). This is usually a sale period for spring and summer apparel. Sale signs are important. Flags or a picnic theme indicating the beginning of summer could be used.

Father's Day (third Sunday in June). Set up three weeks in advance with signs and/or banners. Themes based on sports activities are often used.

Independence Day (July 4). This is the summer clearance period, especially for swimwear, playwear, and items such as sandals, picnic items, and fans. Signs, banners, and flags are usually the only display elements used.

Back-to-school (promotions begin in July and August). This promotion applies to department stores and specialty stores. The total trim is usually related to fall so that there is a tie-in with the overall store theme. Major fall props can be used until the Christmas season, but specific back-to-school signs and trims should be removed by the end of September.

Labor Day (first Monday in September). This is another sale sign and banner display opportunity. Late summer and transitional fashion merchandise will be reduced for clearance.

Halloween (October 31). This involves store displays of pumpkins, costumes, and ghosts to create a festive feeling. Setup is one week prior to the day.

Thanksgiving (fourth Thursday in November). Christmas trim should be in place on the Friday after Thanksgiving, as this day is the beginning of the Christmas season. Specialty stores may wait but should have some decorations in place. These six weeks constitute the strongest selling period of the year. The display task is the largest as well as the most rewarding of the year. It is hard, physical work that is highly creative and involves many extra hours. When there is a Santa, he should be in place and ready to greet children and parents by December 1.

Christmas (December 25). The Christmas season is presented by Thanksgiving or shortly thereafter in most stores. These decorations are often repeated from year to year, with money spent to update and add to the festive look of the store. A major outlay of money is necessary to change the display look of this season, so it is advisable to consider a traditional or old-fashioned Christmas theme rather than a contemporary, short-lived trend in decoration. A traditional look can be freshened for fewer dollars with the use of holiday greenery and flowers, which will add a feeling of realism and life to the decorations. Large amounts of red and green with touches of gold or silver will communicate the holiday mood. Using fabric to recover walls, columns, and valances gives the store a special look. Some of the red can remain for the Valentine promotion period in some departments.

Holiday decorations should remain up until January 1 because of the charming effect created and the expense of the props, as well as the time involved in creating the Christmas theme. Store display departments should not prematurely strip the decorations in order to avoid the store appearing bare and bleak. There will be heavy traffic in the store the two weeks following Christmas because of clearances and exchanges. For example, New York City stores do not remove holiday decorations until early in January, and these are some of the best-displayed stores in the country.

Special Sales

White sales (linen sales over the entire month of January)

New Year's (a continuation of winter clearances)

Lincoln's and Washington's birthday sales (combined for Presidents' Days sale)

Pre-Easter events and/or after-Easter clearances

Founder's Day sale and Anniversary sale (two promotions frequently used for storewide events in the spring and fall)

Themes/ Ideas

The first floor of a large, multilevel department store makes an important impression on the customer. The display theme used here can be carried throughout the store to create a feeling of continuity. Variations of the theme can be used for individual departments. A specialty store should have an overall theme to create a unified store image. Harmonious themes can be achieved by the use of related architectural features, banners, signs, flowers, matching properties, valance colors, matching coverings for mannequin stands, and color-coordinated groups of fashions. In a small store a simple theme should be chosen because it can be altered more often to provide a fresh appearance.

To ensure compatibility, overall trims and decorative colors should be selected after most of the merchandise has been ordered for the season. To select color schemes and trim before placing apparel orders is dangerous because buyers select fashion colors based on the store's regional location and previous selling history with such goods. A common mistake is to select a strong color theme to feature in store presentation where the color is so dominant that the merchandise loses viability.

Visual excitement must be created in each department. Repeating the use of two mannequins and decorative plants at the entrance of every fashion department, for example, is uninteresting. Each area needs visual variety to attract attention.

When selecting a visual theme for a department or shop concept, make sure it is compatible to all the merchandise. For example, a western theme would not be appropriate in a department of young men's clothing if playwear and dresswear are featured in the area. In developing themes for several shops on a floor of a department store, experienced display personnel plan so that the customer will be attracted to all the shops. To accomplish this, they make all themes separate but equal in eye appeal. A conflict of themes will result if one or two are visually stronger than the others.

One source of ideas is the published service "Views and Reviews," provided by the Retail Reporting Bureau, 101 Fifth Avenue, New York, NY 10003. This service regularly issues color pictures showing recent displays of top retailers from everywhere in the country as well as overseas. Another source of ideas are out-of-town stores, which can be visited on market trips. The display person should always be looking for display ideas as well as ideas for new props.

In June and December the display industries have a giant trade fair in New York City to show the newest concepts. Large department stores usually send representatives to these week-long exhibitions to see new display props and fixtures and to look for new ideas in decorations and methods. The display fair is a separate market and takes place at a time when the fashion buyers are not in market. Small stores usually do not have the funds or time to set aside an entire week for display inspiration.

A variety of visual experiences from plays, movies, museums, and magazines provide input to the creative process. Major city and college libraries have publications that are devoted to display creativity. These sources also have books on theater arts that can inspire display ideas. Of special interest are the monthly publications for the visual presentation field, which are full of ideas for window and interior displays.

Another source of ideas is *Show and Sell: A Guidebook for Display Ideas* by Martin M. Pegler (Cincinnati: S.T. Publications, 1970). This book is in the form of a dictionary. Sample entries are: *anniversary, angels, carriage, clearance, dolls, ice cream, chairs, palm trees, paper bags, posters, sun,* and *wagon wheel.*

Colleagues who perform a similar display task in other stores are an excellent resource for ideas. The current lifestyle of the store's target customer can also generate ideas. If the customer loves to spend weekends boating and skiing, props reflecting these activities could be prominent in various displays. The fashion market itself can provide inspiration. Buyers who go into the garment market can glean ideas for themes from the designers. For instance, if a fashion designer is inspired by a nineteenth-century French artist's particular painting style and coloring concepts, the store could use a theme and color scheme inspired by that artist's work. Copies of paintings could be borrowed or rented from a library. One season Ann Klein II named silk prints after Italian museums and cities. For a given season, a store display could include a reproduction of an Italian painting from a gallery or museum to give a feeling of beauty and historic art.

Extensive reading in relation to display ideas means that one is constantly scanning everything in the fashion world. Magazines such as *Better Homes and Gardens* will show ideas for flower arrangements and small props such as antique tables. Fashion magazines such as *Vogue, Harper's Bazaar, Southern Living,* and *Esquire* are good sources of elegant expression.

The merchandise itself will often suggest an associative idea. The plaid lining of a jacket naturally suggests that the display can emphasize a Scottish theme. It could be bagpipes and large pieces of plaid fabric from Scotland or Ireland. Merchandise that has an ethnic print or design would suggest a theme related to the culture that inspired the design. Leather handbags suggest the use of large uncut hides to draw attention to the entire display. Using bales of cotton or cotton bolls with beautiful cotton fashions can remind customers of the qualities of natural fibers.

Life Expectancy of Displays

According to Emily M. Mauger,
   Merchandise definitely should be changed in display areas every 7 to 14 days because:

1. The same people often pass a display area daily and they like to see new or different displays.
2. Periodic changes assure better coordination between departments and emphasize the promotion of merchandise.
3. The customer will become acquainted with more of the varied stock a store has to offer.
4. Items left on display too long soil, fade, rust, become dingy and therefore cannot be sold as first quality merchandise.
5. Displays are the most conspicuous part of the store, and they should be kept interesting at all times.[1]

There are two issues in considering the life expectancy of the display. One is the merchandise; the other is the props. If it is a seasonal idea, such as back-to-school or Christmas, the props may remain the same since they are usually costly and often are difficult to set up. The actual fashion merchandise in front of the props should be changed more frequently. The typical merchandise change schedule a store employs is determined primarily by: (1) the traffic in the store and how frequently the same people visit the store, and (2) how many display staff members are available to change the merchandise. If sales associates can easily change the merchandise, such conversions are convenient. If mannequins are used and skilled display personnel are needed to make changes, paying these personnel to change mannequins every week can become expensive. Consequently, many small stores do not have a large number of mannequins. Also, these stores must display the merchandise so it is immediately accessible for the customer to try on and for the salesperson to sell. There is a trend toward the use of goosenecks or partial mannequins from which garments are easily removed.

   There is commonly a difference in the schedule for changing displays between specialty shops and department stores. Department stores draw on a wider geographic area and generally bring in a greater

---

[1]   Emily M. Mauger, *Modern Display Techniques* (New York: Fairchild Publications, 1980), p. 69

number of people who come less frequently. The specialty store draws on a smaller group and may attract customers who come in more often. It is more important that this type of fashion specialty shop change displays frequently and easily.

Some interior displays are effective in that the merchandise is sold directly from them, and these can be changed daily. It is really a compliment to the person who has installed the display when its merchandise sells very quickly. Frequently changed display areas present more merchandise, give more fashion messages to the customer, and offer more opportunities for the customer to purchase. Freshly merchandised displays also provide the salespeople with opportunities for new ideas of coordination and additional ways to build a sale.

Displays that take a long time to change reduce the selling opportunities, because the longer the display area is vacant, the less usable it is for presenting merchandise. The plan for installing a display should be to finish that area quickly before moving on to another display area. Windows and areas where there are large numbers of potential customers passing by should be changed during the lowest level of customer traffic, such as early in the morning and late at night after the store has closed.

If windows cannot be changed when the traffic is low, a sign should be placed in the window stating when the display windows will be open again. For instance, New York City stores change their displays the same time every week, and there may be a sign that reads: "These displays are being changed and can be viewed tomorrow morning at 10:00." At Christmastime when the elaborate window displays are set up at Lord & Taylor and Saks Fifth Avenue, signs indicate the date and time the windows will open. The windows are so spectacular that people actually line up to see the displays when they are first opened for viewing.

New trends can become short-term displays. The hottest new item that arrives should be quickly inserted into an appropriate display. If the item never develops past a fad, it should be removed as it begins to lose selling momentum.

A display is vulnerable to the traffic in the store. Children can place their soiled hands on the merchandise, or adults may search for the price ticket and pull at the garment until it is no longer attractively arranged. Displays need to be checked each day to be sure they are in good condition. Displayed merchandise is also vulnerable to sunlight fading and dust; colors such as blue, purple, and green used in silks will fade very quickly under strong lights and in daylight. In addition, the public may place shopping bags or throw debris into the displays, so areas should be reviewed regularly to be sure they are tidy and in good repair. Some displays near doors or windows should be checked for dead insects or dust that accumulates.

Types of Displays

Window Displays

Main street or downtown shopping has declined in most cities, so window shopping is rare except in a few large cities. The trend toward malls has almost eliminated the display window that faces out to the street.

A *closed-back window* is a typical window with a large area of plate glass and walls enclosing the remaining three sides. There is a door on one of these walls through which props and merchandise are passed. Many doors are not wide enough for large props, which therefore are commonly made in sections and reassembled in the window.

Some stores have a single display window or a pair of windows separated by the store entrance. Other stores have several windows—four or more. These may be separated by doors or walls. Display windows may also consist of one very long window 20 or more feet in length; the only divider is the metal band that retains the plate glass. Dividers can be added inside such a window to separate its space into smaller units. The display person can mass several mannequins for a major presentation in this type of window or divide it into several smaller individual mannequin displays.[2] (See Color Plate 5.)

The advantages of a closed window are many. The merchandise is protected from shoppers who could touch and disrupt it. The closed-in area makes it possible to present any seasonal fashion or mood within the display. The setting for festive wear can be an intimate candlelit evening even though the store itself may be brightly lit. The walls of the closed window will also block the view into the store and thus keep the merchandise floor from detracting from the impression being created in the window.

Closed windows also have several disadvantages. They are more costly to construct than open windows. They take up valuable floor space that could be used for selling. More time is required to create displays because the entire space must participate in the look of the presentation. More props are used than would be needed in an open window.

Open-back windows do not have a back wall, thus presenting a view into the selling area beyond. Extra effort is required to keep the selling area in the background from distracting the viewer. Screens, plants, or see-through drapery effects can be used to create a backdrop. (See Figure 5.1.) The trend toward opening the store to full view of sidewalk traffic is used in smaller stores as well as many large department stores.

---

[2]   Martin M. Pegler, *Visual Merchandising and Display* (New York: Fairchild Publications, 1983), p. 7.

Figure 5.1. Open window. The black-and-white graphic serves to separate the display area from the store beyond, and the live tropical plants provide the place and the time. (Jaeger's, Manhasset, N.Y. Reproduced by permission of the Retail Reporting Bureau.)

This type of window stimulates and invites the passerby to come in and look around. When accomplished properly, this treatment can be very effective. However, lighting is a problem, as spotlights may accidently be directed to the eye of the customer who approaches the display. Excessive glare and reflection are also problems. Using the display to coordinate with the merchandise directly behind the window will enhance the merchandise being presented and create a less confusing display. Using the same color scheme behind the display is also an effective merchandising and display technique.

Open windows take less space and less money to construct, but they are vulnerable to customers who may disturb the merchandise. Mood setting is difficult because of the store and its distracting lighting in the background.

Partially open windows are very similar to open windows except they use versions of separation. These serve to screen the window space from the selling floor yet do not block the entire view to the store. The partition can be solid or open material such as railings, latticework, or wrought iron. This type of window is a useful compromise between the previously discussed types. The partial divider makes it less likely that customers and small children will disturb the display area, and such a display is not as expensive as the closed window. Furthermore, it does not use as much space.

An *island window* has glass on all four sides so that merchandise can be viewed from all directions. Island windows are often in arcade fronts and are isolated from the rest of the building. Since there is not a solid back, the display person cannot pin, gather, and wire the props and merchandise as in other windows. Fortunately, there is usually a distinct traffic pattern so that the display person can concentrate on one view and reduce the focus on the other views.

Lighting is a problem in an island window since lights will be visible from every direction. Direct the lights to the merchandise and avoid the glass as much as possible because the light can hit the eye of the passerby if not carefully placed. The interference from activities around the island display may be compounded in this type of window.

A *shadow box* is a small elevated window. These windows often are on side streets and may have previously been full-size windows. Shadow boxes are used for smaller items such as folded shirts with ties and sweaters; accessories such as jewelry, handbags, and shoes; children's fashions; and home furnishings such as china and crystal. Because the space is small and shallow, strong color contrasts and dramatic effects are necessary to attract attention.

Interior Displays

Displays inside the store should relate to the displays seen in the windows. Good display effects should continue inside the store to move customer traffic through the store. The aisles, the signs that direct the customer, the walls, and the interior displays are most important to the total visual concept of the store. Each department, shelf, counter, ledge, case, and furnishing in addition to the display areas requires analysis in executing display techniques. The furnishings of the store should be attractive and placed so as to enhance the visual impact on the customer. There should be updating and improvements in fixtures to avoid a stagnant, dated effect. For example, the seasons of the year usually dictate visual changes.

An island display is used at the entrance to a department within the store and is viewable from all sides. It usually is on a raised platform or uses a different flooring material such as an area rug. An island display should present a special fashion story. It may carry a storewide or departmental theme. Most importantly, the merchandise used in the display should be available nearby for the display to be effective. Clear views of island displays are an important consideration.

Ledges are usually the top spaces of a backup storage unit behind a selling counter[3] or a shelf placed above presentations of merchandise. In

[3]   Martin M. Pegler, *Visual Merchandising and Display* (New York: Fairchild Publications, 1983), p. 21.

large stores, the main floor may have such high ceilings that mannequin groups or other props are usable. Macy's in New York usually has very large and elaborate flower arrangements for their annual flower show on such ledges. In elevated ledge locations above the floor traffic, attractive displays provide a cheerful spectacle. Extra lighting is used to focus on the merchandise. (See Figure 5.2.)

Most new or remodeled stores lower the ceilings for better lighting of the merchandise as well as energy efficiency. When large ledges are used with lower ceilings, the mannequins can sit or kneel to fit the narrow space. Partial forms are also a good choice when ledge space is limited in height.

The walls in a store can be an excellent area for display. A flat wall can use fixtures for hanging merchandise. If the top rows are face-outs as opposed to straight rods, productive selling displays result. A flat wall

Figure 5.2. Ledge and floor displays: a menswear shop—for the relaxing type. The shallow shop seems to come to the aisle and brings the light-colored merchandise along with it. Nautical props are combined with the simple white floor fixtures to make a seaworthy setting for Dockers. The well-illuminated back wall carries displays and signage over the wall-hung, folded, and binned garments—above the level of the floor merchandise—and makes ready eye contact with the shopper in the aisle. The coordinated displays explain what is available and what can be teamed up with what. (Foley's, Penn Square, Oklahoma City. Reproduced by permission of the Retail Reporting Bureau.)

with shelves for folded merchandise can be used for such items as shirts, sweaters, table linens, and dishes. Color arrangements can be the key to attracting the customer into the department. The end of a wall that extends toward an aisle can also be used to create a highly visible display area using a T-wall extension.

Display cubes are available in various sizes and of various materials. They are often used in wide aisles to gain attention for a special product or adjacent to the aisle to draw the customer into the department. Cubes can show any goods, from cosmetics to expensive art objects. Shoe departments use them in clusters to show the shoe selection. Houseware departments employ them to display and also to hold stock. The materials used should coordinate with the decoration of the surrounding department and may be natural wood, laminated materials, or colorful fabrics. (See Figure 5.3.)

The Trend away from Isolated Displays

Isolated displays are less frequently used now than in the past, because they require too much time and expensive props such as mannequins. They are often far from the merchandise to which they relate. The

Figure 5.3. Cubes can be used for display or to show quantities for purchase. (Saks Fifth Avenue, New York. Reproduced by permission of the Retail Reporting Bureau.)

customer is stimulated by the display and should have immediate access to the merchandise. For example, when a red dress is on a mannequin, a T-stand should be placed nearby with other sizes of the red dress. Such a display catches the eye of potential customers passing by and draws them into the department. When a display is located near the merchandise, the natural traffic flow is movement from the mannequin to the fixture, which encourages customers to touch, feel, and possibly try on the garments.

The idea is to make it easy for the customer to see the new merchandise and then easily find it without the help of a salesperson. Merchandise can often be presold by the display and the fixture that holds the garments.

Elements of Display

The Merchandise

The most important element of a display is the merchandise. Props are useful but should never be the focus and become more important than the merchandise. To create a good display requires the use of the art principles discussed in Chapter 4 involving line, form, balance, color, and light. The eye appeal of the display is responsible for most impulse sales.

Mannequins and Forms

A mannequin is a three-dimensional form representing the human body. It can be somewhat idealized or stylized to give a certain look, which is often more slender than the average figure. Mannequins vary in size and proportion. They represent all age groups and can be obtained in many positions—standing, kneeling, reclining, and in action positions such as swinging to hit a tennis ball or diving. Some mannequins do not have arms or full torsos. Bust forms are used to give the look of the top part of the body.

The use of mannequins in a display of apparel tells the customer how a person will look in the garment. Mannequins throughout the store can effectively create a positive fashion image. They are often referred to as silent salespeople because they do an excellent job of showing the total garment fashionably accessorized. Every mannequin is designed to express a personality, and it is very important to select an attitude that is compatible with the store's distinctive image. If the store has a light, sunny personality, then a youthful, open-faced mannequin would be a good choice. For an upscale store, a more aloof, sophisticated look to the face and a casual slump to the torso may be appropriate.

Mannequin styles and personalities have changed just like all other aspects of life. They have become more realistic. Even though mannequins still appear very slender, the bustline has become more true to life and a slight "tummy" shape has been added. There are also mannequins representing the large-size customer, although the mannequin industry has had difficulty creating a realistic and pleasing appearance in this category. Male mannequins have become slightly larger. In response to the boom in exercise and bodybuilding, muscles and ripples are appearing on both male and female forms. The facial look is strong, intelligent, and cultured.

Mannequins come in three types: realistic, semirealistic, and abstract. Some do not have faces, just an oval shape for the head without eyelashes. Often this type does not have hair, so it can be sprayed in metallic pigments—black, grey, or whatever color is desired. The realistic type uses simulated hair, eyelashes, colored eyes, and other effects.

A decision on which type of mannequin to use needs to be made by considering the target customer personality and the store image. The realistic mannequin should portray the particular character of target customers. It should have the characteristic smile and posture to be posable in an activity in which the target customer might participate. The selection of mannequins might include the ethnic groups that shop the store. The problem with high-fashion mannequins is that the hairstyle and makeup have to be changed often to stay abreast of fashion. Some mannequins can be sent back to the manufacturer repair specialist to be corrected and have the makeup changed. However, there is lost time during the repairs. Consequently, most of the realistic high-fashion mannequins are used by stores that have expansive budgets for display materials. (See Color Plate 5). New mannequins may cost hundreds of dollars ($800–$1,000). Refurbishing them from time to time is an additional expense.

The abstract mannequin is less expensive to maintain because hairstyle and makeup do not change. It projects a high-tech, severe look that is well suited to attract a particular target group. This would be inappropriate for a traditional store or one that requires a gentle "country look." In these situations a better solution might be a dress form. It is a three-dimensional representation of a part of the human anatomy, which could be the torso, the bust, the area from the shoulder to waist, or the hips to ankles. Since less of the figure is seen, there is less of an apparent mood. The merchandise itself sets the stage.

Mannequins are also selected according to sizing dimensions. For instance, the "missy" mannequin differs from the junior mannequin.

Obviously, there is a difference in the sizing of children and youth mannequins. Care must be taken to be very specific in the sizing of mannequins for use in each fashion department. Purchasers of the mannequins should check the poses to see that different styles of apparel will fit and that enough different postures are possible to show all types of clothing, such as straight skirts, full skirts, and pants.

Skin tones are also important. They should complement the various types of clothing the mannequins will display. Unless the budget allows a variety of makeup styles, a simple but subtle makeup can be chosen rather than a distinctive one so that it can be used with a wide variety of looks. Some manufacturers offer cosmetic touch-ups as part of the service to the purchaser. Retailers should inquire about the availability of this service at the time of purchase.

There are several substitutes for mannequins. Soft-sculptured forms are especially popular for showing children's clothing. They bend easily into many positions with no risk of breakage. They are also easy to dress. Cutouts are even less expensive, can be made with joints that allow different poses, and cutouts are useful especially in children's areas and casual wear departments for men and women. A high-tech look can be achieved with pipe forms.

Forms are the most frequent substitutes for the complete mannequin. They have three advantages: (1) they are less expensive, (2) they are easy to change, and (3) they are less visible because they have fewer distinguishing characteristics. Because they are practical for changing merchandise easily, sales associates can often do this and save the store the extra expense of trained display personnel. The torso form allows the garments to be more readily available for the salesperson to sell to the customer immediately. Less space is required, which can be a consideration for the store with small display areas. They also take less room for storage when not in use.

The dressmaker form does not have arms or legs, but it is flexible in height and can be raised and lowered. Pins can be used to make the garment fit easily, and tissue can be added to stuff the sleeves of the garment for more shaping. It does not have exposed parts such as hands and a head when dressed; therefore, there is no problem of matching shoes. The only part that will be visible is the neck area. Fabrics such as lace, satin, or a scarf that is appropriate to the garment can be used to cover the neck. Some forms have a rich wood finish that has a traditional look. See Figure 5.4 for a form with an upholstered head.

Props

A prop is anything used in the display to help decorate the area and accent the style of the fashion. The term *props* is a contraction of *properties*

Figure 5.4. Use of a form. The striped suit is shown on a dress form with an upholstered head and articulated wooden arms and hands. (Kenzo, Madison Ave., New York. Reproduced by permission of the Retail Reporting Bureau.)

and probably comes from the theater, where props are used to decorate a scene and thus tell a story. The props in a display enhance the fashion message, help to tell the story, and should not compete with the merchandise. They should be interesting and relevant to the merchandise.

Props can be purchased from display manufacturers or made in the store. They can also be borrowed from cooperating neighboring stores. A prop could be a chair, a table, a platform, a plant, a flower, a colorful backdrop, a Santa Claus mannequin, or a stuffed animal. They could include tinsel or glitter. Props are often used to convey the impression of the lifestyle in which the merchandise would be used. For instance, a luggage display could use travel brochures or scenic photographs to suggest the activity in which the customer may be involved when using the merchandise.

The National Association of Design Industries and the Western Association of Visual Merchandising conduct display fairs twice a year. Retailers send their display people to search out new ideas in display and fixtures. At the show are many manufacturers who can show display people various elements for merchandise presentation. These include floor and stock fixtures in addition to props, mannequins, lighting fixtures, and sign making apparatus.

Many props can be locally borrowed or rented. The local hardware store will have ladders, paint cans, and paint brushes that could be used for a spring theme called "A Fresh Start." Bales of straw from a feed store or a local farmer provide interesting props. The local garden supply center can provide crossties, lumber, flower pots, and gardening tools. Picture frames make simple focus props in a display for accessory items. Dried flowers and leaves can be acquired from the countryside and properly treated. Art galleries, museum shops, and handicraft stores may also offer props when promoting the latest art show.

Antique pieces are frequently used as props because they have an attractive quality. The store needs a variety of these so they can be moved about to break large areas into smaller spaces. Avoid the use of the same chair and the same chest in the same window month after month. Such displays begin to look alike and fail to make an impact on the viewer.

Christmas is the time when props can create a special feeling and spirit. At this time there is a tendency to use an abundance of Santas, reindeer, Christmas plants, trees, and tinsel. The customer reacts joyfully to Christmas displays. Instead of just a few flowers on counters and in displays, this time of year demands near saturation of Christmas decor to sell the joy of the season completely.

The art elements and principles mentioned in Chapter 4 should be a guide for arranging props. Once the appropriate props are selected, how they are arranged within the display becomes equally important. Rules of good design should be observed.

Props such as screens or urns are selected because of their versatility. If screens are chosen with grids, garments can be hung from them to create a variety of proportions and shapes. Urns can be spray-painted red for Valentine's Day and green for St. Patrick's Day, or any other color appropriate for a particular theme. Other items such as dried or silk flowers may be used in more than one display during a year by being arranged in different color groupings. Bricks are good props because they can be stacked at different levels or moved about and are fairly indestructible. The buyers in department stores have little input into the props selection, whereas the manager or owner of a specialty shop would have the responsibility of selecting props as well as directing others to arrange the props in displays.

Signage

Signage is a visual and graphic form of communication to the customer by the use of mechanical or hand lettering or any recognizable symbols.

Store signs, whether they are inside or outside, can have a considerable impact on the store's image as well as a customer's understanding of the message. Whether the sign is large or small, it should be evaluated as to its legibility. This legibility is determined by its size, color, and the style of lettering used. An exception is a store with a recognized logo that is not read very easily but is so familiar that it is immediately understood; for example, Lord & Taylor's logo in Figure 4.19.

The color of paper and ink is very important in signs with black on white or white on black being the easiest to read. Creating contrast in the sign will achieve the best results, as it enables the customer to read and understand the message readily. When appropriate, yellow is an excellent color to use in signing because, according to research, it catches the eye and holds the attention better than any other background color. This is especially true when it is used with black lettering. The colors used should be relevant to the character of the store.

There are many styles of type, from block lettering to script. These will be discussed more in Chapter 9. They should be selected to reflect the image of the store and the clientele. A store that caters primarily to juniors could use rounded, simple letters with no capitals to indicate a more casual look (see Figure 4.5). A more sophisticated store would tend to choose an elongated script as in the Lord & Taylor ad, Figure 4.19. All of these choices depend upon the store image. The large department stores with their own sign shops make signs that are hand-lettered and can be laminated. Some artists can do calligraphy; others can silkscreen multiple signs. If a poster is needed, a local artist who does freelance work is a good source.

Signs are used on the exterior to designate the name of the store. They are also used to locate departments in large stores or shops within a section. Signs should also give directions and indicate department locations, such as petites or large women. They can also announce a special event such as a fashion show or a personal appearance by a celebrity. They can indicate locations of fitting rooms and rest room facilities, escalators, and elevators. An important sign category is the directory of where departments can be found. All signs should be coordinated in style and use a similar type of lettering.

Signs can be located in display windows or in display vignettes inside the store. The practice of putting signs with displays has varied over the years, and there have been debates on whether price signs and other messages should be included in displays. This depends on what is appropriate policy for each store. Lord & Taylor usually indicates the designers featured in the windows and the location of the merchandise along with a selling statement.

Too much lettering on a sign will not be read, so determining what goes on a sign requires thought and editing. The most common mistake is too much information as opposed to verbal economy. Some fashion stores rarely indicate the prices of the garments in a display. In a high-fashion operation, price is of little concern to most customers. They are much more interested in the designer, the brand name, or the fashion theme being promoted. Pricing signs are most often used inside of a department, usually on the fixture. However, European shops and stores usually place price cards in windows. Aggressive price-oriented stores such as discounters usually feature prices in their displays.

When signs are used throughout the store, the sign holders are important considerations. They are available in wood, plastic, and metal. The materials and colors should be in keeping with the character of the store and be attractive to the target customer.

Since it takes time to prepare signs even with the mechanical methods available, always take the time and care to request a sign accurately. Write clearly and check all spelling. Most retailers use request forms to ensure care in sign preparation. Such sign request forms can guide the text writer in composing a short message necessary for good signing. See Figure 5.5.

PROFFITT'S
SIGN REQUISITION

DATE ORDERED _____ DATE REQUIRED* _____ AD DATE _____ NAME OF SALE/EVENT _____
ORDERED BY_____ EXT. # _____ DEPT. _____ REPLACEMENT SIGN _____

STORE/QUAN.   STORE/QUAN.   CHECK ONE
01_____   11_____ $3\frac{1}{2}$ X 5 □   Topper □
02_____ $5\frac{1}{2}$ X 7 □   14 X 22 □
03_____   13_____   22 X 28 □
04_____   14_____
05_____   15_____   Reduction taken at register □
06_____   16_____   Priced as marked □

* Signs must be ordered 15 working days in advance of your needs.

Distribute copies as follows: White - Printshop   Yellow - Advertising   Pink - Buyer

For other instructions use back.   Price

MDS-025   Rev. 6/89

Figure 5.5. Sign request form. (Courtesy of Proffitt's Department Stores, Alcoa, Tenn.)

Signs can be on banners made of fabric or paper and hung from ceilings. Other types of signs, such as wooden signs, can be hung from chains. Signs may be attached to columns, placed into slotted wallboards, or used in floor holders. With so many opportunities for signing, there is the danger of oversigning. If there are too many signs coming from the ceiling and hanging on every fixture, even during a sale period, a quality fashion store can look like a low-priced discount store. Too many signs present a cluttered look and project a low-quality image.

Lighting

Lighting is one of the most important elements of display, as discussed in Chapter 4. If properly used it will aid in selling merchandise and thereby add to the profit of the store. Working with light to make displays and merchandise more dramatic is the goal of every display designer. The main design elements of light and shadow are very important. Too much shadow can hide important details of the merchandise and also change the appearance of merchandise colors.

Spots or high-intensity discharge bulbs can be excellent when used correctly. Spots alone in a display unit or window can leave the rest of the display in shadows. A few floodlights can brighten an area and, with the addition of spots, correct lighting and color as well as create visual energy. Pin spots (small spotlights) can be used to accent small areas. Caution is necessary, as the light beam can give off enough heat to fade or even burn merchandise and props. All artificial lighting as well as sunlight can fade fabrics and colors. Bright colors are especially vulnerable to strong light. Blue or purple silks placed near lights or windows are faded very quickly.

Windows require the same amount of lighting in the day as in the evening because the window light will be competing with the bright sunlight outside. At night it is important to make sure that the shadows fall in the correct places in the display. Lights that are directed up from the floor should also be checked, as they can cast unnatural shadows on mannequins. Store management and display staff should constantly reevaluate lighting for correct placement of spots and light bulbs. Each year there are innovations to improve the cost efficiency of the bulbs as well as their color accuracy.

Fluorescent lighting is used for general lighting in store ceilings, showcases, and valances. These lights consist of long tubes and come in colors that can create a natural, cool feeling or a warm, sunny feeling. Fluorescents diffuse light over an area and do not create shadows or accents. Fluorescent lights also create problems of fading. Placing bright-colored merchandise directly under these bulbs, such as on the top rod nearest the light, should be avoided. Bright colors can be placed on a lower level and light colors placed on the top rod.

Mills and Paul state that "proper display lighting is vital to selling."[4] It attracts the customer's eyes to the merchandise and thus persuades them to buy. The important idea for store management to keep in mind is that the purpose of display lighting is to call attention to the merchandise. Lighting can be used to help direct the shoppers through the store, urging them to pause and examine displays of featured goods. People buy because they see the goods and like what they see. There is no magic about the attraction of proper display lighting. To a great extent, buying decisions are a result of seeing. The shopper's eye is automatically drawn to the brightest thing in its field. Therefore, lighting on the display should be two to five times stronger than the room lighting. (Refer again to Table 4.1.) The more difficult it is to see the detail, the more lighting is needed for that particular display.

A common type of lighting for a display are spotlights, which are usually placed on or near the ceiling. These can be turned and should be readjusted after each display is changed. Leaving the spotlights in the position they were in for the previous display often means that they will not accent the focal point in the current display. Repositioning the lighting is the last step in finishing the display. Some areas in a store will be dark, and if spotlights are not available, the display staff should carefully choose the merchandise to be placed in that location. Light-colored merchandise will show up much better.

The issue of lighting was originally left to the architect of the building, but now there are lighting specialists who can be brought into the design of a store. Store personnel can be trained in the day-to-day use of certain types of lighting. The specialists can determine the fixtures to be attached and the wattage to be used, as well as the types of lighting equipment. It is important that the specialist have retail store design experience. Salespeople at retail outlets for lighting can also be helpful. A display manager of a store, who has been participating in designing the store's lighting, may be available to a small store for freelance work in lighting.

Light fixtures and the electricity needed for these fixtures are an expense to consider carefully. Most leading manufacturers of lighting produce energy-saving bulbs. The big three—General Electric, Sylvania, and Westinghouse—as well as several small firms offer low-cost energy-saving bulbs, which can help keep costs down when a large amount of lighting is used.

[4]   Kenneth H. Mills and Judith E. Paul, *Applied Visual Merchandising* (Englewood Cliffs, N.J.: Prentice-Hall, Inc., 1982), p. 76.

Information on lighting is available from the following sources:

SOURCES OF INFORMATION FOR LIGHTING

Illuminating Engineering Society of North America
345 East 47th Street
New York, NY 10017

Sylvania
GTE Product Corp.
2115 Sylvan Rd. SW
Atlanta, GA 30344

General Electric Institute
Nela Park
Cleveland, Ohio 44112
216-266-3900

Common Problems in Display

Many display areas could be improved just by avoiding errors that decrease their effectiveness. One such error is lack of a theme. The customer should be able to understand what the display idea is in just a matter of seconds. Too often merchandise is placed in valuable display space without any kind of message to the viewer. Also, there can be too many themes in the display. Another mistake is the use of approximately the same arrangement in all displays.[5] It is easy to get into the habit of seeing a certain space as accommodating two or three mannequins or three or four items. If the layout remains the same week after week even though the merchandise changes, it can look too much like last week's display to excite the customer. A conscious effort to change the number of mannequins and the number of items placed in the display is needed so that the distribution of space alters in each display period. It will look newer and fresher when extra thought and time is spent.

Too much merchandise in a display is a mistake made by some stores. When the presentation is overcrowded, nothing is noticed, and the passerby disregards the display. Too much merchandise becomes ineffective and may suggest a lower-quality operation. Since there is not a really good rule of how much merchandise to use, the art principles of good design must be applied (Chapter 4). If it is necessary to use a

[5]   Kenneth H. Mills and Judith E. Paul, *Applied Visual Merchandising* (Englewood Cliffs, N.J.: Prentice-Hall, Inc., 1982), p. 115.

large quantity of items, such as belts or handbags, they can be clustered into groups so that they begin to appear as larger units rather than a scattering of many things. In this way the display will look less cluttered.

Use enough props to tell an attractive story. One item may be sufficient if the prop will complete the scene. If props are not used, the display can look as if it has not been finished or as if there are not enough funds to obtain appropriate props. Use of too many props in a display is also a disadvantage because they can overpower the merchandise, reducing the impact of the display. Grouping props to show a certain mood and then putting the merchandise in front of the props can tell the customer the purpose of the display. Inappropriate props can divert the customers' attention away from the merchandise, thus fragmenting the thoughts of the customers.

Another common mistake in display is the failure to change a display frequently enough. Interior displays should be changed as often as possible, preferably weekly. Some displays in stores may need to be worked on daily. If the merchandise has been chosen carefully, replacement should only involve a different size of the garment. For instance, if a medium-size shirt is on display and all the medium shirts in stock are sold, it may be necessary to sell the shirt on display. However, the same shirt in another size can be used. The original display is retained, and the thinking process of what blends in with the department does not have to be reconsidered. During Christmastime, extensive displays with animation usually remain for as long as two months. However, these do not show actual merchandise.

When new merchandise is received, it is necessary to accelerate the changes within a department to display the important new group of merchandise available. In many cases new merchandise can be placed into existing displays and floor arrangements. Periodically a section of a department or a store must be totally revised to keep the fresh, new merchandise out front. The newest fashions should be in the front of each section or department.

Maintenance can be a problem. The display can be set up to be very attractive, but customers may request removal of the merchandise or may simply pull the belt to one side or untie a scarf. The display areas should be checked throughout the day to see that they have not suffered from tamperings.

In putting together an elaborate display, the work should begin well in advance of the date the display is to be completed. Props must be made, repainted, or repaired and all gathered and ready to go to the display area. Merchandise must be selected and approved by the department management so that it is fresh and new. Preparation also includes making sure that certain apparel has been pressed before the time to work on the display. All of this should be ready before the old display is removed to avoid leaving the floor empty or having an area or window half finished for a long period of time. Employees should be assigned to work on the display so it can be installed quickly. Price tags are hidden or removed when this is the policy of the store.

Summary

Visual merchandising can encompass all aspects of the total visual impact of the store and its merchandise. The execution of displays requires advanced planning in order to coordinate the merchandise, props, lighting, and signage. Displays must be changed every 7 to 14 days to create an image of newness. Whether the purpose is to arrange merchandise placement in the department or to create a separate display, the principles of art are incorporated. Visual merchandising is one of the most creative aspects of retailing.

CHAPTER 6

Merchandising Presentation: Tools and Techniques

In this chapter, particular emphasis is placed on fashion merchandise as it is offered directly to prospective customers, who go to a store "to shop...perchance to buy." At this stage of product distribution, articles have been selected by a buyer, sent via established distribution channels to the retail outlet, priced, and delivered to the selling floor.

Techniques

With labor costs continually increasing, the retailer must take advantage of every opportunity to sell merchandise. Appropriate presentation tools placed correctly on selling floors and dressed properly are a successful silent sales force. A primary goal of the fashion retailer is to create and maintain a quality fashion image. Merchandise presented interestingly to the public can contribute greatly to both a store's and a department's image. To achieve this goal, a retailer needs to remember how the customer sees the store and the merchandise displayed in it. Each item of merchandise, properly arranged, is part of the image development process (see Figure 6.1).

Total Look

Customers enjoy shopping in well-arranged departments that present the new fashions in a "total look." This technique can be activated by careful use of mannequins or partial forms to demonstrate the season's new styles in three dimensions. Using mannequins or partial forms will

Figure 6.1. The customer's view of the department as he or she enters. A complete approach to merchandise presentation from entrance through the department and on back to the walls helps to develop the image. (Miller's, Ross Park, Pittsburgh. Reproduced by permission of the Retail Reporting Bureau.)

require salespeople to pull together the needed accessories that accent or highlight the actual items for sale in that specific department. Many experienced retailers suggest that a different version of the total look be presented every week so that the "stroller," "browser," and the "just looking" shopper can look, learn, and become interested in specific merchandise. Repeated exposures to new lines and new designs are pleasing to style-conscious women and men. They are likely to become paying customers because they want something new. This "new style urge" will motivate them to go to a store more often than when their closets indicate a shortage of clothing.

Because fashion is constantly changing, the retailer should feel a constant urgency not only to sell merchandise but also to provide current fashion information to the customer. A good way to offer this education is to be fastidious in the "picture stories" provided within the department. The buyer and other department associates should keep in mind that the customer understands fashion trends more quickly when she sees a total look (see Figure 6.2). Just looking at a smart ski outfit doesn't inform a sports-minded customer how to dress. Looking at a smart ski outfit on a mannequin wearing a ski helmet, palm-lined gloves, and ski boots provides a clearly understood style message.

Colorizing

Be constantly aware of the force of color. Of the art elements, color is the first to attract the viewer's eye. The well-planned, intentional use of colors almost literally carries a customer's gaze across the merchandise. The eye moves more quickly between related colors than between unrelated colors, and a harmonizing arrangement of color is created by a juxtaposed placement of merchandise with related colors. One should refer to the color wheel to maintain chromatic consistency (Color Plate 3). With merchandise in a wide range of colors, merchandise arrangers could start the merchandise on the left with yellows, then proceed to oranges, reds, violets, and blues, ending with greens on the right.

Figure 6.2. A total look can be presented on a shelf or ledge as opposed to hanging of folded merchandise. This type of display helps to bring the merchandise to life for the browsing customer.

With the color wheel opened at yellow, this becomes the lead color for the merchandise on the fixture, with green the final one. If merchandise is in neutral colors, light ones can be placed next to the yellows and dark ones next to the greens. As with all display guidelines, however, variation from color rules can sometimes build interest. Rigid adherence can only lead to monotony, building a negative influence on both customers and salespeople.

For some occasions a better picture is created when the arranger starts with another color. For example, as Valentine's Day approaches, red is a reasonable color to feature. Lead items on all fixtures could have a tint of red, with colors proceeding around the wheel, ending with orange.

The wheel can be entered at any color. An arranger then easily moves from that color to the next most closely related color in stock, continuing until all stock colors have been included.

Self-Selection by Customer

Color catches the customer's eye, but the presentation of the merchandise should be equally appealing so that the customer is drawn to it. The ultimate goal is to help the customer make a satisfactory selection of goods. Because sales personnel are not always available, merchandise presentation on store fixtures should be effective silent salespeople.

Four major factors influence customers as they make preliminary selections: color, design features, size, and price. Fixtures with merchandise first grouped by color, then by size effectively show design features. This arrangement helps customers serve themselves, and fixtures that promote more self-selection aid the customer in finding desired items more quickly, resulting in quicker sales and increased impulse buying.

Fixtures that encourage self-selection generally have the capacity to contain a great deal of merchandise, which results in most of the stock being advantageously housed on the selling floor. It is especially important to have merchandise accessible during sales as well as during other peak traffic periods. When adequate stock is available to the customer in a self-selection format, sales productivity increases; that is, sales per square foot increases, resulting in higher profits.

The Backdrop

Background art is a part of the display picture that is retained for longer periods of time. Backgrounds may be changed only four times a year—at the major seasonal change periods. However, specific merchandise being displayed should change frequently—if possible, every 10 to 14 days. At all times it is good to keep in mind that customers expect something "new and different" whenever they stroll through the store. Their expectations lead them to make trips to a fashion department more often, thereby increasing sales.

Back Walls

Walls serve as backdrops, providing a dramatic environment comparable to a decorated setting in the upstage (rear) part of a stage set. On the walls the name of the department should be clearly visible to store traffic from as far away as 50 yards. Tied in with the department name should be seasonal additions. Examples of seasonal additions are:

In the fall, implications of fall colors, football games, cool-weather sports, harvest themes

In the winter, artistic suggestions of snow skiing, sledding, ice skating; for an upscale appeal slanted to cruise patrons, swimwear, evening wear, and sun sports

In the spring, warm-weather looks shown in motifs of outdoor games, picnics, traveling south for spring break, picking spring flowers

In the summer, a holiday atmosphere expressed by implying fun, travel, outdoor activity, beach pleasures, school vacations, or international jet travel

Often the back wall in an apparel department can be retained throughout one season. Swim shops that are set up in March, for example, can be retained with minor alterations until July.

Side Walls

Side walls also can be likened to the elements of a stage set but can be more intimately arranged, with prime visual appeal to customers with specific interests in one department. Visibility to casual shoppers in other store areas can be much less significant. These walls should be part of the weekly or biweekly merchandise change and should tie in as closely as possible with fashion attire being specifically "limelighted." Side walls of a sportswear department are extensions of back walls with their scenic motifs. They should integrate mannequins or partial forms into the viewing area, as shown in Color Plate 6.

When the back walls and side walls are designed and arranged for display, one general theme should be established in order to create and maintain harmony in the minds of the customers. With unity established, forceful impact can be achieved.

Some retailers take a more aggressive approach to the use of walls and turn them into fixtures that hold as well as display the merchandise. Display wall systems, as seen in Figure 6.3 can utilize almost every inch of wall space.

Ledges and the Tops of Shelves

Taking advantage of the space on ledges and shelf tops can add a visual dimension to well-arranged walls. It should be pointed out that on most ledges, shelves, and cases displays can be effective even when they are above eye level. When space allows, these projecting elements can accommodate mannequins or partial forms that display promoted merchandise in realistic environments. Where space is at a premium, ledges are effective when they hold decorative items such as seasonal greenery placed in front of a wall decoration or behind a suspended element. The combination of near and far elements and stable and moving elements can enliven the visual environment of a department. Use of ledges can be very inexpensive; for example, leaves or chrysanthemums can be pleasingly arranged in front of an Autumn football scene in a sportswear department. Later in the year, Christmas greenery can replace the leaves. As spring arrives, early-blooming flowers or small azaleas are effective and inexpensive. At all times of the year,

Figure 6.3. A display system that turns the wall into a merchandising fixture. (Courtesy of Visu-Wall by H.B.S., Inc.)

ledges are ideal for interweaving the artistic with the real. For example, when a snow skiing motif is shown in one dimension on a side wall, a ski lift print could be attached to the back wall. On the ledge, a set of real skis would add authenticity and three-dimensional appeal along with the skiwear merchandise.

Forms

As one moves from the background to the selling floor, presentation tools become more specifically related to the merchandise.

Mannequins

Of all the presentation tools, mannequins are the most popular. Built in a variety of human forms, mannequins can trigger customers' imaginations, causing them to visualize themselves wearing the merchandise. Also, mannequins can be completely accessorized to provide a total look. They can be used singly or in groups. Currently, most stores use them in groups to strengthen specific fashion statements.

In recent years, mannequins have been designed in wider varieties of the human form, representing a spectrum of ages, sexes, races, body builds, and recreational interests (see Figure 6.4). Mannequins come in basically three types: realistic, semirealistic, and abstract as discussed in Chapter 5. The type used should be determined on the basis of store image and type of merchandise to be displayed. It is important for anyone responsible for purchasing mannequins to consider the appeal of each one under consideration, and also to keep in mind at all times the desired image of the store or department. The total impact of the selling unit should guide the selection; mannequins have become quite expensive, and each mannequin must provide an impression of appropriateness and quality.

Merchandise worn by mannequins in the department should be located adjacent to the display. The location is important so that browsers can easily move from the mannequin that created the fashion impression directly to the displayed items. Easy access to the fashion articles that are dramatically displayed can mean faster inspection of the merchandise and increased sales.

Price tags should be hidden when the merchandise is displayed so there are no distractions cluttering the garment lines for the customer. Having extra stock in clear view quickly provides answers to customers' questions. In this manner, sales are part of a continuous flow of action

Figure 6.4. Mannequins are available representing all age groups, both genders, and different races and can be posed in a variety of positions. (Courtesy of Carlson Store Fixtures.)

from first attraction to fast sale. Experience has shown that a customer who is responsive to a display—often a mannequin—quickly develops an affirmative reaction to the apparel and is ready to consider buying the item even before the salesperson approaches.

Partial Forms

If mannequins prove too expensive or if space will not accommodate them, partial forms can be used (see Figure 6.5). They do not permit the complete fashion look, since they represent only portions of the human form, but they offer a more realistic presentation of the merchandise than a hanger can provide. Partial forms may be adequate to show a jacket, a coordinated blouse, and appropriate neckwear; a skirt, belt, and handbag can be placed next to the form. They are also effective where space is limited, such as on a small ledge or the top of a shelf.

Figure 6.5. Various styles of partial forms are available.

Body Forms

Still less expensive and requiring less display space are various types of body forms, which are effective on ledges, cases, and furniture. They are excellent tools for displaying merchandise in a boutique setting within a department and in specialty stores. Body forms are available in a variety of materials, with rattan being very popular (see Figure 6.6).

Metal forms of chrome are neutral in mood and more versatile for display (see Figure 6.7). More updated display tools are the stylized

Figure 6.6. Rattan body forms are popular in specialty shops with a casual feeling (Courtesy of Carlson Store Fixtures.)

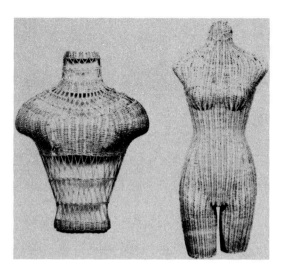

forms such as the one seen in Figure 6.8. Updated and somewhat more animated are the flexible forms illustrated in Figure 6.9.

Plastic forms are flexible and adjustable and may be more desirable for certain merchandise and situations. Swimsuits are a natural for plastic forms, as seen in Figure 6.10.

Mannequin Alternatives

A wide variety of other mannequin alternatives are available and may be a more economical choice for some stores. Some alternatives are dress forms, soft-sculpture mannequins, inflatables, and cutout figures.

Figure 6.7. Chrome T-top and gooseneck with skirt or slack arm, standard equipment in many retail stores.

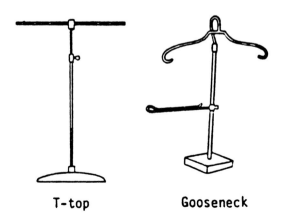

T-top   Gooseneck

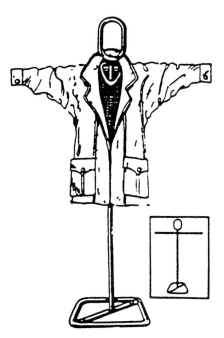

Figure 6.8. Tubular body form
(Courtesy of Carlson Store Fixtures.)

Stuffing garments is effective for children's and casual wear. Other alternatives to mannequins are European display techniques: pinups, flying technique, and laydown (see Figure 6.11).

In addition to mannequins, partial forms, and body forms, other tools of merchandise presentation are floor fixtures and free-standing fix-

Figure 6.9. Flexible body form. (Courtesy of Carlson Store Fixtures.)

Figure 6.10. Plastic body forms. (Courtesy of Fix-Play Inc.)

tures. Most fashion goods look best when carefully and artfully hung. Therefore, one should consider the use of hanging racks, including T-stands, four-ways, rounders, and straight racks. These fixtures are described next.

Figure 6.11. The laydown technique of display is seen here on fixtures that are angled up on the aisle by the Esprit area. (G. Fox, Galleria Mall, Wappinger Falls, N.Y. Reproduced by courtesy of the Retail Reporting Bureau.)

Fixtures

Hanging Fixtures: Bars, Stands, and Racks

Bars, stands, and racks are implements of retail salesmanship designed to provide wearing apparel with a pseudorealistic vertical hang. When properly arranged, the merchandise itself provides a colorful display within a department that has been delineated on three sides by the back and side walls. To continue the theater analogy, with the walls and ledges representing the stage set, the fashion items themselves become the actors. Prospective customers arriving in the department may look at, try on, and buy the merchandise because the atmosphere is conducive to shopping. When well arranged on bars, stands, and racks, items can be easily seen and touched.

T-STANDS   The T-stand is an accent piece used to feature a fashion story or advertised merchandise (see Figure 6.12). T-stands are placed on aisles to indicate to the potential customer the types of merchandise found in the area and what some of the new fashion statements are.

The T-stand, like other fixtures at the front of the selling area, should be at a lower height than the rest of the fixtures and placed so that the lead garment is at least 12 inches from the aisle, with the merchandise face out. In this position, open space around the T-stand helps emphasize the merchandise, keeps the area uncluttered, and draws shoppers

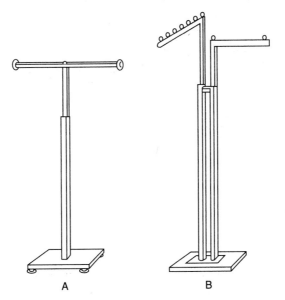

A   B

Figure 6.12.   T-stands. (a) Straight-arm fixture. (b) T-stand with a waterfall on the left and a straight arm on the right. Both arms are adjustable.

into the department. It is effective when located next to a mannequin where shoppers can see merchandise in three dimensions.

Structurally, the T-stand is an upright rod with a heavy base and a crossbar at the top. It has two arms, which are used to show merchandise in two directions. Buyers or display personnel should avoid placing more than two types of items on a T-stand. It is advantageous to put one type on each arm.

For a T-stand with a slanted bar, hangers can be placed in descending order to produce a "waterfall," which can create a dramatic fashion statement. If the bar has notches to hold and space the merchandise, only one hanger should be placed in each notch; otherwise, the rack is unbalanced, cluttered, and is apt to be unappealing to customers. The T-stand is not designed to hold large quantities of merchandise.

Although the T-stand is a versatile fixture, some care should be taken in selecting merchandise to be shown on it. The merchandise should be new, have hanger appeal, and carry out the image of the department. Use of one style and one color makes a very strong fashion statement. Although more than one color can be used effectively, too many colors create a choppy appearance. Sometimes a more forceful presentation of goods can be achieved by maintaining a monochrome color scheme and arranging the bulk of the merchandise on a larger rack.

When coordinates are used, jackets and blouses should be hung on slanted bars, with matching skirts or slacks arranged on back horizontal bars. The first garment on the higher bar should face the front of the department and be accessorized, provided it is not situated next to a mannequin dressed in the same merchandise.

If three or four colors are to be used on a waterfall arm, the darkest or dullest one should be placed on the bottom. Medium values or medium intensities should be in the middle and the light or bright colors on the top.

Skirts, pants, and shorts should not be hung on slant arms. This is to prevent the dominant focus from being on the hangers instead of the clothes. Merchandise on T-stands should be changed often so that the fashion story is always fresh, maintaining the interest of regular customers.

QUAD-RACKS OR FOUR-WAYS   Quad-racks rank next to T-stands in appropriateness for telling a fashion story. Like the T-stand, quad-racks should be arranged near the front of a department. For greater interest, their heights should be varied. Fixtures with lowest height should be nearest the front of the department. Structurally, the quad-rack is a four-armed fixture with arms extending from the middle(see Figure 6.13). Arms can be either straight or slanted to create a waterfall impression. A popular combination has a waterfall in front and straight rods on the back portion of the arrangement. In this four-way config-

Figure 6.13. Four-way racks. (*a*) Fixture with adjustable straight arms. (*b*) Fixture with adjustable waterfall arms. (*c*) Combination of straight arms and a waterfall.

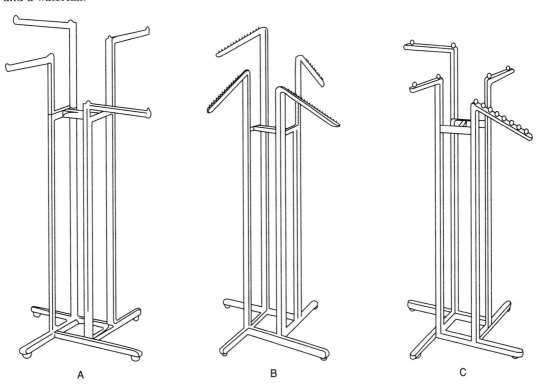

A   B   C

uration, tops should be placed on the waterfall. Coordinate skirts and pants are best shown on the side arms. The waterfall should face the aisle, with the first garment completely accessorized. This arrangement allows shoppers to see a simultaneous front and shoulder view of the merchandise on display.

Arms heights can be adjusted to suit the merchandise; they can be raised to accommodate long pants or dresses and lowered to hold blouses or jackets. The quad-rack holds twice as much merchandise as the T-stand. In addition, it provides four face-out views of the latest fashion statement. For this reason, it is an excellent choice for the display of coordinate groups. Four different pieces—blouse, jacket, skirt, and pants—can be displayed, giving the department an impressive showing of a complete ensemble. Quad-racks also can hold two styles of blouses and two styles of skirts. Usually merchandise on a four-way is presented by color, by style, and by size on each arm. Four-ways can hold one style of blouse in four colors or a variety of blouses in one color. When there are more than four or five items, the merchandise should be hung on larger racks because quad-racks are designed to feature a single style or related items in a group.

SIX-WAYS   The six-way rack has many of the advantageous features of the four-way but is newer and can hold more merchandise. It has six adjustable arms, which can be a combination of straight and slanted (see Figure 6.14). The six-way is effective for larger groups of merchandise including several colors or coordinates with a choice in styles of the various pieces. The rack should be dressed in much the same manner as the four-way. Because of its large size, the six-way should be placed toward the middle of the department, where it will not create a barrier to incoming customer traffic.

MULTIFEATURE FIXTURES   A wide variety of multifeature fixtures are available, such as the one shown in Figure 6.15. It may not hold as much merchandise as the six-way, but it offers more flexibility.

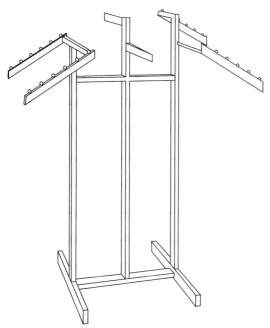

Figure 6.14.   Adjustable six-way rack with slanted arms (waterfalls) at each end and straight arms in the center.

Figure 6.15.   A system for creating a stack arrangement and display within the same unit. (Courtesy of Pipeline Displays and Fixtures, Inc.)

ROUND RACKS Round racks, or rounders, are the "workhorses" of merchandising. They are seldom surpassed in their ability to hold large quantities of merchandise. Structurally, the round rack is a circular rod, usually 32 to 42 inches in diameter, that can be raised and lowered to suit the merchandise (see Figure 6.16). Round racks hold many items but do not display them interestingly because they present the items shoulder out rather than face out. Rounders often have a flat circular surface in the center of the top, which can be used for a display. Round racks can be used for garments of all types and lengths. They are valuable when large quantities of merchandise need to be available for the customer to examine. With the round rack, as with any fixture, a system of "dressing" the rack must be employed if it is to be effective in selling merchandise.

Because brilliant hues are eye stoppers, merchandise is often arranged by color. When several styles are displayed together, they can be hung first by color, then by style and size. For example, when there are four styles of dresses in blue, one should start on the left with the first style and arrange that item from the smallest size to the largest size. Then it is best to take the second style in blue and size it from small to large. After handling the fourth blue style in that manner, a salesperson begins with the first style in the next related color in stock, following the color technique discussed earlier.

When coordinates are hung on a round rack, there are two possible arrangements. The major item, often the jacket, can be on the left, moving right to the blouse, skirt, and pants. Another possibility is to

Figure 6.16. A round rack is often referred to as a "rounder."

arrange by length, either from short to long or from long to short. This procedure prevents an unattractive irregular line at the bottom of the merchandise. Following this principle, if blouses are in front, jackets should be next, followed by skirts and then pants. One color should be dominant in either arrangement. If the group has items featuring print designs and various sets of solid-colored coordinates, the print item can be hung between two selected solids. In this case it might not be possible to arrange colors by the order in the rainbow, that is, by the color wheel.

The order of colors on the rack is often determined by the merchandise available. After an appreciable amount of merchandise has been sold, it may be necessary to regroup the remainder. This rearrangement may be quite unlike the original grouping. Store personnel should be guided by what they feel will create the best picture with the merchandise in stock at the time.

Generally, one does not display more than two or three garments per color per size or style, even on the round rack. Overcrowding usually discourages sales. As the garment hangs on the rounder, shoppers get only a shoulder-out view. Space is needed so that shoppers can separate individual garments and get a clear front view of each item while it is still on the rack.

Because the rounder holds so much stock, it frequently is used to display sale merchandise. In that case, rounders should be placed near the back of the department where they are not a detriment to the fashion image. Also, the customer passes by and views the new full-priced merchandise on the way to the back of the department to the reduced goods. For special events such as semiannual sales, rounders can be advantageously located near the front of the department, but only for brief periods of time.

When possible, sale items should be grouped by color, following the order of the rainbow's spectrum. Clearance items are apt to be widely varied, so as groups become too broken in sportswear, salespeople should rearrange by item, placing all jackets, all skirts, and all sweaters together. As stock sells and the supply begins to appear sparse, it should be moved to smaller racks to avoid the appearance of being picked over.

STRAIGHT RACKS   Straight racks are a good choice when it is desirable to present many similar garments (see Figure 6.17). Long straight racks are placed toward the back of the department. Items should be colorized in the same manner as with the round racks—first by color, then by styles within a color, and finally by size.

Straight racks can be built into perimeter walls and interspersed with face-outs to feature a specific style and to show the fronts of garments (see Figure 6.18). These sloped face-out bars are good because items on

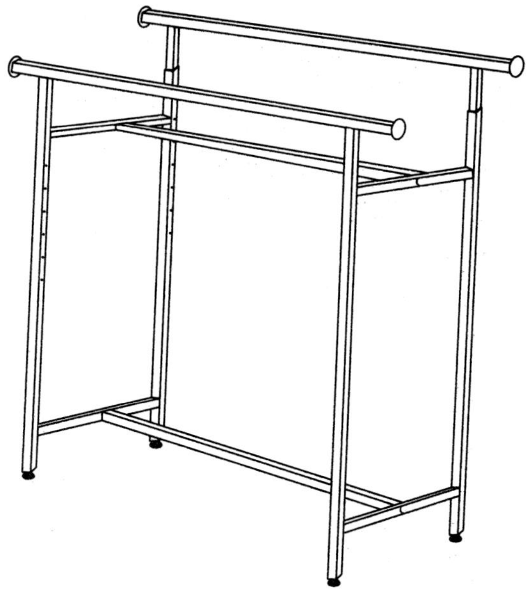

Figure 6.17. A double-rail free-standing straight rack.

Figure 6.18. Built-in straight racks interspersed with a waterfall arm presenting the merchandise "face out."

straight racks hang shoulder out and do not show the garment's features well. Salespeople should resist the temptation to overload straight racks. Crowding is unsightly and often hampers customers in their selection processes.

Nonhanging Fixtures

Of all the described elements of departmental decoration and display, nonhanging fixtures are probably the most traditional. A display counter is good for the actual exchange of money for product. Other shoppers use the counter to touch, feel, inspect, and, in most cases, "try on" the item they are considering purchasing. Primary shoppers are those who have reached the conclusion that they will buy an item; they go to the counter, request a salesperson's assistance, and ask for the item to be wrapped or bagged so that they can pay for it and take it home. Secondary shoppers have not reached a decision to buy. It is this category of store traffic that can be enticed to touch and feel the merchandise by the judicious placement of tables and bins.

TABLES   Tables are a good presentation fixture when the merchandise has little hanger appeal and does not fold or stack neatly, as is often the case with intimate apparel or accessories. Tables are often placed in aisles to feature advertised items. The style of the table should fit the store's mood; for example, high fashion can be accented with a china-red lacquered parson's table or an elegant circular table with a full-length silk cloth.

The salesperson and department manager need to consider the size and shape of the tabletop when planning the arrangement of merchandise. It is wise to establish vertical and horizontal rows by colorizing the merchandise, arranging related colors adjacent to each other, and then sizing the items from small to large.

When merchandise comes in a variety of shapes and colors, as is the case with accessories, it should be arranged with small items in the front and large ones in the back. Items of one shape should be placed together. Salespeople should select some pattern of progression through the various shapes of items, if possible, to achieve an orderly appearance.

When tables are used to display clearance items, salespeople must be alerted to the necessity of keeping the merchandise orderly. On special sale days, a table piled high may well be the right invitation to the bargain hunters. They may enjoy the challenge of finding great buys among dozens of items. But when special sale days are over, a clearance table can be moved to the back or side of the department so that it does not detract from the store's fashion personality.

COUNTERS Counter fixtures serve many purposes. Glass counters safely display out-of-reach small, expensive merchandise, such as jewelry, perfume, and handbags, protecting them from theft or accidental damage. Inside the case merchandise should be arranged to tell a fashion story about color, texture, and name brand. As salespeople or managers plan a display case, they need to keep in mind the shopper's view of the case, from the front and from the top. Start filling the case at the top and work from left to right. Small items show up better on the top, with larger items on the bottom (see Figure 6.19). If all the items are small, they can be arranged in artistic groups for greater impact. When the merchandise is stocked in a wide range of colors, it should be colorized following the color wheel.

Some merchandise can be placed on countertops to invite shoppers to touch it. Countertops are also very effective places for interaction of the salesperson with the customer. In a cosmetics department, the countertop is the actual site of the service rendered to the customer. Therefore, care should be taken to leave an area free of goods. Space for the demonstration and dialogue with the customer is a valuable sales aid. Usually, a mirror and other furnishings such as trays, racks,

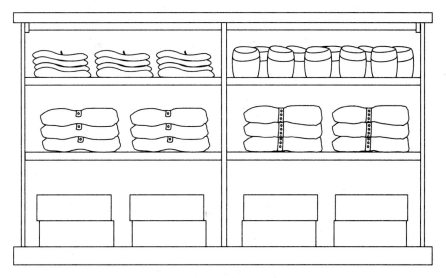

Figure 6.19. Front view of a glass or open showcase.

and holders are useful for counter displays of small articles. Too much merchandise on counters creates a disorderly appearance and destroys a prestige image. At all times, it should be remembered: *The counter is the principal setting for closing a sales transaction.*

BINS AND SHELVES   If shelves are available on the wall behind a case, it is good to use this space for items related to articles found in the case. If the entire perimeter wall contains shelves or bins, the choice of merchandise is less restricted and might include sweaters, tailored blouses, or knit tops. Remembering that a vertical image is strongest, one should stock the merchandise so that each vertical row holds a separate color (see Color Plate 6). The merchandise should be kept within reach of the customer. Goods should not be stacked too high or too low for the average customer to reach easily. In the space above the highest shelf, partial forms can be dressed in the merchandise of the same color as that arranged below. If the merchandise is not available in sufficient depth to arrange vertically by color, it might be arranged by style down through the shelves, with each shelf sized from small to large.

GONDOLAS   Gondolas are basically a series of free-standing shelves and are used primarily for folded and packaged merchandise such as shirts, sweaters, and tights. This merchandise should be colorized vertically and then sized, with small to large arranged from top to bottom. A portion of the top shelf can be used for display, perhaps with a partial form to show shoulders and sleeves. This arrangement lets the customers know about an item's features without their having to open packages or unfold merchandise. These safeguard measures help keep the area neat and attractive and the merchandise correctly sized for easy self-selection by customers.

TRANSPARENT DISPLAY UNITS   These fixtures are basically columns of upright cubes that hold a large quantity of folded merchandise in neat, orderly arrangements (see Figure 6.20). The display unit should be addressed in much the same manner as the gondola. Being made of clear glass or other transparent material, these fixtures allow the merchandise, rather than the fixture, to make the scene. The color of the merchandise is more apparent because of the transparent fixture. Also, this see-through quality makes the area appear less crowded, more open, and lighter. This feeling of spaciousness is very desirable because it lends visual appeal and subsequent status to the store. Again, the color wheel should guide the vertical order of the merchandise. If there is not enough stock to fill an entire column with one color, related colors can be arranged in a systematic manner within the column; for example, lavender on top, then deep pink, and maroon on the bottom.

Figure 6.20. Transparent display units or cubes can be arranged to create fixtures of varying dimensions with space for a display of the merchandise on top. (Saks Fifth Avenue, Mellon Square, Pittsburgh. Reproduced by permission of the Retail Reporting Bureau.)

In addition to holding merchandise, fixtures can guide customers through an area. For this reason, certain combinations and arrangements of fixtures can be far more satisfactory than others. Generally, fixtures should remain in place, and the merchandise should be moved to keep an area interesting and new.

MODULAR UNITS   Fixture systems that can be designed from modular units are a high-tech type of merchandising concept (see Figures 6.21 and 6.22.) Most incorporate a space for stock as well as for display and provide various combinations of units.

Building Uniqueness: The "Shop Concept"

One of the best ways to create a unique fashion image for a store or department is to choose a specific area of merchandising and emphasize it strongly. This activity can create an appealing "shop concept" within the confines of an existing department or specialty store. It can provide a magnet for browsing customers by providing a touch of something

Figure 6.21.   A free standing modular unit. (Courtesy of J.P. Metal Products, Inc.)

unique. Unusual props or displays can be used to build a successful shop concept. Some of the categories that apply well to the shop concept are as follows:

swimwear	special resource or designer
sweaters	business woman's shop
playwear	special occasion shop
sundresses	handmade items
jeans and tops	Valentine shop
sunglasses	stuffed toys
suits	
furs	

Shops can be established in the mind of the customer by locating one type of merchandise, such as a designer brand, in a small area set aside

Figure 6.22. This high-tech fixture is a ceiling to floor system. Tubular display system supplied by Opto International, Inc., Prospect Heights, Ill.

Complete fashion shop in dove grey and yellow.

from the rest of the department. Often, dividers such as clear lucite partitions are brought in to indicate the shop's boundaries and to set the stage for the merchandise. Since shops are miniature departments, T-stands and four-ways, which are designed to show off the merchandise, are used instead of rounders and straight racks, which are designed to hold large quantities of stock.

Timing of Merchandise Rearrangement

Merchandise on the floor is best rearranged on fixtures as soon as new articles arrive in the store or department. For the store to utilize fresh merchandise to the fullest, it should be placed near the front of the department, or in a high-traffic area. The goal should be impressed consistently on salespeople that they are presenting an ever-changing show to their customers. A good customer may frequently make quick trips through a department that offers the new and different, just because she can see new and interesting items. Whenever possible, a flow should be maintained; new items should be brought into visual harmony with related older merchandise. This principle holds true even in specialty stores where mini-departments can be maintained—for example, areas for dresses, other space for sportswear, and a separate place for accessories. The key is to overlay the entire department or store with a flash of something exciting to the customer's eyes; this can be most easily achieved with a colorful arrangement of new items.

In order not to create a jumbled effect or a confusing impact on customers, display persons and salespeople should keep in mind that customers appreciate seeing merchandise in families. To achieve this, a salesperson could put a new group of casual wear in front of older similar items already in the store. It is not wise to spotlight the new items where they would be out of place or in disharmony with other merchandise. (For example, swimsuits should not be displayed in proximity with soft party clothes.)

When new merchandise arrives, often it is necessary to rearrange an entire department. This occurs particularly when there is a major seasonal change. It is sometimes necessary to move an entire swim shop when a large shipment of autumn colors and autumn-weight sweaters arrive and warrant the major focus of display.

Another occasion for complete rearrangement occurs when it is necessary to develop a competitive response to another store. Also, if price-positioning needs to be altered—that is, when there is a change in the proportion of merchandise in a given price range—it is important that the display areas reflect this change. Central to this, salespeople should be alerted to be aware of competitors' activities. They should be encouraged to provide input about competitors in the same market and bring in fresh ideas from other cities—even other countries.

Merchandising Special Types of Goods

Special Purchases

To build and maintain customer traffic, buyers try to find occasional special purchases—not in broken lots or seconds but in fully balanced supplies of sizes and of standard quality. These kinds of merchandise offerings often can be bought at a good value and sold for a low, customer-appealing price, even while achieving a normal or near-normal markup for the store. Buyers who use this merchandising technique will benefit from media backing coupled with conspicuous displays.

These special purchases can be effectively displayed in the second or third rows of fixtures in a department store area. For greatest impact they should be on a separate fixture and colorized and sized like all other new fashion goods. However, even though the item is a highly promotable and timely one, usually it should not replace the standard, expected items in a department. The display needs to be conspicuous, but not completely "out front."

Before arranging the display, the sales associates should be certain that there is an acceptable quantity of the special items. Promotions can entice a customer to come to a department to buy something new and different at a special price. However, if the item is almost sold out, an effective display of that item can create more ill will than good will between customers and the department.

In planning with the visual merchandising personnel, it is important to emphasize that "signing" should be unusual, perhaps of a varied color combination and larger than the regular signs and tags, if possible. When the special sale of this merchandise has run its course, these over-size, overcolorful signs should come down immediately. At this point, if there is a small amount of the merchandise remaining, it can be moved to smaller fixtures and ultimately merged with markdown merchandise.

Advertised Items

It is important for salespeople to have a regular incoming flow of information about advertised items. Because ads can only entice a customer into the store, the sales force must then take over, provide further information, exert selling skills, and close the sale. Various media choices, so common in retailing today, provide a wide spectrum of advertising messages to the public. When the media have been wisely chosen, the selected target markets will be responsive (see Chapter 7). Fashion merchandise should be readily available to customers after an ad has appeared in the paper or after a commercial has been run on televisin or radio. The principal rules for buyers to follow so that money is well spent and produces the greatest profit for the department or specialty shop are the following:

1. Buy advertising time and space only when there is enough merchandise to cover the customer response. When possible, have alternate

merchandise of a satisfactory style and quality that can be moved into the department if the advertised items sell out.

2. Inform the salespeople of the advertising schedule. Often it is advantageous to let them know how much the ads cost. This motivates them to respect the effort necessary to bring customers into their own department or shop.

3. While the ad is running, make sure that the advertised merchandise is in a conspicuous location easily accessible to customers. It is often advisable to place fashion advertised items at the front of the department.

4. Use signs, props, display tools, and mannequins as effectively as possible, to provide quick identification between the advertisement and the item.
   a. T-stands and four-ways holding the advertised items are effective.
   b. Mannequins dressed in the advertised items are forceful eye-catchers.
   c. Signs with advertised items and prices are essential.

Markdowns

An age-old problem in any selling area is the marketability of broken lot, soiled, and slightly outdated merchandise. One effective solution is to mark down the selling price and arrange the leftover items in as attractive a way as possible.

A key to an attractive arrangement is often an awareness of *color.* Some retailers suggest that if a few pieces are left of a sportswear group, these can be merged together with other separates by color and item. For example, if several styles of blouses in one color and a range of sizes are grouped together, this level of organization will ensure that the articles do not look leftover or cheap. This is also possible with pants, sweaters, shirts, or other similar items that share a common color. These color arrangements appear to be well-organized and maintain a quality appeal for customers. The visual appeal is also quite aesthetic and does not offer a "clearance sale" atmosphere, even when the items are being cleared from the department. Frequently, fashion items that are out-of-season can be presented attractively when fanned out in analogous color formations.

If color arrangements are difficult, suggest that salespeople choose *sizes* as the next possible organizing factor. However, since different brands have different size specifications, it is limiting to use a size arrangement very often. Manufacturers cut garments to many specifications, achieving different looks, different styles, and varying degrees of snugness or looseness—all of which affect the size of a garment. There-fore, there are limitations to merchandizing size over style or color.

During a fullscale markdown event in a department, when items with slashed prices are in great quantity, signage needs to reflect this situa-tion. At these times, it can be advantageous to use pennant-size signs or banners to impart a mood of excitement to shoppers.

During major clearance events, such as after Christmas, after the Fourth of July, or after Thanksgiving, displaying marked-down mer-chandise in the second and third rows of a fashion department has proven effective. After much of this merchandise is sold, it is time to move what is left, the clearance merchandise, nearer the back of the department. Items of similar categories can gradually be merged to-gether when they become few in number. For example, swim suits can be merchandized with playwear. This is particularly true in the month of August, when summerwear reaches the point of declining sales.

Despite the value of selling merchandise at markdown prices, it is important not to allow the second-in-importance merchandise to work against the image-building forces of the new, exciting first-rate goods. A store or department must maintain its fashion look and continue to play up the newest look in all areas except the ones designated for markdowns.

Sometimes it is particularly difficult to protect this image in a small department or in a specialty store. In some cases, successful specialty stores will elect to give clearance apparel to charity, rather than mar the overall image of the shop. Another alternative is to find a compatible store or department in another location and supply it with the clearance merchandise. There are jobbers who provide the service of removing old apparel and placing it in other selling locations. At all costs and by whatever means, it is important to keep the major selling space exciting and full of new, current styles.

Summary

The presentation of merchandise is essential to the fashion story and the selling process. Since the advent of mall stores, emphasis has moved from isolated display windows to merchandise presentation throughout the store. A wide variety of fixtures, forms, and techniques are available to entice the browser to buy. It is not sufficient just to make merchandise available; it must be presented in a manner that stimulates and excites the customer. Effective merchandise presentation not only contributes to the store image, but it can persuade customers to make more purchase decisions.

CHAPTER 7

Media Mix

Introduction

Media mix is the term given to the strategy of allocating advertising and promotion budget funds for the most effective and efficient usage. The ingredients for the media mix include all media that many stores or advertisers will use. Some advertisers will use just some of the media possibilities that are available, while others may use all of these media possibilities, but to each advertiser the media mix is the key to spending advertising and promotion money efficiently. Elements of a media mix consists of (1) newspaper advertising, (2) direct mail advertising, (3) broadcast advertising, which is divided into radio and TV, and (4) magazine advertising, along with expenditures for billboards and handbills.

The concept of media mix assumes that a selected combination of the different media will have a beneficial synergistic result not attainable with only one medium. Obviously, the media mix can vary from one promotion to another, depending upon what is more effective for a particular promotional effort and a particular time of the year or season. One medium is not likely to reach all of the prospective customers; therefore, to reach a larger percentage of the market, supplemental media may be added. The media that are added depend upon the strength of the primary medium.

To formulate a promotion plan, retail management should make assessments of the function of each medium in reaching various segments of the market. For example, retailers, whose principal medium is the newspaper because it has significant circulation in the region, might supplement their media selection with TV ads. Television advertising usually reaches more people than newspaper advertising. A value-packed storewide event is a likely candidate for this planning because the store's objective is increased volume. Budget permitting, the retailers can also consider direct mail advertising to the store's active charge account customers with emphasis on a "preferred customer" *advance preview* of this special event.

With such planning of the media mix, the advertiser has notified a maximum number of customer prospects, including its most loyal charge account patrons, of the store's excellent values. If it is affordable, radio can be added to the mix. The final days of the event should get plenty of radio time to continually remind listeners not to miss the value opportunities. Good usage of the principles of media mix does not necessarily mean simultaneous use of each medium.

Thorough use of the principles of media mix assures the advertiser that the various segments of the market are receiving the appropriate messages. Because of the characteristics of each medium, some of the message may be carried better in one medium than another. Consequently, to deliver the ad messages to the widest consumer market, it is important that the retailer be aware of the strengths of each medium.

When selecting the proper media mix, one should focus advertising attention on the most important medium and use the other media to supplement, not duplicate, the message. Use the secondary media to do something that has not been done or cannot be well done by the major medium. When this takes place, the store has achieved a variety of messages on the same subject. For instance, radio or TV make ideal supplements to the promotion program by calling attention to the promotion that is running in the newspaper. As an example, a newspaper ad featuring a fur sale could be highlighted by a radio ad saying, "Macy's semi-annual fur sale. Mr. Jones, our fur specialist, will be in our fur salon at 3:00 tomorrow to help you select your fur fashion." When voiced on the radio, the message should have the spirit of urgency.

No one mix of media guarantees success; however, it is helpful to know what has occurred in the past. Table 7.1 presents the percentages allocated to the various media by stores with sales volume between $20 and $50 million; Table 7.2 presents figures for specialty stores with sales over $5 million. The figures are reported voluntarily to the National Retail Federation (formerly NRMA); therefore, the same store may not report every year. These figures are not necessarily desirable goals for stores of this size; they are simply what occurred during the respective years.

An obvious trend in Table 7.1 is the decrease in the advertising dollars spent in newspapers. Historically, the newspaper has been the retailer's best medium for advertising, and it still receives the single largest allocation. Decline in newspaper circulation has diminished its success in getting the retailer's message to prospective customers. Radio has received only a small percentage of the advertising dollars over the years and is usually a secondary medium for the retailer. Television's allocation peaked in the early 1980s and has declined since. The expected

Table 7.1. Percentage of Expense by Medium for Department Stores—Sales $20–$50 Million.

Year	Newspaper	Radio	Television	Direct Mail	Other
1967	87	4*		5	3
1973	83	10		4	3
1974	81	10		5	3
1978	74	7	6	7	5
1980	70	5	9	6	10
1982	69	6	11	12	2
1986	64	8	5	17	7
1987	66	5	5	16	9

SOURCE: Percentages calculated from figures in the National Retail
Merchants Association, *Financial and Operating Results of Department and
Specialty Stores,* 1967, 1973, 1974, 1978, 1980, 1983, 1987, and 1988.
* Expenses for radio and television were grouped together before 1978.

potential of television for the retailer does not seem to have been realized by many stores. Perhaps this is due to its increasingly high cost or lack of confidence with a newer medium. At the same time, allocations for direct mail have increased due in part to its ability to selectively target the audience.

These trends appear to be typical of retailing in general; however, any specific store's allocation may deviate from these percentages without indicating a lack of advertising success. This is possible because the mix of media should derive from the store's merchandising philosophy,

Table 7.2. Percentage of Expense by Medium for Specialty Stores—Sales Over $5 Million.

Year	Newspaper	Radio	Television	Direct Mail	Other
1967	88	1*		6	5
1973	82	2		11	6
1974	67	8		21	3
1978	64	8	11	11	6
1980	64	4	12	14	6
1982	57	4	16	18	5
1986	66	8	2	14	10
1987	66	5	5	16	9

SOURCE: Percentages calculated from figures in the National Retail
Merchants Association, *Financial and Operating Results of Department and
Specialty Stores,* 1967, 1973, 1974, 1978, 1980, 1983, 1987, and 1988.
* Expenses for radio and television were grouped together before 1978.

its image, and the advertising competition. It is generally agreed that advertising is more productive when it occurs in fewer media regularly than in a wider variety of media infrequently.

No single combination of media is best for every store or even for a category of stores. In the early stages of planning a media mix, retailers usually plan for a wide mix, often choosing major usage of newspapers, plus planning some broadcast, and buying a limited amount of direct mail. A history of sales can indicate that a store's selected broadcast medium has not delivered results commensurate with costs. However, results from the modest use of direct mail indicate that the medium would be more successful if more dollars were budgeted. Retailers are continually analyzing the results of various elements that make up their media mixes. Consequently, there are continual changes in what is budgeted for each medium. Effective media mix planning relies on many factors, the most important being the analysis of sales results delivered by each of the several media the store uses.

Responsibility for Determining the Media Mix

The specific media mix to be used by a store is determined in large part by the size of the organization and by its policies. In most organizations the decision is a shared responsibility and occurs only after much discussion. For example, in a small department store the decision is often made during the deliberations leading up to the six-month advertising plan. During these meetings, the head of advertising presents information and statistics on the national and regional trends for the customer profile of the store's target customer. The general merchandise manager and the division manager discuss these trends with others in the advertising department and with the buyers, who are usually in attendance. After much discussion and sometimes much debate, a decision is reached by consensus as to the specific media mix for that six-month period. Sometimes the weight of the responsibility for the decision is determined by the individual's skill in debating or strength of personality. The decision will be evaluated after each month of advertising and may be changed, if the results have been unsatisfactory.

Influences on Media Mix

Importance of Marketing Information

When they are making a media selection advertisers must know who the customer is. Is it a newspaper-reading audience? Which segment of the customer group reads certain magazines? Who in the customer group has charge accounts with the store? When they are making media selections, advertisers should be aware of new areas where people will be moving, and the possibilities of using supplemental media circulation, such as local community papers, to reach outlying regions where the customers of the store could be living. Each medium—radio, television and newspaper—will have such marketing information available.

Influences of Lifestyle Factors

The best media will have data on the lifestyle of the customers in the market; such information is very important in making effective use of the media. This information tells the advertiser what is most important about how the customer lives in terms of the merchandise that is being advertised. It helps advertisers direct their expenditures through the specific medium that is relevant to the customer's way of living. Not only does it help advertisers to select media, but it is vital to the creative character of the advertising. Lifestyle data tells the creative people who produce the advertisements the important facts that determine the nature of copy and illustrations. Such data also guides the creative processes for broadcast media.

For example, if the target customer is in the "societal conscious" lifestyle group they are described by Mitchell as people who are "affluent, highly educated, politically liberal, self-confident, high degree of interest in consumer issues, enjoy healthful outdoor sports such as jogging. Above average readers of newspapers, magazines and books...."[1] This information suggests that newspapers or magazines are good media for these target customers, and that the copy or script should be sophisticated, possibly with a reference to outdoor sports activities.

Store Volume and Location

Store volume, of course, determines the advertising dollars spent to reach such sales. More dollars will be spent to attract more frequent traffic with higher sales volume. Specialty stores will need a lower frequency of advertising than department stores. The department store has a broad range of customers from a large geographic area, whereas the specialty shop has a narrow, specific customer in mind. So, the two will differ in their approach to the mix of media for their promotions. For example, the department store might spend more on television to

[1] Arnold Mitchell, *The Nine American Lifestyles* (New York: Macmillan, 1983), pp. 61–71.

a large geographic area, whereas the specialty store might spend more on direct mail to loyal customers.

Location of the store is a significant factor in how decisions on media mix are made. When a store is in a mall, the mall itself is an attraction and other stores help to draw customers to the mall, so there is less need for external advertising. Consequently, the retailer can focus on just one medium to attract more traffic to itself. In some cases the mall stores will use in-store advertising more, because they want to draw passing customers in and sell them, once they get them in the door. Stores that are in free standing buildings will need to advertise more than those in a shopping center or mall, because they must attract the customer to their location.

Competitive Situations

In planning their media mix, retailers evaluate the nature of the advertising of their competitors. When an important number of their competitors appear in a certain medium, it may be desirable to join with these competitors. A retailer's being absent from a medium in which its competition is visible may leave potential customers thinking the store does not offer comparable goods or perhaps does not offer as good a level of quality or price. This does not mean that a retailer should automatically advertise in the medium in which the competitor advertisers, but it does mean that the retailer should assess the situation in every case and see if it is wise to omit that medium.

When the retailer advertises in a community of competitors, (e.g., on the same page in a newspaper) there are certain beneficial effects. The customer is offered choices and finds such exposure of options to buy intriguing or stimulating. However, once a retailer decides to advertise where the competition appears, it must consider developing its own distinct style of advertising in order to achieve identity (see Figure 8.6).

Media Availability

Not every community has all media available. Most communities have efficient, effective newspapers and radio stations, but may not have a TV station. When there is no TV availability in the community, many retailers will use a neighboring city's TV station. This means the retailer is paying to reach some viewers who are not in the target group. However, if the store's target group is reached effectively, the TV ad can be justified.

Some newspapers produce special sections that are allocated to reach certain circulation zones that are important to the retailer. These zoned sections may appear on a weekly, biweekly, or daily basis, depending on the size of the newspaper. If zoned situations are available, the newspaper is a more attractive medium for small stores.

Thoughtful consideration of the various elements of the media mix is important, to be sure that the retailer is reaching all of the customers. Each element in the media mix cannot reach all customers; therefore a careful selection of the various media helps to fill the gaps found in each of the various media. For example, newspaper circulation often does not reach the outer areas of the market. These can be reached by using either radio, TV, or a special mailing list for direct mailings to the prospective customers living in these geographic areas.

Each medium has strengths and weaknesses. For example, direct mail is very effective for reaching specific customers whose names and addresses are available from a charge account or special mailing list. However, it cannot reach new customers when they are not on the mailing list. A balance may be achieved with the addition of radio and newspaper. Newspapers are an excellent medium for advertising since they reach a broad range of potential customers; however, there are those groups in the target market who do not buy or read newspapers. In some cases, the radio would be appropriate to add to the newspaper market in order to cover that portion such as young people, who typically do not read the newspaper.

Media Costs

Each medium varies in cost for reaching the customer; therefore, budgetary considerations must be involved in preparing a store's media mix. When making budgetary considerations, advertisers should evaluate media in terms of efficiency (the cost of reaching a member of the target market). Newspaper efficiency is measured by the milline rate, which reflects both the cost per agate line (there are fourteen agate lines to an inch of space, one column wide) and the newspaper's circulation:

$$\text{Milline rate} = \frac{\text{Cost per agate line} \times 1,000,000}{\text{Circulation}}$$

The *milline rate* represents the cost to a retailer of one agate line per million circulation. A newspaper with a circulation of 400,000 and an agate-line rate of $5.25 has a milline rate of $14.38.

Magazine efficiency is based on cost per thousand (CPM):

$$\text{Cost per thousand} = \frac{\text{Cost per page} \times 1,000}{\text{Circulation}}$$

A magazine with a circulation of two million and a per-page rate of $24,000 has a cost per thousand of $12.00. However, not all of the people who receive the magazine or newspaper will be target customers, so this should be included in the calculations. For example, if 65% of the magazine's readers are the retailer's target customers, the actual CPM is

$$\text{Cost per thousand} = \frac{\text{Cost per page} \times 1{,}000}{\text{Circulation} \times \dfrac{\text{Target market}}{\text{Circulation}}}$$

$$= \frac{\$24{,}000 \times 1{,}000}{2{,}000{,}000 \times .65}$$

$$= \frac{24{,}000{,}000}{1{,}300{,}000} = \$18.46$$

A small store dependent on obtaining the most for its advertising money may necessarily use the most expensive medium if that medium is attractive to its best customers. Mass merchandisers such as department stores and discount stores depend on the lower cost media in order to reach more people. Certain media may be ruled out on the basis of cost. For instance, a television advertisement could cost more than a small store would have in its total advertising allocation; therefore, that medium would not be available to that particular store. High postage and printing cost may lower the frequency of direct mail that a small retailer can use. Small retailers may also choose to use preprinted postcards or mailers from vendors when the price is acceptable. Preprinted mailers should be considered, because the costs for producing a mailer are expensive due to model's fees, photographer's fees, and other production costs.

Newspapers may be costly in reaching specific customers for a specialty store; however, there may be certain times of the year during which newspapers publish certain special sections that will benefit the store. Even though the cost may appear too expensive at first glance, these special sections of the newspaper are well read; hence their cost may be acceptable. For instance, many newspapers have fashion sections that are widely read and appear during major fashion peaks. An ad in that section is very visible, and it may be the only time of the year that the specialty store is in the newspaper.

Mechanical Considerations

In determining media mix the retailer must keep in mind the technical capabilities available for the various media that will be selected.

Most newspapers are competent in producing the retailer's advertisements. Most radio stations offer reasonably competent creative services in terms of script writing or voice techniques; however, preparation of television advertising can present problems. The bigger stations offer production services that consist of photography, script writing, editing, and voice and sound libraries for selecting music or sound effects. However, small stations may have few services to offer the advertiser. Direct mail requires skilled printing and typography capabilities. Many printers offer a good selection of interesting paper stocks that add quality impressions to the printed product. Many large communities offer services for retail advertisers that involve addressing direct mail and performing all the services that will help the post office keep postal costs at a minimum.

AVAILABILITY OF SKILLED PERSONNEL   The level of skill in all of these creative areas may vary from city to city. It is desirable for a city to offer a range of capabilities so that various stores in the community can have different images, different voices, and different models. If one medium offers a greater choice in these areas, with all other things being equal, the store could select that medium. Although most of the larger cities offer the retail advertiser creative services such as photography and fashion art, it is important for the smaller advertiser in smaller cities to be aware of these services available in nearby larger communities.

TIME REQUIREMENTS   Another consideration in media mix is time. If the retailer has forgotten to prepare an ad ahead of time or forgotten to advertise something that is very important, speed of production may determine the medium used. Often radio is the fastest medium, unless the ad is a very simple newspaper ad. TV production cannot be executed quickly. Likewise direct mail is very difficult, because time is required for printing, for addressing the mail pieces, and for delivering them to the post office for mailing.

Even when the store has an advertising department, time is still a consideration. How much production is already on their calendar? How much time will be required for them to complete the necessary parts of the advertisement? They may already have a full schedule even though the buyer has planned well in advance.

It is important for the retailer to be open-minded about making changes in the allocation of advertising dollars to the various media. There is a tendency to avoid the risk of doing something different from the past years. This can lead to sameness in advertising, year after year, and can cause the retailer to miss new creative opportunities. Even if an effort failed in the past, the situation may be right for success this time.

Principles for Achieving Effective Mix of Media

After carefully thinking out the ingredients of the media mix, the advertiser should apply the following principles.

Balance Principle

A principle of balance in media mix is to maximize the positives of a medium and to minimize the negatives. It is important for the retailer to understand that the preparation of the media mix should be directed toward balancing the weaknesses and the strengths that are inherent in all media.

An example of an excellent media mix is the well known Secret Sale promotion. All charge accounts on the store's mailing list receive secret sale announcement cards offering special discounts (see Figure 7.1). Many stores follow this up with a small newspaper ad that reproduces the post card and asks the question, "Have you received your secret sale postcard? If not, come in and place your name on our mailing list. We will give you a card for this sale. You will then receive our Secret Sale Card during these special promotions." In this situation the media mix provides more customers than those who get the card and adds valuable names to the mailing list. The ad also reminds customers who have the card to take advantage of the special offer.

Style Principle

No matter what medium is used, whether it is newspaper, direct mail, radio, or television, it is important that the store create a distinctive, consistent advertising style. Such an advertising style is essentially the total impression of the various units that make up store advertising.

Effective use of media mix depends on good advertising style. Careful selection of the various elements that go into the media mix is not enough. The retailer must communicate to the audience in a style that is consistently compatible with the character of the store and is consistent across all media. This means that the advertising, whether it is in print or in broadcast, must have an interrelationship. To be very blatant in radio or television advertising and to be more elegant or refined in print media presents a contradiction that will confuse the audience. If the advertising has an elegance in print media, the verbal messages for radio and TV must also use terms that are appropriately elegant.

These various media units must work together to emphasize the store's personality, describe its merchandise, and invite a customer to

P.O. Box 388 / Alcoa, TN 37701

Postmaster: Please deliver March 31, April 2 & 3
and <u>do not</u> deliver after April 7.

**FOR OUR
VALUED
CHARGE
CUSTOMERS**

would you like a
**SECRET
DISCOUNT**
on everything
you buy

SALE STARTS WED., APRIL 4

• WEST TOWN • EAST TOWNE • FOOTHILLS • OAK RIDGE • ATHENS • HAMILTON PLACE •
• MARKET STREET • EASTGATE • NORTHGATE • WALNUT SQUARE • BILTMORE SQUARE

Proffitt's **SECRET SALE**

**STARTS WEDNESDAY, APRIL 4
5 BIG DAYS: WEDNESDAY THROUGH SUNDAY
APRIL 4, 5, 6, 7 & 8**

Here's how to get your Secret Sale discount on everything you buy except Gucci Watches, all
Liz Claiborne merchandise, Fine Jewelry Watches, Designer Furs, Lalique and Hartmann Luggage.
• You may shop at Proffitt's all five days.
• Save all of your receipts.
• Bring this card and your receipts to any Proffitt's on or before Sun., April 8, 1990.
• Secret Sale cashier will reveal your discount after all your purchases are completed.
• Then, you'll receive a cash refund on your cash purchases and charge credits on your
charge purchases for 15%, 20% or 30%.
• Secret Sale discount cannot be applied to purchase of gift certificates.
• Fine Jewelry Secret Sale also in progress at West Town, East Towne,
Foothills, Hamilton Place and Eastgate.
• 8,100 cards will have a 30% discount • 16,200 cards will have a 20% discount.
• 50 cards will say "FREE" giving you all your purchases free up to $1,000 limit.
• 149,700 cards will have at least a 15% discount.

**YOUR DISCOUNT
WILL BE**

15% 20% 30% OR **FREE***

ON YOUR
TOTAL PURCHASES

VOID
IF
TAMPERED
WITH

YOUR
"HIDDEN"
DISCOUNT
IS
BELOW

CASHIER'S
MAGIC PEN
MAKES YOUR
DISCOUNT
APPEAR

YOUR
DISCOUNT IS
HIDDEN HERE

* $1,000 limit.

Figure 7.1. Secret sale postcard sent by direct mail. (Courtesy of Proffitt's, Alcoa, Tenn.)

make a purchase decision. Advertising style reinforces these varied elements in such a way that they build instant recognition and identity for the store. In print media these elements are a store's signature. The store's selling message is composed of headlines, copy, and illustrations, whether drawings or photography, that are placed together in an attractive layout. They become the advertising style that is effective.

In broadcast media, especially radio, the audio is very important. The sound of the message must be distinctive and represent the store's personality. The elements that are used to develop an audio personality are the voice, music, and possible sound effects. An aggressive retailer seeking immediate response will use a highly persuasive voice, perhaps march music, and most likely sound effects such as a fire bell or a trumpet. Since television is a welding of picture with sound, the photographic use of the camera is very important. Picture and sound must blend in feeling to express the store image. For instance, a fashion store can express the dynamics of a sportswear presentation by using quick cuts, with upbeat audio as an accompaniment.

The logo that is very important in all print media must also be thoughtfully developed. In radio the audio sound can easily be the logo for the store. It can be a trumpet announcing the store name or a piano rhythm that is part of a jingle that uses the store name. In television the logo can be an adaptation of the print media logo using the various graphic devices that can animate the store name visually. A store that caters to the upscale customer will use fashion illustrations or photos that suggest the character of customer, and its advertising text would use sophisticated terminology. Elegant photography situations for television should be accompanied by equally elegant sound effects in the audio portions.

Continuity Principle

CONTINUITY OF IMPRESSION   Continuity of impression is one of the most valuable assets of the advertising planning process. Retailers achieve identity and customer loyalty when their advertising is instantly recognized regardless of the medium being used. The repetition that is based on continuity of impression is most important, because all of the store's customers do not see or hear all of the advertising in any one medium all the time. Such repetition keeps the store's name in the mind of the customer, so that when customers want to fill a need, they will shop at that store.

Alert retailers spend a lot of money to achieve continuity of impression and receive the valuable rewards of instant identity. It is almost as if they have a presence in the mind of the customer. An interesting example of the importance of continuity of impression is of a well-known store in the middle west. This store ran frequent ads in the newspaper with a distinctive border and logo plus the store's special illustration style. One day, in advertising an important sale event, the retailer omitted the store logo, yet there was a satisfactory response as if the logo had appeared. The readers had recognized the total style of the ad, because of the continual repetition of the various elements that made up the ad format.

CONTINUITY OF EXPRESSION   In order to strengthen the continuity of impression, stores strive for continuity of expression. The advertising style, copy, layout, type style, and logo should have a similarity in all print media. The illustration style should be similar as well. There can be subtle differences between drawings for newspapers and for better-printed direct mail. However, TV advertising demands its own special style that reflects the dynamics of TV. Copy is shorter and should aim to establish a mood, since the video, in effect, describes the merchandise. The store's print logo should be used on TV. However, the logo does not have to be a static element tacked on the video sections. The TV logo should have a video style, yet resemble its print version. Various computer-generated graphic effects for animating the print media logo are available. By using such effects the logo can increase its size to dominate the picture at the end of the message. Commercials can end with multiple logos covering the screen to create a graphic pattern, or the logo can dance across the screen to a musical beat. Relevant continuity of expression can be used in radio advertising. Certainly the mood-inspiring copy style for TV can be expanded for radio usage. The voice should reflect the personality of the persons that are used in the illustrations of print media. The music that is used can, in its own subtle way, create added enhancement to the verbal message. Such music can vary from the classics for a quality fashion store, to stirring march music played by a brass band for a mass-merchandising operation featuring low, discount prices.

Flexibility Principle

It is important to be flexible with the dollar allocation to various media. Effective media mixes will change as new technology offers greater capabilities in terms of targeting individual people by demographics and lifestyle. The media mix must reflect such changes. When a mass merchandiser changed its merchandising policies from frequent sales to "everyday low" prices, it also changed its advertising plans, particularly in newspapers. Fewer major tabloid insertions were used, whereas the number of day-to-day R.O.P. (run-of-paper) pages was increased. In this way, the mass merchandiser was making sure that its lower prices were seen often, instead of having a special sale for one week only.

Media mix decisions will change as the store grows in its market. For instance, a new operation may choose to use a lot of radio to get its message out quickly, using the newspaper to back up radio. As the store develops and establishes a loyal customer clientele, the mix may move to a higher percent for direct mail to capitalize on promoting to the growing list of customers. A good part of the radio budget would then be transferred to the direct mail budget.

CONTINUAL EVALUATION PRINCIPLE   Constant review of the media mix is necessary to determine the most effective combination of media. First, the sales results from each medium should be analyzed. Second, the sales results of promotions involving more than one medium should be studied.

The "Blitz" Principle

Basically a "Blitz" media mix extends the store's advertising to all possible phases of expression. The retailer tries to reach all of the customers in its target group. Such tactics completely saturate the awareness of the customers. This practice, however costly, can be used for unusual special events such as opening a new store or a new important department.

Media Mix Example

Retail stores will vary in their mix, making it difficult to cite a typical example; however, Figure 7.2 shows some frequently used combinations of media.

Buyer's Responsibility

The buyer's responsibility in regard to media and media mix includes being a collaborator with the advertising management.

The buyer should:

1. Inform the advertising department of the results of all ads. Assessing the success of each medium is essential for future planning and media selection.

2. The buyer should relate to the advertising department who the customer is and whether customers' needs are constantly changing. This

a, b, c

e

```
PROFFITT'S RADIO

SUBJ:        Founder's Sale
LENGTH:      :30
RUN DATES:   5/8-13/90
STATIONS:    WYXI, WYMU (Tues., May 9 & Thurs., May 11 only)
WRITER:      Pete

MUSIC:       PROFFITT'S JINGLE, JUNIOR VERSION-CUT #16

WOMAN:   At Proffitt's, we honor the founder of our store with
         our biggest and best sale of the season!

MAN:     It's Proffitt's Founder's Sale, going on now through
         Sunday!

WOMAN:   You'll find exceptional savings on the latest fashions
         for men, women, and children from all your favorite
         names!

MAN:     Plus, you'll save big on a great selection of
         housewares, gifts, and much more!

WOMAN:   Many items are at our lowest prices of the season,
         so it's a perfect time to buy those Mother's Day and
         graduation gifts!

MAN:     Hurry in for fabulous savings now through Sunday
         during Proffitt's Founder's Sale!

WOMAN:   Our biggest and best sale of the season!
```

d

Figure 7.2. An example of a promotion with mixed media, newspaper ad, newspaper insert, and radio script. A direct mail piece and in-store signage was also used but not pictured. (Courtesy of Proffitt's, Alcoa, Tenn.)

requires the creation of a motivation profile of the customer who will buy the merchandise advertised. The buyer should offer detailed information that helps the advertising answer the customer's questions.

3. The buyer should inform the advertising department how much money, at retail, is invested in the stock of the goods being advertised. The advertising staff can then evaluate how much money should be spent either on advertising space in the newspaper, or on cost of production in direct mail, or on time expenses in broadcast media. This is important in order to avoid making a large investment in advertising money to sell a small investment in merchandise.

4. The buyer, and also the advertising department, should know the purpose of the department's advertising at a particular time of year, and whether the store considers that department to be a growing department, a promotional department, or a fashion forward department. What is the department's purpose? Is it to build the image of the store? Is it to promote and increase volume immediately? Depending on store policy, the buyer can request variations in media mix depending upon the objectives for that department at the time.

5. The buyer should be aware of competitor advertising in order to be able to inform the advertising department of the methods and media selection of competitors. A buyer should be aware not only of competitor advertising, but also advertising of similar retailers in other communities. Aware buyers will usually get the best advertising for their department, if they remember the sign that first appeared in a major New York department store's ad department, "When you want advertising that sells, you must first sell the advertising department."

Summary

No one medium is effective in reaching all the potential customers; therefore, a mix of media is employed to balance the strengths and weaknesses of the media used. Continual evaluation of the media mix is essential. The mix may need to be changed occasionally, because the effectiveness of each medium has a potential to change over time. Influences on media mix include lifestyle factors, store volume and location, competitive situation, media availability and cost, availability of skilled personnel in the medium, and preparation time. The principles for achieving effective media mix are balance, style, continuity, flexibility, continual evaluation, and the "Blitz" principle. The decision to use a certain mix of media is often reached by consensus. Care should be taken to maintain a continuity of style across all media for instant recognition.

CHAPTER 8

Advertising Principles: Print Media

Introduction

Advertising is the prime sales promotion tool that retailers use to attract the customer's attention and to bring the consumer to the point of sale. Advertising is a paid message in a public medium such as newspaper, magazine, radio, television, direct mail, or billboards to persuade the customer to take favorable action on the retailer's offering. Advertising is from the Latin *ad vertere*, which simply means "to turn toward." Good advertising *turns the reader's attention toward* the sales promotion proposition. It either praises the benefits of the merchandise involved, or it emphasizes the cost advantages of the merchandise to the consumer. Those are advertising's principle functions. The secondary function is to focus the reader's attention on the special characteristics of the advertiser such as a quality personality or an aggressive price-oriented personality. Advertising activity has one more objective: to be retained in the prospective customer's memory by being meaningful to him or her. Advertising, to be effective, needs staying power in the customer's mind. All this advertising activity must be positive enough to persuade the customer to respond favorably by shopping in the establishment and making purchases.

Advertising Objectives/Purpose

1. A prime objective of advertising is to *increase sales transactions and volume,* thus adding to the net profit of the store.
2. A goal of advertising is to *contribute to the store's image* and develop a reputation for the store. The retailer must promote the store as a

desirable place in which to trade before the store can hope to sell its merchandise.

3. A purpose of good advertising is to *speed the turnover* of goods.

4. An objective of effective advertising is to *stabilize the sales volume* by increasing sales volume of the store during months when business would normally be weak and during periods of general business depression.

When the advertising of timely desirable goods achieves these objectives, it becomes a powerful asset in building a store's sales and profitability.

Types of Retail Advertising

Advertising can be broken down into types based on merchandising objectives, by using this A.B.C. formula:

A is for Action, *aggressive* action. This advertising should be directed towards obtaining *immediate* maximum customer response (see Figure 8.1).

B is for Building *impressions*. This advertising should build *favorable attitudes* about the store's fashion product leadership, merchandise values, famous brands, assortments, and innovative ideas (see Figure 8.2 for an example of a "B" ad).

C is for developing the Character of the store. Often called *institutional advertising*, this type of advertising is concerned with creating goodwill for the store. This category focuses on the store's special character and services. (See Figure 8.3 for an example of a C ad.)

Print Media

Advertising media are categorized in groups. The first category is print media, which consists of newspaper advertising, magazine advertising, direct mailings, catalogs, sales letters, postcards, hand bills, package stuffers, billboards, outdoor signing, and in-store media such as posters, signs, and price cards. Packaging can also be included when there are shopping bags or wrappings used by customers. The other category of advertising media is broadcast, often called the electronic media. This consists of radio, television, in-store announcements over a public address system, and in-store video presentations. Even though the electronic media has grown in importance over many years and seems to dominate the customers' attention, print media receives a leading share of the ad budgets. Because of the increased use of color-printed inserts, newspapers are still the prime medium for most fashion advertisers, although this medium's importance has diminished somewhat since its peak use in the 1960s.

Newspapers

ADVANTAGES   Because most fashion retailers wish to reach the largest number of potential customers, they use newspapers more than any other advertising media. Nearly everyone reads a daily newspaper, and readers are accustomed to shopping newspaper advertising to get information on the merchandise they want to purchase. Most homes receive a newspaper, usually a morning newspaper, since there are more morning newspapers than evening newspapers. The number of evening papers has been decreasing for many years mostly because of high production costs in the face of shrinking circulation of evening papers.

Flexibility;   Using newspapers allows advertisers to set definite times for the advertising because they can choose the days that are best for them. Such flexibility of choice is a significant advantage. For example, some retailers may prefer to introduce new items early in the week in a "B" (building impressions) ad and publish immediate response "A" (aggressive action) advertising at the end of the week, when most customer shopping takes place. Newspaper advertising also permits the advertiser to be flexible in the use of space. The store can run a quarter page ad one day and use twice as much space on another day.

Repetition of Ad Position;   The advertiser can usually have the advertisements placed on the same page on specific days. For example, a store can select page five on Thursdays. Readers then will become accustomed to looking for the ad when they turn to this page. The best page position can be determined only by experimentation. Men's clothing or active sportswear for men is often placed in the sports section of a newspaper.

Special Interest Sections;   Most newspapers publish special sections, such as brides' supplements, back-to-school fashion guides, or vacation sections, that help the retailer reach special groups at a time when there is a demand for such merchandise. These sections often have a higher readership and may not be discarded immediately, thus having the potential of being read several times.

Relatively Low Cost;   Newspaper ad rates are less costly than the rates for television or radio. The number of TV viewers or radio listeners reached may be larger, but these audiences may contain people who

Figure 8.1. Coat promotions *aggressively* advertised in different creative styles in the "A" category. (Courtesy of Globman's, Martinsville, Va. and Macy's, New York.)

Figure 8.1. (*continued*)

Figure 8.2. The objective of this "B" ad is to *build* a favorable impression of the advertisers. Lord & Taylor uses a double page to focus on its comprehensive selection of lace fashions. (Courtesy of Lord & Taylor, New York.)

are not valuable enough prospects for the advertiser; hence, the ad may not be worth the expense.

Retrievability; A major advantage of newspaper advertising is that the information is retrievable. If customers are interested after they have seen an advertisement in a newspaper, they can go back to the page and read it again. The ad can be clipped by the customer and taken to the store as a shopping aid. This does not happen when electronic media are used. The message has evaporated soon after it is presented.

DISADVANTAGES

Competition for Reader's Attention; An important disadvantage of newspaper advertising is the intense competition of other advertisers in the paper for the reader's attention. A newspaper full of advertising is very much like a busy marketplace with many vendors loudly hawking their wares.

Short Life; The short life of the ad page is a consideration. It lives for a few hours, and the next day it may line the bottom of a bird cage.

Poor Reproduction Ability; Due to the speed of the printing press and the poor quality of the paper stocks, illustrations of merchandise often may not print well. This is especially true when photos or subtly toned drawings are used. However, in several cities, the local newspapers are now using the newest printing methods, based on laser and computer technology, to improve their printing quality. *USA Today* is a fine example of such improvement.

Limited Reading Time; People have limited time for newspaper reading because of distractions such as television, participation in community activities, and spectator sports.

Long Preparation Time; Another disadvantage is that it takes a retailer more time to prepare effective ads for newspapers than formerly. Not too long ago retailers could prepare a newspaper ad in three to four days. Now it can take a week or more. In contrast, a retailer can get advertising on the radio in a few hours.

Wasted Circulation; Retailers often question how big their local paper's audience is in relation to their particular market segments. It is possible that a store's advertising will appeal to a very small part of

Figure 8.3a. In the "C" category, Bloomingdale's double-page ad strengthens the store's fashion impression by focusing on California lifestyles. (Courtesy of Bloomingdale's, New York.)

Figure 8.3*b*. Macy's "C" ad welcomes another leading store to the New Jersey community where Macy's is a popular retailer. (Courtesy of Macy's, New York.)

the newspaper's total circulation. Furthermore, advertisers may not be reaching customer prospects because of the paper's limited distribution in growing suburban or rural areas.

WHO CAN BEST USE NEWSPAPERS   Many experts consider newspapers an important medium for those retailers who thrive on immediate customer action. These stores focus on aggressive promotional merchandising practices. They feature attractive competitive pricing often resulting from merchandising opportunities provided by resources. These can be special purchases at a price advantage or closeouts of seasonal stocks. Usually these advertisers use discount prices, short markups, or deep markdowns to stimulate quick customer response. "A" for action is the prime category of advertising used by these advertisers.

Newspapers are also useful to fashion retailers who wish to occupy a niche in terms of filling the customer's special fashion needs. These niches vary from store to store or even within a store. These retailers find newspaper advertising valuable in reaching their particular market segments, especially when the paper publishes a special section of interest to fashion aware readers. This advertising, usually in the "B" category, employs various techniques to make a favorable impression on the prospective customers. These ads appear mostly in the Sunday editions, when the readers have more time to study the advertisements. The fashion aware customer eagerly awaits the Sunday newspaper to find out what's new. At the end of the week the same reader looks for advertising that features price promotions from the same stores.

BUYING NEWSPAPER SPACE

Selection of Newspaper;   When there is more than one newspaper in a community, the advertiser's first consideration should be the quality of circulation. Such circulation information is available at the newspapers involved. Largeness of the newspaper's circulation, is not necessarily the most important consideration. What is important is how many potential readers within the circulation area of the newspaper who can be the store's customers. It is important that the advertiser determine which newspaper has the biggest circulation among the store's type of customers.

When stores are considering a newspaper, they also look at the character of the newspaper in terms of its readership. They refer to circulation data on who buys or subscribes to the newspaper. If one newspaper is more conservative in its editorial policy, its readers are probably going to be equally conservative. A very good example of the need for evaluating circulation is demonstrated in New York City. *The New York Times,* a leading newspaper in this market, reaches all customers, but its circulation emphasis is toward the better educated, more affluent reader. However, *The New York Times* circulation is not necessarily the biggest circulation. *The Daily News,* a tabloid, has a bigger circulation in the New York market and is read by many middle income readers as well as more blue collar readers. The creative techniques for advertising in *The New York Times* are different than those employed in *The Daily News.*

Evaluating Newspaper's Circulation; Before making any decisions regarding newspaper advertising, store management should be familiar with data concerning the extent and character of the circulation. Answers to these questions are significant: What percentage of the total circulation is in the immediate metropolitan city? How much of the circulation is in the suburban areas, and how much of it goes out into the bordering counties?

Circulation demographics data are valuable in the decision process. These demographics describe the income level of the readership in each of the above categories. It is important to know whether the readers own or rent houses and what these cost. Demographic data from a newspaper should discuss the educational and social levels of its readers as well. (See Figure 8.4 for a sample of demographic data.)

Along with such demographic information the retailer should know about the various editorial features of the newspapers. Many newspapers owe a large part of their circulation to these special features of the newspaper. Those retailers who wish to impress special groups of customers will find such editorial features a valuable accompaniment to their advertising. Some newspapers, because of certain creative talents on the staff, produce excellent home fashion pages of interest to the home furnishings customer, whereas others have interesting apparel fashion sections that draw the attention of the alert fashion customer. Many papers devote their editorial attention to various elements of children's activities, thus becoming an important medium for stores that cater to the family.

There is an easy way of determining the relationship of various newspapers that have different size circulations and different space rates. Many retailers use a common denominator known as the milline rate, which is the cost of reaching one million readers with one agate line of advertising. Milline rate is determined by multiplying the rate per agate line by one million and dividing the result by the circulation (see Chapter 7, "Media Cost"). *Agate line* is an oldtime printers' term used by newspapers for measuring advertising space. An agate line is exactly 1/14 of an inch. Fourteen agate lines equal one column inch. Most newspaper pages are six columns wide and three hundred agate lines deep. Over the years, the word agate has been dropped, and newspaper space is measured by *lines* and *columns.* (See Figure 8.5 for an example of a newspaper rate card.)

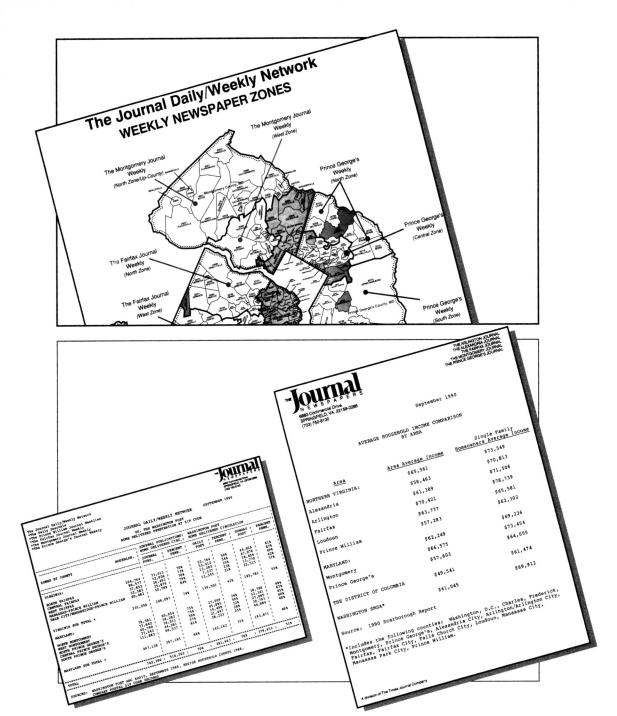

Figure 8.4. Typical demographic data supplied by most leading newspapers. Such information usually includes circulation maps, consumer income data for each circulation region, and the newspaper's circulation penetration in each region. Often, some papers include comparison figures for competing media. (Courtesy of The Journal Newspapers, Springfield, Va.)

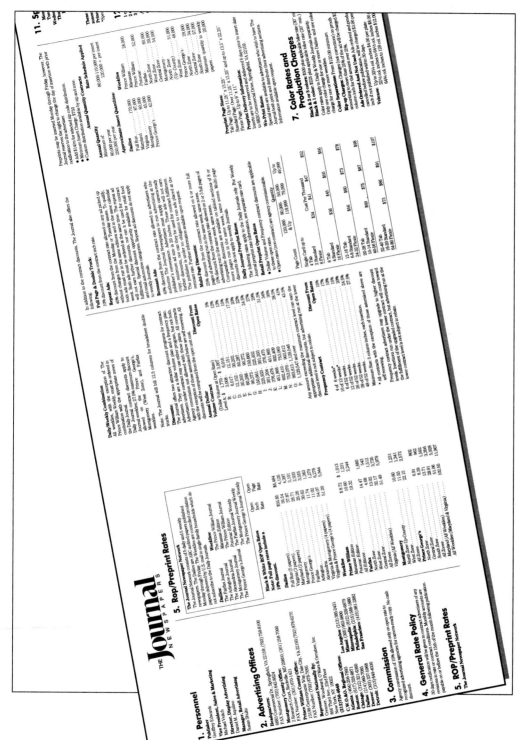

Figure 8.5. Commonly called the "rate card," this detailed rate schedule offers much information that is useful to the retailer. Advertising in newspapers is subject to the terms and conditions that are specified in such rate schedules. (Courtesy of The Journal Newspapers, Springfield, Va.)

Sunday Versus Daily Newspaper; It is important to be aware of the relative merits of Sunday or daily newspapers. Such information guides the advertiser in making media decisions, which are based on the different categories of goods being advertised.

This process determines to a great degree what types of merchandise are best for a Sunday newspaper, a morning newspaper, or an evening newspaper. When the entire family is at home, they can enjoy a Sunday newspaper at leisure. They are not hurried by the typical daily occupations. Therefore, it is a more pleasurable experience to read the paper. Because of its larger circulation and potential of reaching every member of the family that can read, the Sunday papers have many feature sections of interest to specific members of the family. For the younger adults there are sections that concentrate on fashion and entertainment, and for the children there are always the comics. This is evidenced by the ever-increasing weight of the Sunday paper. Advertisers are attracted by the Sunday newspaper's ability to reach the various members of the family plus the additional advantage of the widest possible circulation.

Sunday newspaper circulation in most communities extends beyond the distribution of the daily newspaper. Consequently, this market reach is very important to retailers. Because of this, in many communities Sunday space costs more than daily morning or evening. In making a decision to use Sunday or daily morning or evening, the retailer must consider the advantages and disadvantages of each. Morning newspapers are usually home delivered to a greater extent than evening papers, and because morning editions are delivered, it is easy to evaluate the accuracy of the circulation figures. Evening newspapers often sell at newsstands, and it is difficult to trace the circulation except from day to day, because circulation may depend on the weather or some other event.

Morning newspapers are best for "B" advertising. Because it is usually delivered to homes, the morning newspaper offers a splendid opportunity to build an advertising impression of quality, fashion leadership, or brand identity. The morning newspaper can also be used for "A" advertising for major sale events. An aggressive action promotion can begin the day the advertising appears. For the past few years evening papers have been declining in circulation, and many communities no longer have evening papers for reasons that are related to publishers' costs or needs. The few evening papers that may be available can be important to the aggressive retailer. For example, the advertiser can publish advertising in an evening paper that says, "starting tomorrow, a very special event."

Which Day of the Week? When retailers consider the objectives of their advertising, they must also consider the days of the week. An important decision that is made when retailers consider daily circulation is whether to run on Monday, Tuesday, Wednesday, Thursday, or Friday. Many stores stay out of the newspaper on Monday because they have planned an extensive Sunday paper program that has a strong effect on Monday sales. Tuesday is not necessarily a good day because as a retail sales day it is usually weak. On Wednesday, many fashion retailers omit the newspaper because it is usually full of food and supermarket advertising. Thursday and Friday are very strong advertising days because sales results indicate that the peak of selling usually takes place Friday and Saturday. Saturday morning newspapers have been used by smaller retailers to stimulate extra Saturday volume on top of what is usually a good business day.

Sunday is very good for "B" advertising when the plan is to feature fashion themes, new ideas in fashion, famous brand names, or a very special week-long price-oriented promotion. Thursday and Friday newspaper advertisers usually publish aggressive immediate-action ads to achieve the heavy sales that take place over Friday and Saturday. Such advertising is usually in the "A" category.

There are exceptions of course. Some stores will advertise on Monday and Tuesday because the space rates may be lower than Sunday rates so they can use "A" advertising earlier in the week to achieve a longer sale period. There is less retail advertising published on these days, and the store's ad can receive more visibility in a smaller space.

The Advertisement Position in the Newspaper; Position of the ad refers to the page on which it appears in the newspaper, and to the placement on that page. *Placement* refers to whether the ad is on the left or right or on top or the bottom of the page. There is a continual debate among advertising professionals as to whether a right-hand page or a left-hand page is better. There are some advantages to a right-hand page. Customers are apt to see a right-hand page before a left-hand page. Before the center fold under certain conditions the right-hand page prints a little clearer because there is a printing strike-through on the left-hand page. Past the center fold of the paper the reverse printing effect takes place. However, if the promotion is strong and the advertising message is very attractive and moves readers to action, then left-hand pages have been equally productive.

Often advertisers have some historical control over the position of an ad. There is a "grandfather clause" in which certain pages, in effect, belong to long-time advertisers because they have always used those pages. These stores do a large amount of advertising; consequently, they are important to the newspaper. However, this "grandfathering" is slowly disappearing due to publishing necessities. As a result, a store may have little control over where the advertisement appears in the newspapers, with a new advertiser having the least control. These ads get the *Run-of-Paper (ROP)* position, that is, any place the newspaper management decides.

There are newspapers who offer advertisers *preferred positions* at a premium cost. This means the store pays extra to get on a specific page. The increase varies from 10% to 25%. In many newspapers "preferred position" is considered as follows: The back page of the first section of a newspaper is a prime preferred position, and in the opinion of many retailers and publishers it is the second most important page, with the front page being the most important. Pages two and three are also considered valuable preferred positions. For this reason, in many communities, upscale quality merchants run small ads for which they pay extra, that enable them to get on page two or three. Consequently, a community of retail advertisers on pages two and three has grown to be an advertising feature in most newspapers. On these pages are several stores that are competitors appearing together to share the same category of customer. (See Figure 8.6.)

Special Sections; Certain sections in a newspaper are important to some advertisers. The sports section is significant for retail advertisers who sell action sportswear to men. The various special newspaper sections of interest to homemakers are of interest to most home fashion advertisers. Many newspapers publish special sections of interest to brides that offer retailers a splendid opportunity not only to sell bridal costumes but fashions that appeal to the mother of the bride, as well as bridesmaids.

Also, there is a special section each week in many newspapers that focuses on local television programs. This is called the *television log* and is printed in a tabloid form or smaller. The contents of this special section are devoted to programming and interesting information about television programs or performers. The back page of this section is considered very valuable for advertising to a younger market. Many stores use this back page, paying a premium price, to advertise to juniors or the high school crowd. This advertising has a week-long life around the house, particularly in the vicinity of the television set. Often this ad is highly visible because the front page is frequently face down on the television set. Many retailers have been advised to use this advertising opportunity to promote their brand name strengths. Because it is expensive and because color is often used, this advertising may be funded by cooperative advertising programs from leading resources.

Inserts in Newspaper

PRE-PRINTED COLOR INSERTS Many retailers, particularly the aggressive promotional stores, use this type of color insert to gain maximum

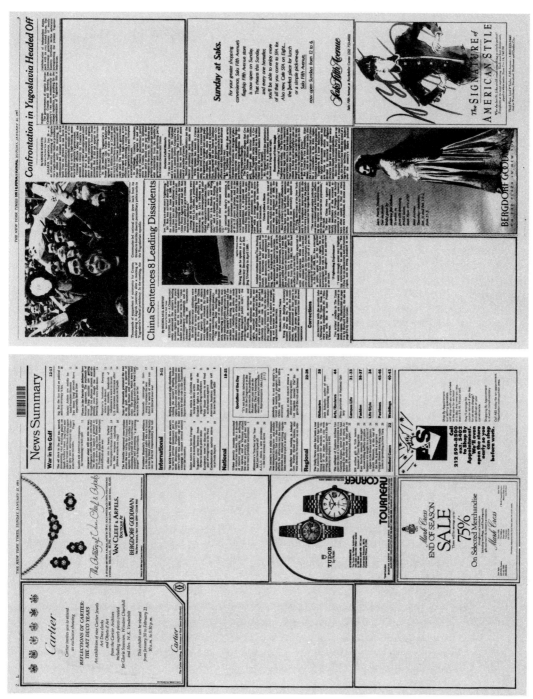

Figure 8.6. The small-space advertisements of many fashion retailers are effectively grouped together on pages two and three of the *New York Sunday Times*. Such preferred positioning is available in many markets. (Courtesy of *New York Times* and the advertisers.)

181

advertising impact in the newspaper. Its form is usually tabloid size ($10'' \times 15''$), and it is inserted into the folds of a standard size newspaper. With the addition of full color, the insert becomes, in effect, a special section. With the improvement in offset color printing techniques, more retailers are using full color inserts to increase the advertising impact on the customer. This type of insert is usually printed days or weeks ahead of the normal printing schedule of the newspaper. All things being equal in terms of circulation and market penetration, the advertiser now has the advantage of using color and, often, better paper stocks in preparing such inserts. The color insert, whether it is "A," "B," or even "C" advertising, gives the retailer splendid opportunities to establish an effective advertising personality.

ADVANTAGES   Inserts are best expressed with color photography, but when color photography is not available, or it is too costly, color illustrations drawn by skilled artists are very effective and often very distinctive. Inserts printed in black and white are less effective. The prime benefit of color inserts is that the customer is quite impressed because such advertising closely resembles magazine advertising. Secondly, the quality of the paper adds to the upscale impression that the retailer aims to give to the reader. Thirdly, the clarity of the illustration, whether it is photographic or drawn, helps improve the sale of the merchandise.

Manufacturers, particularly in the fashion field, may supply such inserts as part of their cooperative ad plans. Retailers that are members of buying offices will often acquire from these offices attractive color inserts for special promotions. The cost of these inserts is lower than it would be if the store produced its own insert material.

DISADVANTAGES   Such inserts are costly to prepare, to print, and to insert into the newspaper. The cost of insertion is often as much as the cost of a black and white ad that runs ROP. Inserts often fall out of the paper, and many customers never get to see them. Because inserts are very popular with retailers, many newspapers schedule too many inserts for one edition. Some newspapers can have as many as eight to ten inserts, leaving fashion competitors sharing the same insert schedule with hardware stores and supermarkets. The disinterested reader often disposes of inserts before glancing at them, especially if there are too many. In newspaper ROP advertising, the reader must continue to turn pages to get the text of the news matter. Thus, the ROP ad has a good chance of being seen, possibly read.

Magazines

At one time there were only national circulation fashion magazines such as *Vogue, Vanity Fair, Harper's Bazaar.* Only major retailers in large cities could afford to advertise in these. These stores had branches in many states, thus making such national circulations worthwhile. Stores such as Lord & Taylor, headquartered in New York, have branches in Atlanta, Chicago, Dallas, Los Angeles, Boston, and other cities. Other major stores acquired a nationwide reputation although located in one region. A good example is Neiman-Marcus, which originally was located in Texas.

Later, several magazines published regional editions that had special sections for the advertising of stores in a particular region. For example, *Seventeen* magazine publishes a southeast regional section that is used by stores in Georgia, South Carolina, Tennessee, Virginia, and North Carolina. Retailers with branches that are in most of these states can profitably place their advertising in such regional editions. These regional editions do not appear every month, they usually are seasonal. At the same time, *Seventeen* publishes similar sections for circulation in other regions of the country.

There are more national magazines published now that are targeted sharply to the various readers' lifestyles. These include publications of interest to working women. *Self* and *Mademoiselle* serve various career-motivated age groups, whereas *Elle* is for the young professional woman. *Lears* is read by the more mature fashion-aware reader. Even the larger size woman has her own publication, *Big Beautiful Woman*.

There is an important phenomenon in magazine publishing. There are magazines that focus on matters of interest to the citizens of various major cities. The contents of these publications reflect the lifestyle of these communities. Leaders in such publishing are *The New Yorker* and *New York Magazine*. Washington D.C. has its own magazine, *The Washingtonian*. Philadelphia and Chicago readers have their own magazines. So do citizens of Atlanta, Boston, Dallas, and other cities. These magazines, whether they are national or regional, offer splendid opportunities for fashion specialty stores to advertise their merchandise. The multi-department store can advertise certain categories of merchandise that relate to the editorial thrust of the magazine. The young and upwardly mobile would be an ideal customer prospect for advertising in *The New Yorker,* or *The Washingtonian* or any similar magazine (see Figure 8.7).

Many newspapers offer their readers magazine formats in the form of inserts that look like magazines but are distributed as newspaper inserts. *Parade* and *USA Weekend* are typical of this category. *The New York Times* publishes its own fine magazine as a Sunday insert. These newspaper supplements are considered choice media for national retailers as well as local stores.

LEVELS OF MAGAZINE DISTRIBUTION   National advertising is published in magazines whose circulations cover all 50 states as well as the rest of

Figure 8.7. Some of the magazines that focus on matters of interest to the people in various communities. Local fashion advertisers find such media are useful in enhancing their personality. (Courtesy of *San Diego, New York,* and *Washingtonian.*)

the world. This advertising reaches its nationwide audience simultaneously. There are also regional media that cover sections of the country composed of several states and appeal to the readers of the region. Included in this classification is the local magazine that reaches the readers who live in a big metropolitan city and its peripheral areas. An exception is *The New Yorker,* which is read all over the country and is a truly national magazine with its contents that reflect New York's culture.

There is little advantage for a small specialty department store to place advertising in a national magazine. On the other hand, Bloomingdale's achieved a national reputation in spite of the fact that it had stores only in a few major cities in the east. Sales were made mainly to eastern customers, while its reputation was impressed on possible customers who would visit New York. As a result, such national advertising contributed to Bloomingdale's nationwide reputation.

There is an important requirement for stores who advertise in national magazines. There should be an adequate merchandise supply, because wherever these stores are located, unless they are in a national chain, they must be able to serve the customer who travels a distance because of the reputation the store has earned.

ADVANTAGES   The leading advantage of magazine advertising is that stores can use it to concentrate on the advertising that creates a store's character or image. The reproduction of color or black and white illustrations or photos is superior to the printing of similar advertising in the newspaper. Important to the retailer is that the circulation opportunities are often larger than those of the local newspaper. Manufacturers' cooperative money is more readily available, because such advertising offers the bigger audience valued by the manufacturer. An advantage, similar to newspaper advertising, is that the information published is retrievable by the reader. Magazine advertising often lasts longer than newspaper advertising in the mind of the reader. Furthermore, the prestige of the magazine is shared by the advertiser.

Very special forms of national advertising are often used when a nationally known fashion manufacturer places its own advertising in a magazine to promote its label. Within the body of the ad are listed several stores, all noncompeting, that will offer this merchandise. The manufacturer often will devote the entire ad to one or two stores. This advertising is 100% paid for by the manufacturer, and the retailers have the advantage of appearing in this space. However, some vendors will publish the names of too many stores in such small type that it is very difficult to read, thus minimizing the advantages to the stores.

DISADVANTAGES   Whether it is a national advertising program or a regional advertising program there can be wasted magazine circulation.

The entire circulation, nationally or regionally, may not be representative of the customers of the store. Although the magazine has a large circulation, the advertising can fail because it was not productive enough to pay the high ad cost, especially when there are not enough goods available to offer customers who may respond to the advertising weeks after the magazine is issued.

Because of the longer life cycle of magazine advertising as compared to newspaper advertising, it is important that the supply of advertised merchandise be sufficient to meet the needs of the customer during this period. This means the retailer should have enough open-to-buy to stock deeply enough to cover the demand over a fairly long period of time. This eliminates shallowly stocked items from consideration for magazine advertising.

A distinct disadvantage is that, whether it's a regional, local, or national publication, the advertising cost is usually more per thousand customers than the cost for newspaper space.

Like newspaper advertising, there is the disadvantage of advertising clutter in magazines. The most important magazines can have page after page of retailer advertising mixed in with the national advertising of manufacturers. The competition for attention is intense. However, some of the better magazines, or more successful magazines, make sure to avoid such clutter by mixing small space advertising with "run-over" editorial matter so that the reader is carried through many pages of smaller ads.

STORES THAT BENEFIT MOST FROM MAGAZINE ADS   Magazine ads are most useful to the specialty shop that is directing its merchandising towards a particular group of people, whether they are grouped by how affluent they are, what their lifestyle preferences are, or where they live. The demands of regional customers vary from market to market as climatic changes occur. For example, regional magazines are best for the outdoor sportswear specialist that operates several stores in sections of the country with different climates. What is appropriate advertising for the cold north central states would not be effective in a warmer region such as the southeast. The merchandise in the advertising would be changed from region to region even though the format could be the same.

Magazine advertising for the multi-department retailer is best when used to establish leadership in certain special categories of merchandise. To project the total image of a multi-department operation is extremely costly in magazines. This would require a series of many pages following each other in the magazine. In effect, the retailer would be advertising in its own special section. The expense for this is prohibitive. A few of the biggest retail advertisers such as J.C. Penney have done this. This treatment is often used during a significant anniversary event.

If a magazine is publishing a cruise edition, it is important to advertise active sportswear or swimwear in that edition. When a magazine is publishing a special edition on gourmet cooking, it is best to advertise those categories of merchandise that are appropriate, such as table linens, glassware, or formal party fashions. An outstanding example of special interest magazines are the various bridal publications. These magazines have become very effective advertising media because this important event in a woman's life offers profitable opportunities for the retailer. Wedding fashions, of course, are especially appropriate for such magazine ads. A wedding is a significant event for a family, and this type of magazine is used to promote practically everything any store sells from bridal fashions to china, glassware, and the luggage the honeymoon couple will use.

Magazines are best for "B" advertising because of their long life cycle, prestige, and better printing quality. "C" advertising is particularly worthwhile in magazines. A retailer can promote the unique character of the store, especially when the store offers special services. Retailers who are opening a new branch in a certain region can schedule, in a regional magazine, "C" advertising that institutionalizes the new store.

"A" category advertising has its place in magazine advertising. Certain seasonal price promotions find magazine advertising very useful. A typical example would be the classic pre-season coat sale in August, which can last from a month to six weeks. Because of the excellent reproduction quality of the illustrations in magazines this promotion can be very appealing to the eye. The periodic White Sale and Sale for the Home are also worthwhile candidates for magazine advertising.

The editorial content of regional magazines can range from items of community interest to articles on fashion trends and health matters, whereas other magazines appeal to the more cultured reader. The readers are attracted to advertising efforts that are compatible and relevant to the editorial content of the magazines. Good practitioners of advertising always consider the importance of the lifestyle interests of the readers of the various magazines and often use a literary style similar to the magazine that the readers favor. In New York City there are two magazines appealing to the lifestyles of the same New Yorkers, but their literary styles vary. *The New Yorker* literary style is slightly cynical and frequently uses jesting terminology. On the other hand, *New York Magazine*'s style is much breezier, is written in a journalistic manner, and uses flip phrases and more contemporary slang. Consequently, the advertising language of a retailer might well vary for each of these magazines.

BUYING MAGAZINE SPACE   Advertising space is rigidly allocated. The biggest space available is a full page, double page or several full pages in sequence. Most magazines offer quarter pages or half pages, many have eighth pages, and some offer space as small as a sixteenth of a page, which is approximately the size of classified advertising in a newspaper. Some publications will sell the retail advertiser preferred positions that are usually in front of the issue. A preferred position may cost more than an unassigned position. This does not apply to all magazines.

Direct Mail

All advertising is divided into two categories, *indirect and direct.* Newspaper and magazine advertising are considered to be indirect advertising because the advertising reaches all readers of these media without any discriminating choice on the part of the advertiser. Many of the recipients of this kind of advertising have little or no interest in the merchandise being offered. Retailers have more control over how much of their market they reach when they use direct advertising. The most prominent method of reaching specific audiences is *direct mail.* The advertiser can aim fairly accurately at specific target customers with carefully chosen mailing lists. When using newspaper, magazine, or broadcast media advertising, the retailer is never sure if enough customers see or hear this advertising. They may have skipped past the newspaper ad, or their radio or TV sets may not have been turned on when the retailer's advertising was on the air. Furthermore, there is wasted circulation in reaching people who are not interested in what the retailer is selling. *Not everyone in the total market can be a retailer's customer.* With direct advertising the retailer can more accurately select the appropriate groups of people who may be the best prospects. The retailers can directly deliver the advertising message to these special segments.

There are many categories of advertising media that can be used for direct mailing. Most important are the various multi-category catalogs and the special brochures that advertise a specific class of merchandise such as a hosiery sale or a coat promotion. There can be the direct selling letter announcing a special service such as jewelry repair or fur storage. A popular category is the statement enclosure or "stuffer" to charge account customers. There are also broadsides, which are the large folded pieces that are mailed or distributed door-to-door.

ADVANTAGES OF DIRECT MAIL

Selectivity; The principal advantage of direct mail is that this advertising is audience-selective if the retailer makes judicious use of lists of customer names that have been compiled based on a skillful segmentation of the market. Consequently, there is little wasted circulation in communicating with people who are not interested in what the advertiser is offering.

One-on-One Relationship; Direct mail that is addressed to the individual and sent to the home has a more personal relationship with the customer than other media. When the recipient opens the mail and is ready to read the message, a one-on-one relationship is established. The retailer is talking directly to the customer, and the customer is reacting directly to the persuasive arguments of the retailer. There are no distractions as in the broadcast media, newspapers, or magazines.

Versatility in Form; Direct mail offers many advantages in terms of variety of physical form. It can be a simple postcard, or can fit into an ordinary envelope. Direct mail can be printed on one sheet, letterhead size like the sales letter, or it can be folded into a three section unit or even an accordion fold that, when unfolded, can be as wide as eighteen inches. There is also the big fold-out, a form of the broadside, that opens up to newspaper-page size or bigger (see Figure 8.8).

Variety of Paper; The advertiser can choose a glossy paper or select rough textured paper. There are perfumed papers or papers with colorful borders to create a happy mood. Even confetti speckled papers have been creatively used by fashion advertisers. Pictorial quality can be varied depending on the paper selected. Color photography can be employed as well as the simplest line drawing or colorful illustrations.

Variety in Creativity; Many forms of typographic creativity can be used to create special moods. Various paper stocks can be cut in interesting shapes, and some advertisers even use direct mail that has a hole cut in it to focus on an illustration or a significant phrase.

Wide Range of Preparation Cost; One advantage of direct mail is that the cost of production can be thriftily low or luxuriously high depending on the objectives and budget of the retailer.

DISADVANTAGES OF DIRECT MAIL

Relatively High Cost of Mailing; Postage rates are continually on the increase, and the mailing cost for each name on the list gets higher and higher. This may seem extravagant when compared with newspaper costs. However, constant examination and culling of the mailing list can help limit rising postal costs by insuring that the advertising is reaching the best prospects.

Relatively High Cost of Preparation; Printing and paper costs keep moving up, and the more elaborate the mail unit is, the more the budget

Figure 8.8. An important advantage of direct mail is that the advertiser can choose from a variety of forms and shapes, from the simple postcard to variations of folded pieces. These choices are usually determined by the budget. (Courtesy of Globman's, Martinsville, Va.; Lady Miriam's, Bellflower, Calif.; Heironimus, Roanoke, Va.; Bergman's, Kingston, Pa.; and Gail's, Columbus, Ohio.)

can be affected. Some of these costs can be mitigated when vendors can be persuaded to cooperate to share some of the expense.

Length of Preparation Time;   A major disadvantage of direct mail is the length of preparation time needed to produce the mailing and deliver it to the recipient. The piece must first be designed, then printed, then addressed, and finally delivered to the postal service.

Unpredictable Delivery;   Also, direct mail that is not sent as first class is often not delivered at predictable times, so that the sender cannot control the exact date upon which the addressee receives it. Using the more economical rates of postage may further delay the timely delivery of the mailing piece. Customers may receive the mailing in one day, five days, or longer.

The Cost of Maintenance of Mailing Lists;   Households move, people die, or families separate. Therefore, customer mailing lists must be reexamined regularly and culled for the deceased or those who have moved. This process can incur modest costs. To cull their mailing lists, advertisers usually send out special mailings that require "return to sender" cooperation from the post office. This procedure should take place every six months. The returned mail usually indicates that the addressee is no longer at the address. Often, forwarding addresses are added to the returned mailing piece. After two mailings are returned, the advertiser should eliminate the name from the list.

Failure to Generate New Prospective Customers;   One function that a mailing list cannot accomplish is to include the names of newly arrived people. Because these names are usually not yet on any mailing list, reaching newer prospects is limited. This is an important disadvantage when contrasted with newspapers, which can be purchased by anyone who is visiting or who has recently moved to a community.

Rejection by Recipients;   A lesser disadvantage of direct mail is that it is subject to the whims and attitudes of the public at the time the mail is being delivered. A very well executed, attractive direct mail piece will be acceptable and welcomed by one customer, and another customer may reject it without even looking at it. If several pieces of direct mail simultaneously arrive at the home, mailbox clutter can occur with a negative impact, and the recipient may throw out all advertising without looking at it.

THE MAILING LIST   One of the most valuable advertising assets of a retailer is the mailing list of the store. It must be regularly examined, culled, and targeted. Direct mail advertising is only as good as the mailing list. The mailing list of a store that has charge accounts possesses a particularly valuable advertising tool. This charge account mailing list is composed mostly of the customers who already know the store and are the most loyal purchasers of the store's merchandise. These names are the prime component of any retailer's mailing list. A good list should be dominant in the type of customers for which the store's merchandise is most useful. The list should be accurate and current enough to avoid wasted preparation and postage expense. Frequent scrutiny is important to eliminate inactive customers or customers who have moved or deceased. Retailers should be extremely cautious in purchasing lists because many lists being offered are outdated. Many retailers initiate various in-store staff competitions to acquire names of new customer prospects for their mailing list.

Stores can make more efficient use of their charge account lists by isolating groups of names into various purchasing categories. Each purchase made by a charge customer is recorded by department into the computer. This procedure is usually called "profiling." Thus the total mailing list of a store is segmented into target profiles based on customers' charge purchase history. For example, to profile a list for a back-to-school special sale, the procedure would focus on all customers who make frequent purchases in the girls and boys departments. Retailers find this is an excellent method of targeting advertising directly to specific groups without wasting money reaching disinterested customers.

Another example would focus on the designer fashion customer. The profile would include not only data on purchases from the designer fashion department but information on purchases in sportswear, dresses, fine jewelry, better costume jewelry, and certain lines of cosmetics. This method highlights the names of the best customers for better merchandise. Other sources are the professional list suppliers, who develop current lists from data provided by the motor vehicle bureau in many states. Many mailing lists are compiled from the lists of other retailers, who often sell their names. Many reliable credit bureaus also sell their own customers lists of their best credit-rated names.

THE IMPORTANCE OF TARGETING MAILING LISTS Specialty shops, particularly those that have active charge accounts, are among the best users of direct mail since their merchandising policies are directed toward selection of merchandise that appeals to special groups of customers. Some specialty stores will direct their mailings to certain economic groups such as the more affluent customer or the middle income customer. Retailers who merchandise to special sizes, such as petites or the larger size woman or man, will use direct mail to communicate to their specific group of customers.

Many retailers, especially the larger ones, use the computer to segment their extensive mailing list to fit particular customer profiles. For example, a store with a mailing list of approximately 70,000 names segments its mailing list to define customers that bought gifts for children, customers for large-size apparel, and customers who have bought shoes. Their list can be used for advertising just to customers of table linens, china, and glassware. Customers who have made many purchases during highly promotable periods are this store's candidates for an effective mailing list for storewide promotions. A limited mailing list of baby-interested customers would have rather inexpensive postal costs when compared with mailing baby fashion advertising to the full list of 70,000. Such a mailing can be more productive at a low cost when compared to a major mailing to all the customers, many of whom are not interested in promotions for babies.

On the other hand, discounters who are devotees of broadsides can present an urgent promotion without employing a special mailing list. Using the "Householder" mailing procedure will suffice. The advertising budget of a discounter or bargain operation can rarely support the higher cost of addressed postage and the higher cost of preparation of special mailing lists. Therefore, they prefer to use scatter method of distribution because all segments of the public are, in some form or other, their customers.

TYPES OF DIRECT MAIL PIECES

Sales Letters;   The sales letter is the easiest of the direct mail pieces to prepare. It can be a simple message on the store's letterhead that can be produced quickly. It is particularly effective when it has a dramatic message or dramatic offering to attract the attention of the customer, such as a pre-season coat event, or a sale for children's wear. Special services such as fur storage or jewelry repair are ideal promotions for the sales letter. Because the sales letter comes in an envelope, it is a more private and personal message (see Figure 8.9).

Postcards;   The postcard is also easy to produce. Postcards can be in the standard postal service size or larger. Retailers find the postal service cards are a satisfactory inexpensive medium for sending brief advertising messages to selected customers to announce special sales, store birthday discounts, and new merchandise. Frugal retailers favor this type of postcard because there is a moderate price for both the postage and the card, yet it is often handled by the post office as first-class mail. Printing a message on this card is a modest additional cost. A distinct advantage of this particular direct mail medium is that the advertising message is read instantly without the recipient having to

Proffitt's

October 1990

Dear Preferred Customer:

In keeping with Proffitt's tradition of offering you the finest in quality and value, I am delighted to announce a very special sale of Fine Jewelry. You will have the opportunity to select from our spectacular $5,500,000 collection of diamond, 14K gold, cultured pearl and gemstone jewelry at 40% savings. In addition, we'll take an extra 10% off sale prices on your private courtesy days, Friday and Saturday, October 5th and 6th.

This entire fine jewelry collection includes hundreds of cluster rings, cocktail rings, gold and diamond rings, as well as necklaces, pendants, bracelets and earrings, all with diamonds or precious rubies, sapphires and emeralds. Also included is our lustrous cultured and fresh water pearl strands and jewelry, even our popular Tennessee pearl collection will be on sale. Save on gemstone designs and all our 14K and 18K gold including our collection of 14K white gold and Black Hills gold. We're sorry, but diamond solitaires are not included in this sale.

Please bring this letter with you to the Fine Jewelry Department to identify you as a valued customer of Proffitt's. The sales associates will take an extra 10% off the sale price at your time of purchase, above and beyond the 40% savings offered.

Sincerely,

R. Brad Martin
Chairman of the Board

Figure 8.9. The sales letter, typed on the store's letterhead and signed by an important executive, is an effective, low-cost form of direct mail promotion. Note at the bottom the special discount for the customer who brings this letter to the store. (Courtesy of Proffitt's, Alcoa, Tenn.)

open an envelope. Many stores prefer larger forms of the simple postal card to be able to have interesting graphics to dramatize the advertising story. Postal service cards lack prestige and space for dramatic graphics (see Figure 8.10).

Statement Enclosures;   A prime advantage of the statement enclosure "stuffer" is that when it is printed on lightweight paper, it does not increase the weight of the accompanying material in the envelope. It gets a "free ride" because the envelope contains the monthly invoice to the customer. Many manufacturers, as well as buying offices, supply these for no cost or at a reasonably low cost. Some of these often use color photographs that are very attractive to the customers (see Figure 8.11).

Broadsides;   These are large-size folders or brochures. They are impressive because of their size and can be attention-getting because of their dramatic use of illustrations, typography, and color. These are often printed on large sheets of paper and folded to fit into the mailbox. They are usually used for the promotion of discounts and other bargains. They are rarely addressed to any particular person but are delivered by the postal carrier to every address on the route or by private distributors. Broadsides are best used by advertisers who rely on "A" action items.

Dramatic Brochures;   This is a more distinctive form of the broadside. Using an equally large expanse of paper, the dramatic brochure is used by quality fashion retailers to make a dramatic statement to impress the fashion aware customer. Retailers usually mail this brochure to their better charge accounts since it is best used to launch a fashion season or establish the store's leadership in presenting quality brands. Such direct mailings are classified as "B" advertising directed to build the retailer's reputation for fashion merchandise. Many retailers use this direct mail style for aggressively promoting an important sale event. The dramatic brochure format permits emphasis on assortments and price impact along with a quality fashion impression in the style of effective "A" promotions. See Color Plate 7 for examples.

Catalogs and Booklets;   These offer opportunities for exciting graphics and elaborate presentations of merchandise. They are produced with many pages of fashions, while the other forms of direct mail are more limited in the number of pages. Catalogs are generally used for gift periods such as Christmas, Mother's Day, and Father's Day as well as for special seasonal presentations of new fashions that focus on the spring, summer, fall, or cruise merchandise. Sometimes they present groups of related merchandise such as in a catalog for Home Fashion Sales. See Color Plate 8 for an example of a fashion catalog.

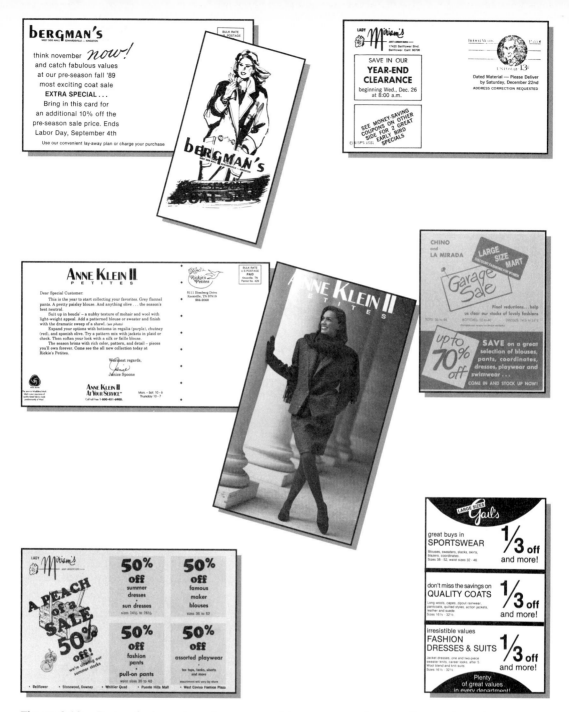

Figure 8.10. Postcards, in various sizes, are useful to cost-conscious retailers and can be prepared quicker than other direct mail media. Note the standard postal service card with postage already preprinted (upper right-hand corner). This card can cost less to produce than the others. (Courtesy of Bergman's, Kingston, Pa.; Rickie's Petites, Knoxville, Tenn.; Anne Klein II, New York [Christina Cuscardi, model]; Lady Miriam's, Bellflower, Calif.; and Gail's, Columbus, Ohio.)

Figure 8.11. The statement enclosure or "stuffer" is the least costly of any direct mailings because it is free of postage costs since it is inserted into an envelope containing the store's bill to its charge customers. Many such inserts are supplied by manufacturers. When the store provides its own special insert, the costs are minimal. (Courtesy of Rheinauer's, Winter Haven, Fla.)

The catalog's principal objective is to demonstrate completeness of stocks within the store. In order to do this, catalogs can contain from twenty-four to over two hundred pages. The page size is usually $8\,1/2 \times 11$ or 11×14 inches depending on the budget.

A booklet is a smaller version of the catalog family. It is usually from eight pages to sixty-four pages in a smaller size that can be from 3×5 up to 7×9 inches. The booklet is most often used to present merchandise in one narrow category such as casual shoes, larger-size fashions, sportswear, jewelry, or it can be used to present merchandise in a limited fashion group such as T-shirts or sweaters for men and women. Manufacturers as well as buying offices often provide such seasonal booklets and catalogs.

Cost of Direct Mail   There are many variations in preparation costs. These depend on who the printer is, what paper is used, how many pages are in the mailing, and how much time is allocated for preparation because a rush job may incur extra time costs. Shortcuts in expense can be achieved by "tailgating" on another printing job. The cost of delivery using the post office is a given, but the cost for producing the mailing piece is controlled by the retailer. Sound direct mail planning must budget the preparation costs as well as the postal costs because preparation costs vary from piece to piece. Cost variance usually depends on the quality of paper. Expensive papers may look better, but may cost more than the budget allows. Another variation in costs will be in the style of illustration. Color photography costs much more to print than black and white photography. The cost of color photography depends on how much each available photographer can charge. Added to all these production costs is the cost of advertising creativity. The fees for writing the text will vary from project to project as copywriters' compensation scale can differ from person to person. Layout preparation of the graphic design will vary in cost depending on the skills of the person engaged for this work.

Many retailers pursue certain disciplines to control costs by insisting on obtaining estimates on all printing. It is best to have an estimate from three suppliers. To control costs many advertisers will accept second quality paper rather than first quality stock. Frequently, lower quality paper will be as useful in the final product as prime quality paper. The negotiating skills used in making any purchase of merchandise are useful in purchasing printing.

Handbills and Package Stuffers

Another area of advertising directly to the consumer is the handbill. This advertising material is delivered directly to the customer by means other than the post office. Handbills can be handed out by special distribution services or by local people employed for this purpose. With limited cost, the advertiser can focus the message toward markets especially near the store. Such distribution avoids the waste of circulation to people who may not be interested in the store's promotion or are too far away from the premises. It is particularly useful when the store is located in a heavily populated area and there is plenty of public traffic (see Figure 8.12).

An important advantage is that the costs of distribution are much lower than for newspapers or post office-delivered direct mail. Furthermore, there is the opportunity for quick production of these handbills because they can be printed a few hours after the work is initiated. Another

Figure 8.12. A handbill that was very productive. It cost very little and was distributed inside the store as well as in the vicinity of the location. The promotion added extra sales with limited ad expense. (Courtesy of Lady Miriam's, Bellflower, Calif.)

important point of distribution for the handbill is at or near the doorway of the store involved.

A leading benefit of the handbill that is distributed outside the store is that it can also be inserted into every store package. As a package stuffer it gets important circulation. Promotional and semi-promotional stores have found handbills and package stuffers to be very productive since the principal objective of such handbills is to generate immediate customer action. Not all recipients of handbills, whether they are distributed in a neighborhood or in the store, react positively and make purchase decisions because of the handbill. However, since the cost of production is so low and the wasted circulation is negligible, the advertising budget is not strained.

Billboards

Newspaper, magazines, direct mail advertisements, and broadcast media advertisements can be supplemented by billboards if this cost does not weaken the budget of a basic media program. Billboards are costly and must be used with discretion. They should be located on well-traveled roads that lead to the store, whether in the city, suburbs, or rural areas. They should also be placed where there are not a large number of other billboards. A location with too much visual clutter reduces the effectiveness of most billboards. Furthermore, the location must give the viewer sufficient time to absorb the message and make a decision about it. It is important that the message be very brief and the graphic design be colorful with an attractive pictorial idea. Because billboards should look fresh and clean at all times, billboard users should plan to change them frequently.

Billboards are used best when they advertise well-known brands, when they advertise easy-to-read directions to reach the store, or when they promote a special event. Many billboards are supplied by manufacturers to advertise the store as well as their brand of merchandise. The best candidates for billboards are free-standing stores conveniently located off an interstate or a major highway. Stores that are not located in a popular mall can also use billboards for advertising their locations. See Color Plate 9 for an example.

In-Store Media

Stores spend a lot of money and energy to get shoppers into the store. Once they are there, the customers should be persuaded to make purchase decisions. Good interior display technique will go a long way toward attracting the customer. Even though the display may be very attractive and may hold the attention of the customer, a selling message must be communicated to the viewer at the same time. A store should not permit its interior displays to be mute. Interior as well as window displays should have verbal communication to persuade the customer. A simple clever message, or a straightforward statement is acceptable as long as it motivates the shoppers to purchase the articles.

THE IMPORTANCE OF SIGNS   According to Lee Dubow, formerly Marketing Vice President, Belk Stores: "Signing is the most inexpensive way to create more sales per square foot. Good benefit signing should be regarded as the fourth media...the final link in sales promotion. The customers in the store are the retailer's best prospects. Good signing will convert this traffic into prompt purchase decisions."

The smallest sign card no bigger than 5×7 inches or the large 22×28 inch store poster are equally important promotion tools for the retailer. Signs placed over merchandise racks or on counters should contain an important headline with the name of the item followed by two or three benefits and the price of the item. Comparative price information can be added to the benefits, if necessary. Amateurishly scribbled signs will not sell goods and cannot express the store's image appropriately. There are several sign-making machines available for small stores as well as large stores that can be used by any employee after a short instruction session. Now there is computerized sign apparatus that can produce signs very easily, in multiples, using quick-drying inks. The negatives of the long wait for the signs to dry and the labor involved in producing the signs on a printing press no longer apply (see Figure 8.13).

An important type of sign that is often neglected is the directional sign. These signs should be located near specific areas. Large signs are helpful at the entrance of stores, especially if they show a map of the location of various departments. Many stores use extra-large posters to promote special events. Important information such as special store hours and opening and closing hours should appear on signs. Stores should include, as a part of their visual presentation equipment, simple easels on which to place such signs.

Boxes, Packages and Shopping Bags

Often retailers do not think that store packaging such as the shopping bag is a part of their advertising program, yet these carry the store name and reflect the image of the store to the general public. Often, this packaging is retained by the customer for frequent reuse. The familiar shopping bag is an effective advertising medium, especially for the smaller retailer.

Figure 8.13. Using computer and laser printing technology, this versatile Printasign equipment produces a variety of signs. (Courtesy of The Reynold's Group, Torrance, Ca.)

According to Wagner and Closen, "Sidewalks of major cities throughout the world have become kinetic exhibitions of graphic art. Everywhere you look you see a parade of art of every imaginable subject and style adorning bags carried by shoppers."[1] When the shopping bag is cleverly designed using distinctive graphics and attractive colors, it becomes a walking billboard. These bags quickly identify the store and project the store's image to a large audience since they are used over and over. There are many successful small stores whose total advertising effort depends on unusually attractive, well-constructed shopping bags. The well-known Cooper-Hewitt Museum on Fifth Avenue in New York had a very impressive presentation of the art of the shopping bag in which almost 100 creatively designed bags were displayed.

Many stores do not pay enough attention to the design of their ordinary bags, papers, and boxes that are used to wrap merchandise. Creative graphics in these areas are also very important. The design can be very simple and should reflect the image of the store. Good packaging is an excellent form of "C" advertising because it helps to project the store's character. The package program should be consistent, from the smallest box to the largest shopping bag. There should be graphic continuity and color interrelationship. Each unit in the total program should, in effect, be a cousin of the other units (see Color Plate 10).

Another opportunity for an alert store to extend its advertising personality is in the area of the store's regular letterhead and envelopes. This material should be well designed to impress the recipients favorably. Major corporations such as General Electric and General Motors spend a lot of money on corporate identity programs. Many retailers, especially promotional stores, have extended their corporate advertising image into areas such as price tags and hang tags. They often use distinctive colors, special dye cut shapes, and distinctive typographic continuity to add to the advertising personality already published in newspapers or in direct mail.

Summary

Advertising is the important tool retailers use to persuade customers to take favorable action on the store's offerings. The prime objectives are (a) increased sales transactions and volume, (b) development of favorable reputation for the advertiser, (c) acceleration of the turnover of goods, and (d) stabilization of sales volume. The various categories of print media include newspapers, magazines, direct mailings, catalogs,

---

[1]   Wagner and Closen, *The Shopping Bag ... Portable Art* (New York: Crown Publishers, 1986), p. 11.

sales letters, postcards, handbills, package stuffers, billboards, in-store signs, and packaging.

The principal function of good print advertising is to (a) turn the reader's attention to the benefits of the merchandise, (b) focus the reader's attention on the special characteristics of the store, and (c) develop an easily remembered image that is meaningful to the reader.

CHAPTER 9

Mechanics of Building an Ad: Print Media

Introduction

The retailer's task in creating effective print advertising involves bringing together the various units that compose this advertising. These are the visual elements and the verbal messages that together will persuade the customer to take action.

Customers usually react to newspaper advertising in one of three ways: (1) They really do not see it, even though they may glance at it. (2) They do not like it and reject it. (3) They like what they see and are attracted to the message. According to the Newspaper Advertising Bureau, Inc., "the most important single factor determining how many people will read any newspaper ad is *the skill and technique used in preparing the ad.*"

The basic ingredients that are employed to create such advertising are (1) the layout, (2) the written word (copy), and (3) the illustration. How well these are creatively coordinated will determine how effective the advertising will be. Furthermore, all the units must work together to express the advertiser's personality. They should reinforce each other to create the advertising style that best represents the advertiser.

Buyer's Ad Request

The creation of the advertisement begins with the buyer's request for the ad. (See Figure 9.1 for an example of an advertising request form.) Each store creates its own form, so the forms vary accordingly. However, there

Proffitt's

( ) ROP
( ) DIRECT MAIL

( ) RADIO
( ) TELEVISION

ADVERTISING REQUEST

Buyer: _____

Ext: _____

Div: _____

Ad Run Date: _____

Ad Size: _____

( ) Black & white

( ) Color

Specify: _____

_____

Advertising requests are due in the Advertising Department 4 weeks out from the run date, except for full color ROP ads which are due 5 weeks out from their run date. Direct mail is due 12 weeks out from run date.

MERCHANDISE INFORMATION:

Brand Name: _____ Item: _____

( ) Brand name must be used   ( ) Can be used   ( ) Don't use

Sizes: _____ Colors: _____

Fabrics: _____ Sale Dates: _____

Reg. Price: _____ Sale Price: _____

( ) Reg. - returns to retail   ( ) Orig. - stays marked down

( ) Special purchase   ( ) Other

List other important information below:

NEWSPAPERS:

_____ Knox News-Sentinel
_____ Knox Journal
_____ Knox Combo
_____ Maryville Daily Times
_____ Oak Ridger
_____ Daily Post Athenian
_____ Chat. News-Free Press
_____ Chat. Morning Times
_____ Chat. Combo
_____ Dalton Adv. (W&F)
_____ Dalton Citizen News
_____ Cleveland Daily Ban.
_____ Morristown Cit. Tri.
_____ Asheville Citizen
_____ Other

_____

Signs ordered?   ( )   Yes   ( )   No

IF MORE SPACE IS NEEDED USE THE BACK OF THIS FORM

MERCH. LOCATIONS:

_____ Foothills (01)
_____ Athens (02)
_____ West Town (03)
_____ Oak Ridge (04)
_____ East Towne (05)
_____ Highland Plaza (12)
_____ Market Street (13)
_____ Eastgate (14)
_____ Dalton (15)
_____ Hamilton Place (16)
_____ Biltmore Square
_____ Other

_____

ART AND LAYOUT INFORMATION:

New Art: ( ) Yes ( ) No Merch. Here? ( ) Yes ( ) No If 'no' when? _____

Pick-up Art: ( ) Yes ( ) No   If 'yes' what date? _____

Feature Art: ( ) Yes ( ) No   Sub-feature: ( ) Yes ( ) No   Box ( )   Liner ( )

Use vendor logo ( ) Yes ( ) No   Return slicks to buyer ( ) Yes ( ) No

List other important art features below:

IF MORE SPACE IS NEEDED USE THE BACK OF THIS FORM

BROADCAST:

_____ Radio   _____ TV

Spot Length _____

Run Dates: _____

Promotional Theme: _____

Target Customer: _____

CO-OP INFORMATION:

Co-op: ( ) Yes ( ) No   Co-op "$": _____

Co-op Requirements: _____

_____

_____

Vendor#: _____ Dept.#: _____ Class#: _____

BE SURE TO FILL OUT PROFFITT'S CO-OP CONTRACT

MPS-017 Rev. 5/88

Figure 9.1. Most retailers use advertising request forms similar to this one. Note how this form is planned to include all information needed to prepare advertising in any medium this store uses. (Courtesy of Proffitt's Department Store, Alcoa, Tenn.)

are components that are common to most advertising request forms. Generally included are the following: medium for the advertisement, description of merchandise, price of merchandise, type of art and layout desired, and co-op information. It is with this request that the ad begins, and the starting point is usually the layout.

The Layout

Definition

The layout is a well-planned diagram of the arrangements of the elements of an ad; that is, the copy, the illustration, and the white space. The layout is essentially the blueprint for building print advertising, whether it is for newspaper, magazine, or direct mail. Without the layout, there is no way to tell the artist, photographers, copywriters, typesetters, and printers exactly how the advertising should look (see Figure 9.2).

Purpose

The layout indicates the size and the placement of the illustration within the ad as well as the location of the store name (logo). An important function of the layout is to show the location of headline, subheading, and text in the advertisement. This results in determining the amount and the shape of the white space. In addition, the layout gives management an opportunity to see what the print advertising will look like in the early preparation stages so that corrections can be made before costly expenses occur. At the layout stage, management can change and adjust the various elements of the advertising to make a better advertisement. The layout is the best way to tell the artists, photographers, copywriters, typesetters, or printers exactly what is expected of them.

The first layout sketch is usually a rough concept. However, it should begin to project the energy of the final product. Revisions may be made again and again, always improving on the rough draft until it is finally approved. In a department store this approval is given by the ad manager as well as the buyer or buyers involved with the particular ad. In a specialty store approval is often given by the owner or the manager.

In print advertising, the picture is usually the most important element since it is the featured attention-getter. Illustrations that attract the reader's eye will also build interest and confidence in the product. The customer then goes on to read the selling message.

The layout usually creates an overall impression that tells the reader much about the store. For example, the retail ad with a large

Figure 9.2. A typical layout that can guide the artist and the typesetters. The text can be written to fit the dimensions indicated on the layout. At this stage the buyer or department head can review the layout. (Courtesy of Globman's, Martinsville, Va.)

attractive illustration and plenty of white space can tell the reader the ad represents a fine fashion store. When the ad is crowded with type and illustrations, the reader is given the impression that the store is highly promotional and is packed with bargains. Mass merchandisers often use this layout style.

The Importance of Focus and Optical Movement

FOCUS   The layout should contain elements that catch the reader's eye. The ad should arrest the reader's attention and direct the eyes to that part of the layout that conveys the dominant message. It is at this focus point that the ad takes its first step in telling the story.

Good advertising layout quickly directs the eye to the focus point of the ad. These focus points can be the headline of the illustration, even the price depending on the merchandising objectives of the ad (see Figure 9.3).

When the headline is the focus point, the size or color of the type can emphasize it. Type can be heavy or light in appearance. Type can be set in many distinctive styles. Often a script lettering is used to create headline focus. Even one word can be a focus point. When the price is the focus point, the exaggerated size of the price serves as an excellent attention-getter.

Focus can be achieved by the size as well as the content of the illustration. A dramatic picture in a small space can be more effective as a focus point than a larger picture that has no action. The forms of the illustration either as circles or unusually shaped units can serve to attract attention.

Another device for developing a focus point is the tilting of headlines on the illustration. Placing the headline in a panel is often used to add to the focus function of a headline or price.

OPTICAL MOVEMENT   A prime objective of the layout is to take the reader's eye quickly to the various elements of the ad after the focus point has attracted the reader. This optical movement is critical. Layouts that do not properly use the principles of optical movement can reduce the impact of the advertising.

The process involved in an effective optical movement is fairly logical. The various stages of such movement start with whatever the focus point is on the layout. When the headline is the focus, the eye should then be directed to the illustration, then to the price, then to the text, and finally to the store name (logo). When the price is the focus point, the eye should then be directed to the headline, then to the illustration, then to the text and logo (see Figure 9.4). Movement/gaze motion has been discussed under the topic "Rhythm" in Chapter 4 and illustrated in Figure 4.18.

Figure 9.3. Headlines and large-sized copy are used to *focus* the reader's attention to this "A" type dress ad. (Courtesy of Herbergers, Grand Forks, N.Dak.)

Figure 9.4. Optical *movement* is demonstrated in this accessories advertising. After the reader's attention is focused at the top by the attractive head wearing the toque, the eye quickly moves down to the bottom of the page. The curving of the belt at the bottom leads the reader back to the copy area. (Courtesy of Lord & Taylor, New York.)

When the illustration is the most important focus point, the eye should then move to the headline, then to the price, then to the text and the store name to complete the reading process.

White Space

The headline, illustration, price, text, and logo are not the only important ingredients in the layout; the amount and shape of the unprinted area is also important to the look of the advertisement. This area is called the white space. The white space should be considered as a picture frame that highlights the pictorial or typographic areas in the ad. White space helps to focus the reader's eye on these units (see Figure 9.5). Without white space, small-space advertising would run into the neighboring ads in the newspaper. In a magazine ad without adequate white space, the various elements within the ad run into each other.

White space gives further emphasis and contrast to the other elements in the ad and can be used to attract attention to copy and art and also to provide distinction in visual style.

Layouts Reflect Store Personality

Ads with simple layouts and eye-catching treatments are doing only half the job. The layout must also represent the personality of the advertiser. A highly promotional store should use layouts that reflect its price appeal character in a bold, aggressive style. A quality fashion store must impart its special flavor in its layout, or it can lose readership.

The best advertising tools for projecting a store's personality properly are the signature, the type faces, the borders, and the character of the illustrations. How the layout assembles these units into an arrangement that best suits the store's character will determine how well the ad is identified with the store.

The layout should maintain *continuity of impression*. The format should be versatile enough to maintain the store's distinctive ad style no matter what task it has to perform. It should be able to introduce new fashions and clear old stock without sacrificing its basic character and advertising identity (see Figure 9.6).

Qualities of a Good Layout

According to *Independent Retailing* by Shaffer and Greenwald, an effective newspaper layout should contain four basic qualities.[1] "Layouts

[1]   Shaffer, Harold and Greenwald, Herbert, *Independent Retailing*, (Englewood Cliffs, N.J.: Prentice Hall, Inc., 1976), p. 165.

Figure 9.5. The white space in this ad helps to attract the customer's eye to the headline and the photos. (Courtesy of Macy's, New York.)

Figure 9.6. This quality retailer's advertising consistently retains its *continuity of impression* whether it is used to present new fashions or emphasize price promotion. Note how its distinctive ad style is effective in small space. (Courtesy of Lord & Taylor, New York.)

Figure 9.6. (*continued*)

215

The SIGNATURE of AMERICAN STYLE

Pared down and perfect...the artful simplicity of the suit. There's not one unnecessary detail on this impeccably conceived suit by Mary Ann Restivo. Of cavalry wool twill, in rich chocolate. The belted jacket, sizes 4 to 12, 500.00; the matching slim skirt, sizes 4 to 14, 200.00

Figure 9.6. (*continued*)

Figure 9.6. (*continued*)

should (1) be simple in arrangement and easy to read, (2) contain visual elements that catch the reader's eye, (3) reflect the store's personality, (4) maintain continuity of impression, and (5) have a versatility that allows them to be developed in the largest and smallest spaces. Regardless of size, ads that lack these qualities usually fail to get sufficient reader attention." Simplicity in arrangement requires an orderly layout of the various elements (signature, type, illustration, and white space) so that the main idea of the message is effortlessly understood. Ads that are easy to read are easy to buy from. Complicated layouts usually repel the reader.

Bergdorf Goodman's advertising employs a distinctive layout style that demonstrates advertising versatility as shown in Figure 9.7.

This style serves the various merchandising objectives of this retailer and maintains continuity of identity whether the store is launching new fashions or offering sale-priced merchandise. The layout style is just as distinctive in small-space ads as it is in dramatic full-page ads.

Buyer Responsibility

The buyer or the manager's responsibility will depend upon the store policy. Store management has a responsibility to represent the customer when evaluating the layout. At this point, management must subjectively think about the advertising but objectively study it in terms of customer needs. Buyers can properly evaluate layouts they review by asking:

1. Does the layout visually present the elements in a manner to attract the customer's eye?
2. Does the layout have the movement required to carry the customer's eye to the significant points of the ad such as illustration or price?
3. Are the logo and store name appropriately placed so that they are not buried within the advertising?

At this early stage in advertising preparation, buyers can prevent costly mistakes.

The Written Word

Persuading the reader to purchase the merchandise advertised is the principal function of the written word. Advertising that attracts the eye but fails to persuade will be a waste of the advertiser's money.

The written word of an ad is usually divided into basically three parts. The first is the logo or the advertiser's name. The second is the headline. The third part is the copy (or body copy). Ad practitioners usually refer to the text of the ad as copy.

Logo or Store Name

"The name of the store is the most important item the retailer has to sell."[2] Therefore, the store name, or logo, is a most important part of a retailer's ad. Not only must the logo have high visibility in all print media, but it should be distinctive and clearly reflect the store's personality.

---

[2]   Shaffer, Harold and Greenwald, Herbert, *Independent Retailing*, (Englewood Cliffs, N.J.: Prentice Hall, Inc., 1976), p. 165.

Did someone say beware the ides of March? What about the blahs of March? Thirtysomething is on break, you couldn't possibly sit through any more arias at the Met and you've already seen every movie that won't win an Oscar this year, precisely because you picked them to! You thumb through the newspapers for a little stimulation and suddenly the headlines are shouting good news: the French are positively sizzling with hot new fashions for next Fall. Leave it to Claude, Karl and Christian, among others, to pick up everyone's spirits.

Lest you begin to lament not being part of the fashion pack in Paris, take flight to **Bergdorf Goodman**'s own new boulevard of boutiques, mostly French, on Two for a little inspiration that's closer to home. Excusez moi, but the new **Karl Lagerfeld** shop couldn't be more chic if Karl himself were there to wait on you personally (don't put it past him, he adores Bergdorf's as much as you do). After all, he did design the shop's wonderfully baroque chairs, and that fringe on the clothing racks is a touch only Mr. Lagerfeld would add. Only he could work black crepe into a fitted, dropped waist jacket trimmed with center pleats of georgette – yes, yes, georgette – that he likes worn over a white georgette slip dress. You'll love the way the cuffs flare, the allure of a higher armhole and narrow, feminine shoulders…just the thing for making a long day's journey into night. Then again, that's what we love about Lagerfeld, the way he blurs day and evening dressing. To wit: his sleeveless V-neck pleated crepe tunics in black or white worn over leggings. Or that red linen dress with attached sleeveless vest.

Bergdorf's is so full of Spring ideas that a trip to Paris is hardly necessary.

Karl Lagerfeld

BERGDORF GOODMAN
ON THE PLAZA IN NEW YORK

Linen suits with scalloped hem and neckline and nautilus shell buttons by **Workers for Freedom**. **Future Ozbek**'s multicolored, psychedelic, deliriously checked, fringed jacket with matching shorts and denim (yes!) bra top. Or that zany **Franco Moschino**'s red twill jacket embroidered around the nipped-in waist with the message "Waist of Money." We don't think so. Neither will you. Find these and a host of others in our designer collections on Three and Five. In a word, whew!

Our sentiments exactly for the stunning collection of shoes by **Manolo Blahnik** in his very own shop on Two. Just in: his D'Orsay pump in black and white calfskin and the trussed, laced-toe shoes in a combination of linen and suede that are truly remarkable. Hmm. After a rousing tour of Bergdorf's, March doesn't seem so blah after all.

Evening Shimmer on Four

Spring sparklers by Neil Bieff. Sequin T-dress in blue or green sparked with gold or silver. Also in metallics of brass or pewter. Plaza Boutique, Fourth Floor. 872-8951.

BERGDORF GOODMAN
ON THE PLAZA IN NEW YORK

Figure 9.7. The *versatility* of the distinctive advertising format of this well-know fashion retailer demonstrates how the format of its large-space ads can be equally effective in small space. (Courtesy of Bergdorf Goodman, New York.)

Furthermore, the logo should not resemble that of any other stores in the community.

When the logo appears in any print media (even on TV) it should, because of its design, quickly suggest to the customer whether the advertiser is a high fashion merchant or an aggressive promotional operation. When well designed, a logo is more than a signature. Its actual graphic qualities can deliver a positive message relating to the personality of the store.

The graphic style of the logo should be carefully planned to achieve all the objectives stated previously. Many good logos use distinctive type styles. Others simulate hand script or calligraphy to project the effect of an actual personal signature. An effective logo style many advertisers use is duplication of the store name that is on the front of the store. This particular style of logo has the advantage of being familiar to the community, thus getting high recognition benefits (see Figure 9.8).

Headlines

PURPOSE   Because one of the headline's functions is to arrest attention and direct the reader to the body of the copy, a good headline will appeal to the reader's self-interest. Effective headlines are usually short and direct to get the reader's attention.

Figure 9.8.   These logos indicate the many different graphic styles used to reflect these fashion stores' personalities. (Courtesy of Lord & Taylor, New York; Saks Fifth Avenue, New York; Anne Taylor, New York; Rizik's, Washington D.C; and Wagener, La Jolla, Calif.)

TYPES OF APPEALS   Retail advertising copy is essentially composed of
certain facts about the merchandise as well as verbal appeal to the self
interests of the customer. The customer wants answers to these questions: *What is it? Why is it good? How much is it? What will it do for ME?*
The answers to these deal mostly with the facts about the merchandise.
The answers to "What is it?" and "How much does it cost?" are obvious.
"Why is it good?" will be answered by facts such as the fashion is an all
wool coat, or one that is made of an easy-care polyester fabric, or that
is in the newest colors. The answer to the last question, "What will it
do for ME?" appeals to various emotional or practical needs of the customer. If the reader is looking for merchandise that will last for many
years, the copy will explain and persuade with text that appeal to the
customer's need for longevity in merchandise. For customers who seek
up-to-the-minute fashion the answer to the last question, "What will it
do for ME?" will emphasize the newness with simple phrases that emphasize that this is the new fashion to add to the customer's wardrobe
this season (see Figure 9.9).

Researchers at Yale University once listed the 12 most persuasive words
in the English language, which are good selling words to help to answer the question, "What will it do for ME?" These are save, money, you,
new, results, help, easy, safety, love, discovery, proves, and guarantee.

Emotional Appeal;   Most fashion merchandise is bought to satisfy
customers' emotional needs. These needs can apply to women and men.
Among the basic emotional needs that are significant to the retail advertiser are the need to be attractive, the need for something new, the
need to be first, the need for innovation in color, and the need for
changes in lifestyle. Effective ad copy should focus on why the fashions
advertised will satisfy any one of these emotional needs. Essentially, text,
which is really printed salesmanship, is the verbal basis in answering the
question, "What will it do for ME?" For example, when the customer is
seeking a fashion that will satisfy the need to look attractive, he or she
can find the answer to this question in copy that headlines: "The New,
Beautiful You." Another headline could say, "Flattering Fashion... Just
for You!" Such phrases usually develop easily when the emotional need
of the customer is identified.

Rational Appeal;   Many fashion goods are bought to satisfy certain
rational needs that all customers have. Some are based on actual *physical demands*. Among these are the need to be comfortable, the need for
warmth, the need for ease of action, and the need for safety. An important rational need has an *economic basis*. The need to save money is one
of the most important needs to which advertisers can appeal. In fact, the

Figure 9.9. This ad is effectively directed to the self-interest of the customer. The headline and copy text clearly answer the questions: What is it? What does it do for me? How much is it? Why is it good? (Courtesy of Bolton's, New York.)

need to save can also be identified as a significant *emotional* need. The appeal of the need to save when coupled with an appropriate emotional need can stimulate effective headlines and copy.

TYPES OF HEADLINES   Since the prime objectives of the headline are to attract attention and begin to persuade the reader, the advertiser should avoid the simple label-like statement. A static headline that says "the longer jacket is here" will not arrest the reader's attention. Instead, there are several categories of verbal styles that can be adapted for writing the headline. The styles that most advertising writers find useful are the declarative, the interrogative, the exclamatory, and the alliterative.

The Declarative;   This form of headline is essentially a straightforward statement that carries a persuasive, informative message. The best headlines are based on customers' rational needs or emotional needs, frequently both. An example of such a headline could read, "Weekend fashions that work while you play." Another headline could say, "Body-skimming sweater dresses at a skimpy price." Such headlines are most effective when everyday terms are used. Choose "people-talk" terms for best communication.

The Interrogative;   The headline that asks a questions is an effective copy style, especially if the question is based on the rational or emotional needs of customers. Such a headline could read, "What's new in sweater savings?" Another headline that also appeals to emotional and rational needs is, "Do you love BIG luxuries at LITTLE prices?"

The Exclamatory;   This style of headline is most effective when limited to one or two words. The exclamation point is an important asset in this headline style. This headline features a word that captures the attention of the reader:

IRRESISTIBLE!
Don't miss these dress-up savings!

Appealing to rational and emotional needs is the objective of this headline:

WARM UP!
Special savings on famous maker jog suits

Study how these headlines use people-talk terminology.

The Alliterative; This distinct style of headline requires considerable skill in writing because the alliterative heading should use familiar words such as: "Fall's Fabulous Fashion Favorites." Another headline demonstrates skilled use of alliteration: "Petites Prefer Patterned Sweaters."

The Copy

PURPOSE   Since the prime objectives of the headline are to arrest attention and begin the process of persuading the customer, the copy should give specific information about the fashions being advertised. Copy should not deal in generalities because it also must supply the answers to the customer's questions: *What is it? Why is it good? How much is it? What will it do for me (the customer)?* The copy does not necessarily have to answer these questions in this order. The message also should be directed to appeal to the customer's needs. The text, too, should reflect the advertiser's knowledge of the various emotional and rational appeals discussed in Chapter 2. The more the writer knows about the customer's needs, the more persuasive the copy will be.

Good copy is based on thorough product information. The more the writer knows about the goods, the better the advertisement. Avoiding exaggeration will keep the copy believable. According to Shaffer and Greenwald (p. 167), "Words like *stupendous, spectacular,, amazing, incredible,* even if true, are rarely believed by readers because they have been continually exposed to all kinds of high-pressure advertising that uses these overworked words."[3] Avoid trying to include all merchandise features in the copy. Instead focus on the most important answers to the customers' questions. Excess detail can cause customers to lose interest.

TYPES OF COPY   Copy styles are divided into three types: *Reason Why, Praise,* and *"You"-directed.* These types define the styles used in writing text. Although good copy can concentrate on any one of these styles, equally effective copy can use any combination of these types.

Reason Why; This type of text focuses on the reasons why the merchandise is good, and what it will do to satisfy the customer's emotional and rational needs. It explains the benefits to the customer (see Figure 9.10).

Praise; This style of copy, usually added or inserted into Reason Why text, essentially praises the benefits of the merchandise. Phrases

---

[3]   Shaffer, Harold and Greenwald, Herbert, *Independent Retailing*, (Englewood Cliffs, N.J.: Prentice Hall, Inc., 1976), p. 167.

Figure 9.10.   Reason-why ad copy that deftly lists the merchandise details that give the reader reasons to make a purchase decision.

A RALPH LAUREN SUMMER.

THE CASUAL MADE CONSUMMATE

IN AIRBORNE LINENS

There will always be a time and place for

clothes like these — the peaked lapel,

double-breasted blazer in cream linen.

The silk patio print blouse in pale

yellow, burgundy and dove grey.

And trousers, cuffed and pleated,

in cream linen.

and words that praise the goods add more persuasive energy to the copy (see Figure 9.11).

"You"-Directed;   Basically, this is copy that addresses the message directly to the customer. The word *you* appears frequently in the text This can be very persuasive because it can be based on customer needs. For example, customers who need a *warm* stadium coat at a *value* price will respond to copy that states: "You asked for a cozy, warm coat for cold stadium days. And you want it at a thrifty price. We have that coat just in time for the big game this week. Remember STORE NAME is always thinking of you." The "You"-directed style, in effect, represents a one-on-one relationship between the customer and the store (see Figure 9.12).

Figure 9.11. Note the use of words that *praise* such as striking, flattering, dazzle, perfect, rich, and romantic.

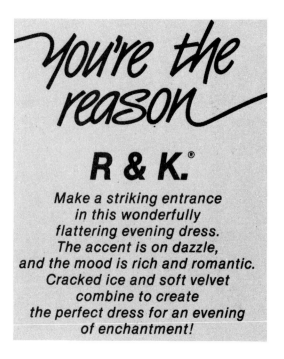

The Importance of Typography

Proper selection of the typography styles that are used for the headlines and the copy areas is most vital in giving the readers the correct impression of the advertiser's personality. The visual characteristics of the many type styles available can help retailers reflect their merchandising image.

Type faces come in many styles that vary in design. Some faces stand upright (Roman). Other are tilted at an angle (*Italic*). Type faces come in all sizes and weights from very light to very heavy. With so many type styles available, advertisers have splendid opportunities to add to the distinctive flavor of their advertising (see Figure 9.13).

CHOOSING TYPE STYLES   Carefully selecting a type face by size and weight can give the reader the best impression of the store's advertising personality.

LARGE SIZE
HEAVY TYPE

quickly tells the reader the store is an aggressive price-promotion operation

LIGHT TYPE
LARGE SIZE

is appropriate for a prestigious store known for quality fashions. Stores that emphasize fashion can select type styles that project

Femininity

Other available type styles easily suggest

MASCULINITY

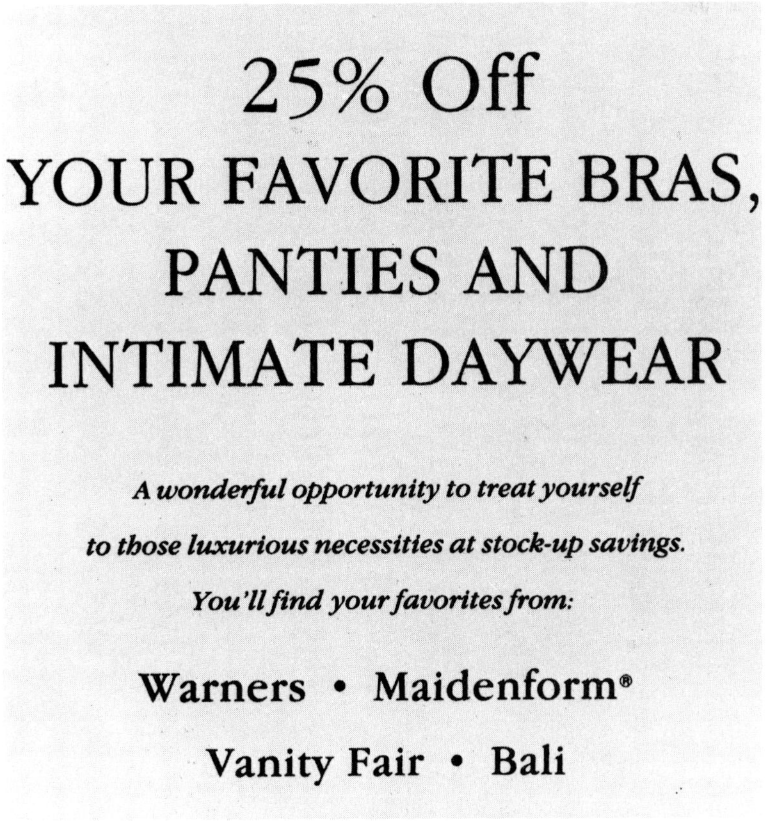

25% Off
YOUR FAVORITE BRAS,
PANTIES AND
INTIMATE DAYWEAR

A wonderful opportunity to treat yourself

to those luxurious necessities at stock-up savings.

You'll find your favorites from:

Warners • Maidenform®

Vanity Fair • Bali

Figure 9.12. "You"-directed advertising that demonstrates how the advertiser is talking directly to the reader on a one-to-one basis.

This is Font 1 News No. 3

This is Font 2 News Bold No. 3

This is Font 3 Universe 65

This is Font 4 Universe 75

This is Font 5 Futura Medium

This is Font 6 Futura Demi Bold

This is Font 7 Futura Bold

This is Font 8 Sans No. 1

This is Font 9 Gothic No. 1

This is Font 10 Helios II

This is Font 12 Bodoni Bold

This is Font 13, Futura Bold Condensed

This is Font 14, Futura Bold Italic II

This is Font 15, Sans Heavy No. 1

This is Font 16, Sans No. 2

Figure 9.13. A selection of various type styles available to advertisers in a small city newspaper. Commercial typesetting shops offer more variety.

Illustration   *229*

VARIETY IN TYPE STYLES   It is not necessary to limit type selection to one face alone. Choose one or two that are best able to present the store's advertising character. Leading advertisers avoid using too many type face styles to avoid confusing the reader. There are many attractive type combinations that stores employ to define their advertising character:

small light type

combined with a

HEAVY TYPE IN A LARGE SIZE

can present headline excitement for promotional stores with an aggressive advertising style.

Quality fashion stores could use the reverse of this formula.

A tasteful type in a light style

combined with a small heavy type

Illustration

Purpose

The illustration serves two purposes. First, it serves to attract the reader's eye. In this context, the illustration can move the reader to another part of the ad just by the direction it takes within the layout. It can be posed in such a way that it arrests the reader's wandering attention. The illustration can also add attractive color qualities to the total layout. Second, it demonstrates the merchandise. The illustration should define the merchandise by portraying the fashion personality of the item. This also establishes a personal relationship with the reader when it illustrates the type of person who wears such fashions.

By demonstrating the fashion in use, the illustration can graphically show the necessary details that will encourage the customer to want to buy the garment. An effective illustration is a visual message that helps to select the audience for the advertisement. The actual illustration, whether a photograph or an expertly executed drawing, should portray the type of customer that will be interested in the merchandise advertised. Such an illustration should reflect the personality of this customer. A well-known fashion retailer uses drawings and illustrations that portray a certain type of woman who reflects classic features. The subtle portraiture of the model used in the illustration style implies its customers' social breeding. Another store uses a photographic style and appropriate models that suggest a quality lifestyle of wealth and position. Another retailer, famous for its unique advertising style, uses illustrations that suggest a very fashion-aware customer doing all the new "in" things. Because of the potential to create such psychological impressions, it is important that advertisers consider very carefully the "portraiture" values of the illustrations that they use in advertising.

In fashion advertising, the picture is one of the most important elements because it usually is the featured attention-getter. When properly done, illustrations that attract the reader's eye build interest and confidence in the product and influence the reader to read the selling message. The illustration not only can faithfully represent the merchandise but when artfully done can create a mood that reflects the quality of the merchandise. At the same time it will also reflect the image and personality of the store. Furthermore, such illustrations, whether they are drawings or photographs, can enhance the distinctive image of the store. Distinctive drawings or high-quality photography, when used continually, can create further advertising identity that adds to the advertising's continuity of impression.

When advertising is too complex and confusing it discourages the reader from reading the ad. It must always be assumed that the reader is a busy person and not all readers are interested. Everything in the ad must be prepared to make the ad pleasant, easy to read, and perhaps be entertaining to the reader. Stores that sell up-scale fashion merchandise should use illustrations that portray the type of customer they wish to attract and should take advantage of the growing improvement in color printing. On the other hand, mass merchandisers such as discounters and certain department stores should use illustrations that emphasize the details of the merchandise because their patrons make purchase decisions based on realistic impressions of the fashions (see Figure 9.14).

Types of Illustrations

There are two types of illustrations used in print advertisements: line or wash drawings and photographs.

DRAWINGS

Line Drawings; The simplest drawing is the line drawing created by a skilled artist using pen and ink or brush and ink. Line drawings are

Illustration   *231*

usually reproduced or printed in black and white. A line drawing can be used in a large size as the main illustration in the advertisement or in a small size as a diagram to explain a detail of a fashion. A line drawing can be a direct report of the merchandise, or can have subtleties that enhance the style and character of the merchandise. Using variations of drawing tools, the artist can make the line drawing very subtle by using thin lines or can make it broad and dramatic by using brush and ink. The advantages of the line drawing are that it prints very well and shows details very accurately. The drawing is ideal for fashion advertising when it is necessary to show a very small fashion illustration in a small-space ad. A disadvantage of the line drawing is that it does not show subtle draping or soft textures. Another important disadvantage is that it does not present the figure's dimensions satisfactorily. (See Figure 9.15*a* for an example of a line drawing.)

Wash Drawing;   The wash drawing uses a combination of pen and ink or brush and ink in combination with grey to black watercolor tones to develop texture effects. This also permits the creation of dimension effects to give a better portrayal of the human body. Techniques in the wash drawings vary from the use of simple mixtures of water with black paint or ink to the use of charcoal to create subtle smudges. The principles of the wash drawing can apply to water color usage wherein colors are used in combination with black ink or black paint to produce a color illustration that has texture and dimension.

The advantages of wash drawings are that they show texture and draping plus the dimensional quality of the merchandise. The wash drawing is better than the line drawing for indicating the subtleties of personalities and character of the human figure. Wash drawings often act as an excellent substitute for photography when photography is not available. (See Figure 9.15*b* for an example of a wash drawing.)

PHOTOGRAPHY   Due to significant improvement in film and camera technology, photography has become a very important form of presenting fashion merchandise to the customer. It is excellent for newspaper and magazine advertising as well as for direct mail brochures. (See Color Plate 11). Most leading newspapers are now able to print fairly good color photos.

Advantages of Photography;   An advantage of photography is that it can show detail in a realistic manner. Photography's ability to picture merchandise realistically, particularly in action, helps to create a positive and often glamorous impression of the fashions advertised. Photographs can establish an advertising personality through correct use of lighting and good selection of models. Because of motion pictures

Figure 9.14a.   One retailer, known for its photographic ad style, uses an eye-catching layout to promote its swimwear assortments aggressively. (Courtesy of Bloomingdale's, New York.)

Figure 9.14b. Another retailer uses drawings to strongly present a wide selection of values. (Courtesy Filene's Basement, Wellesly, Mass.)

Figure 9.15a. The line drawing is best for showing merchandise details but is limited in its ability to indicate textures and the draping of garments.

Figure 9.15b. On the other hand, the wash drawing can effectively show the textures and the draping of a fashion as well as the details of the merchandise. (Artwork by Randy Clay, Advertising Manager, Globman's, Martinsville, Va.)

234

Illustration   *235*

and television the customer now has a photographic awareness capability. The customer has developed a photographic mind-set and can relate directly to any message that uses photographic illustrations. Another advantage of photography is that it is considered a contemporary art technique. Once art galleries showed only paintings or sculptures, but now there are art galleries that feature exhibitions of the best in photography. (See Figure 9.16).

Disadvantages of Photography;   Good photography costs more than either line or wash drawings. In addition to the photographer's fee there is the cost of models. Good models are paid for fitting time, for the time involved with makeup and hairstyling, and for the time in front of the camera. Models are paid by the hour or by the day. In the largest cities, the best models can earn one thousand dollars a day. Furthermore, the actual merchandise must be available for photography in the store or at the studio.

Because photography is a faithful reproduction of actual fashions, there isn't opportunity for exaggeration as in line or wash drawing. Photography reports faithfully, with little subtlety, the actual merchandise, whereas an artist's drawing can exaggerate the sweep of a skirt, the length of a sleeve. This can be a disadvantage when a new style is being introduced in a photographic ad because the distinct fashion features cannot be emphasized beyond the emphasis that it actually is in the merchandise. In a drawing, the distinct feature in the fashion can be oversized or drawn with a heavier, bolder drawing style. Certain style features can be exaggerated for emphasis particularly in silhouette areas of a drawing. However, in both black and white photography and in color photos, the photographs can be retouched to highlight, to a degree, a silhouette and other details. In certain photography situations, photo retouching can also help eliminate many unattractive details. A black and white photograph can be retouched to emphasize further the details of the garment. In color photography, photographs can be retouched to intensify or correct colors. However, such retouching is an added cost.

Major stores, especially the mass merchandisers, find fashion photography best for their advertising because photos accurately show the merchandise they are offering. These stores usually have their own studios because they produce so much photography for their various print media. These photographs can often be used in their various stores for display purposes. Their items can be realistically depicted in a photograph, whereas high-fashion stores prefer to promote the total look that reflects the store's image. The high-fashion store, usually a specialty shop, will find that drawings not only portray the merchandise well but

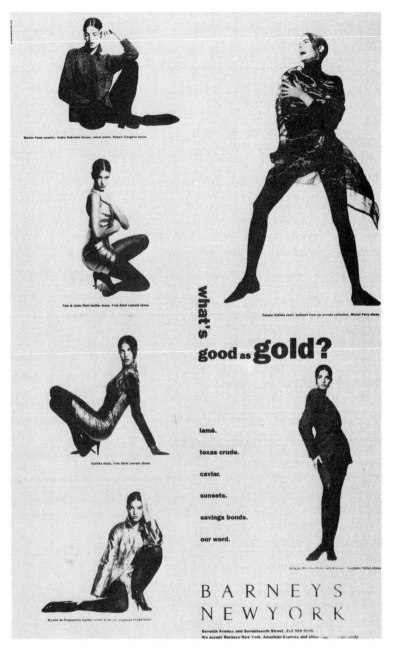

Figure 9.16a. Many retailers choose photography because of its ability to show merchandise realistically in dynamic action or to create a glamorous impression of a fashion. Barney's uses action photos to arrest the customer's attention. (Courtesy of Barneys New York.)

Commanding presence.

Wearing the pants and looking more feminine than ever, it's fall's well-tailored white flannels with a touch of top brass. Just the kind of standout dressing to keep you on top of things, and just the kind of well-thought-out style you know you'll find in the collections at Saks Fifth Avenue.

By Linda Allard for Ellen Tracy: the white emblem-sleeve jacket in cashmere and wool flannel, $355, matching relaxed pants, $225, and white silk charmeuse blouse, $265, all for sizes 2 to 16. Designer Sportswear Collections on Two.

With our complimentary One on One Service, our shopping coordinators will escort you through the store, help with gift selections, write everything on one check and provide gift wrapping. (212) 940-4145. New York, inquiries: (212) 753-4000. Open Monday through Saturday, 10 am to 6:30 pm; Thursday 'til 8 pm • White Plains, Springfield & Garden City open Monday & Thursday 'til 9 pm. Bergen open weekdays 'til 9:30 pm. Stamford 'til 9 pm; Saturday 'til 6 pm • Springfield, Garden City & Stamford open Sunday, 2 to 5 pm; White Plains, 12 to 6 pm • Also available in Boston, Chevy Chase, Tysons II, Owings Mills.

Figure 9.16*b*. The Saks Fifth Avenue photo creates a stylish impression and emphatically portrays the tailoring of the jacket. (Courtesy of Saks Fifth Avenue, New York.)

are able to express a distinctive fashion personality that represents the character of the store.

Photography usually limits the small specialty shop's ability to express its special personality since all photography seems to look alike to the reader. Photography allows the store to set a mood in a picture, but there is not as much variety in impression as there is in a drawing. In a major city, many of the high-fashion stores use very attractive photography in their ads. However, if one were to remove the logos and any other mention of the names of the various stores, it would be very difficult for the average newspaper reader to identify a specific store. This condition can apply to other print media.

Because many mass merchandisers prefer to use photography for their ads, some retailers that offer up-scale fashions choose to add distinction in their advertising by using especially distinctive line or wash drawings.

Qualities to Be Sought in Photography;   Mass merchandisers, especially discounters, who choose to appeal to the less sophisticated customer, should use photography that emphasizes fashion details such as silhouette and texture. Photography for this type of store, whether it is for R.O.P. newspaper advertising or a color insert, should clearly show the merchandise. A fashion forward store should use photography that portrays the personality of the merchandise and the model. Projecting a fashionable impression through lighting and background properties will further add to the elegant quality of the fashions. For example, some stores have used an orchestra background such as violins or photographing a model near a harp to accentuate the quality impression of an elegant gown.

When a special impression background is desired, the photographer can choose a distinctive location such as an art gallery, an elaborate fountain, a dramatic staircase, or elegant furniture. A store that attracts the younger fashion customer can also use musical instruments to express the mood. One imaginative store showed several musicians playing the saxophone, trumpets, and drums in the background to establish a contemporary mood relevant to their merchandise. Such props and background used to dramatize the mood of the fashion can be costly.

Color photography, planned for print media, has an additional bonus value to the advertiser who also uses television, because it can be adapted for television commercials. Various graphic technologies can animate such photographs so that they seem to "zoom" in and out of the screen to the beat of selected music. Photographs have added value in magazines because they print excellently. Photographs in magazine ads are generally more appealing and "sell" better than drawings.

Illustration 239

Special Considerations for the Layout and the Written Word in Direct Mail

LOGO Depending on what physical form a direct mail piece employs, the logo can be a splendid way to increase visual impact. In a folded piece of direct mail, the logo can appear on several folds to add the value of repetition. In a one-sheet unit of direct mail that is printed on both sides, the logo should appear prominently on each side. When any direct mail unit uses an envelope for mailing, the logo should be importantly positioned on the envelope.

When the direct mail piece is in several colors (from two to four colors) the opportunities for color emphasis are numerous. If the main text is printed in black ink it is well to consider printing the logo in one of the other colors. If the direct mail unit is a brochure that uses four-color photography for the merchandise, where possible, a four-color version of the logo should be printed. Many stores will photograph, in color, the sign on the outside of the store so they can use this sign as an effective print logo because it is familiar to their customers.

HEADLINES AND COPY STYLE The headline style in direct mail can be similar to headlines for newspaper advertising. The customer appeals are essentially the same as in any print media. However, the physical design of the headline depends on the nature of the direct mail piece. In a folder or brochure, the headline should appear on the first page and the rest of the text on the other sections of the folder. When multi-color printing is used, the headline can be strengthened by using an alternate color to those of the main text.

The style of body copy, in direct mail, is similar to the body copy of any print media. However, it can be presented in more dramatic ways by using various folds of the printed piece to separate the parts of the text for emphasis.

THE ILLUSTRATION The various purposes of an illustration for newspaper advertising also apply to usage in direct mail. However, direct mail permits separating many of the photographic situations into separate elements. For instance, in a three-unit folder the photograph showing a close-up of the model can be on the first unit. A full-length photo of the model can be shown inside and another picture can show close-up sections of the garment.

Line or wash drawings are appropriate in small-size folders. Photography is best for large-size brochures that can be flat sheet or folded. Colorful drawings are also useful. Because direct mail is printed by a printing specialist, opportunities to use more varied selection of type are available to the advertiser. Since the paper quality offered by such printers is better than newspapers supply, photography can enjoy much better reproduction.

LAYOUT   Direct mail pieces come in many forms, from the simplest standard postcard to the big fold-out brochure and the large size multipage catalogue. Each of these units present creative opportunities for layout specialists. These opportunities offer possibilities for dramatic use of typography. Some advertisers make dramatic use of illustrations that cover the entire sheet of paper. Regardless of the size of the direct mail piece, variations in techniques are as vast as the imaginations of the talented graphic designers.

At the early stages of creating the layout of the direct mail piece, it is best that the designers actually prepare what is called the "dummy." This is created by cutting the paper and folding it to resemble the final form of the direct mail piece. Doing this will start the creative process. Just as in newspaper advertising the creative person should sketch the various elements of the ad on the blank "dummy." Designing direct mail often takes more time and much more skill than is used in preparing newspaper advertising.

SELECTION OF PAPER   Advertising printed in the newspaper or magazines offer very little option in the choice of paper. However, direct mail presents to the advertiser so many choices in paper quality that the paper itself can serve as creative inspiration for the mailing piece. The various textures available often are a significant consideration in the first creative steps in preparing direct mail. For example, the sleek, clean look of coated paper inspires the quality emotions that must be expressed in the other elements that will go into the direct mail unit. Care in illustration style or photography is required, as well as the thoughtful selection of type faces, so that these elements print well on such inspirational paper stocks.

When selecting appropriate paper, keep in mind the personality and character of the advertiser. The aggressive, highly promotional store rarely would use a high-gloss, sleek paper stock for any direct mail. Instead it would select a paper that contains a rougher texture. There are "hard sell" discount stores that actually print their direct mail pieces on ordinary brown wrapping paper to suggest a low-price image to the reader. Promotional stores often print special direct mail announcing a 20% to 40% off discount sale in an unusually dramatic way. The message is printed in poster style on an actual brown paper bag used by grocery stores.

Many retailers have created part of their distinctive advertising personality through thoughtful selection of the paper used in their mailings to the fashion customer.

Summary

The basic ingredients that are employed to create a print ad are (1) the layout, (2) the written word, and (3) the illustration. The qualities of a good layout are simplicity in arrangement, strong visual focus elements, reflection of the store personality, and maintaining a continuity of impression. The principal function of the copy is to persuade the reader to make a purchase. Illustrations serve two main purposes. They should attract the eye of the reader and identify and demonstrate the merchandise. The layout, the written word, and the illustration must reflect the image and personality of the store.

Color Plate 1. Mood lighting is ideal for a window of evening wear. Also note the bright spot on the women's torso to focus the viewer's attention. (Lord & Taylor, New York. Reproduced by permission of the Retail Reporting Bureau.)

Color Plate 2. This display of oriental splendor creates excitement through the use of various textures. The shiny, smooth surfaces of the picture frame and the skirt are set off by being placed near the rougher texture of the beaded jacket. (Saks Fifth Avenue, New York. Reproduced by permission of the Retail Reporting Bureau.)

Color Plate 3. Munsell color chart showing hue, value, and intensity. (Courtesy of Munsell Color, 2441 N. Calvert St., Baltimore, Md. 21218.)

Color Plate 4. The repetition of diagonal lines in fixtures and mannequins unifies this young men's department. (Dayton's, St. Paul. Reproduced by permission of the Retail Reporting Bureau.)

Color Plate 5. Closed window. The double window has a black background and a shiny white floor. The abstract wave pattern that sweeps across the wide expanse of glass ties the several groups and clusters up into a single story, and the expert lighting sets the sunny scene. (Bergdorf Goodman, New York. Reproduced by permission of the Retail Reporting Bureau.)

Color Plate 6. The wall space is a background for this Ralph Lauren shop, providing display and stock space. It also helps to identify the department as well as present merchandise. (G. Fox, Farmington, Conn. Reproduced by permission of the Retail Reporting Bureau.)

Color Plate 7. Dramatically sized brochures that make an important fashion statement. Such brochures can focus on fashion news or promote a value and assortment impression. (Courtesy of Lady Miriam's, Bellflower, Calif. and Les Magasins Taylor, St. Lambert, Quebec.)

Color Plate 8. Seasonal fashion catalogues are an important part of many retailers' promotional programs. This store's fall catalogue features fashion trends (Courtesy of Les Magasins Taylor, St. Lambert, Quebec.)

Color Plate 9. A striking billboard that features a famous fashion maker. (Courtesy of Robinson's, Los Angeles, Calif.)

Color Plate 10. Attractively coordinated packaging that reflects the fashion character of a quality store. Note the graphic variety that symbolizes the store's name. (Courtesy of Fayetteville Tulips, Inc., Fayetteville, N.C.)

Color Plate 11. In producing photos for use in a sale brochure mailed to about 100,000 names, 20 exposures of each fashion group are needed to provide the advertiser with sufficient choices for the best selection of poses. Note how the simple color backgrounds are used for superimposing the typography message. (Courtesy of Les Magasins Taylor, St. Lambert, Quebec.)

CHAPTER 10

Advertising Principles: Broadcast Media

Advertising Objectives/Purposes

Broadcast media advertising shares the same advertising objectives as print media (Chapter 8). Because many advertisers believe that the most essential ingredient of broadcast advertising is entertainment, they fail to review their radio and television ads to determine whether this material has met their advertising objectives.

Broadcast media is the term used to describe the various methods of communicating to a listening or viewing audience. Radio and its companion television are the most-used media for the dissemination of various messages. They sell to the consumer, who will purchase various categories of goods from autos or breakfast foods to every type of fashion merchandise.

Less important categories of broadcast media include interior store announcements over public address systems and in-store television projections placed in important sections of the selling floor. Loudspeakers outside of a store broadcasting announcements or music to attract a passerby's attention are other examples of broadcast media.

Retailers use broadcast media for aggressive selling of fashion goods as well as for projecting a store's fashion image. Many successful large and small retailers such as Casual Corner and Mandee's use radio broadcasting and television exclusively and have enjoyed significant impact on the public by using these media. By employing excellent showmanship in their messages these advertisers have created distinctive personalities for their businesses.

Radio

The Advantages of Radio

WIDE AUDIENCE   Radio provides the advertisers with a wide audience so that the retailer can reach more customer prospects than newspapers or direct mail. The extent of a radio station's audience coverage usually determines the advertising rate—the bigger the geographical range and the larger the number of listeners, the higher the rate.

FLEXIBILITY   The advertiser has considerable flexibility in selecting the time when it is best for the advertising. Radio permits the retailer to choose any day of the week as well as the time period of each day that is best for the store to reach its audiences. A significant advantage of the flexibility of radio is its ability to make quick changes in the timing of the message as well as in the selection of the merchandise that is being advertised. The ability to switch the message and the timing of the broadcast permits the advertiser to met special emergencies such as changes in the weather or situations when merchandise fails to arrive in time for the broadcast. Such quick changes are not possible in print media.

LIVE HUMAN VOICE   A very important advantage of radio is that by tone of voice it can persuade the listener to come to the store and make a purchase decision. In effect, it's one human being, on the air, talking persuasively to another on a one-to-one basis. The human voice can praise the merchandise using certain intonations or urgently persuade simply by changing the tone of voice and the text of the message.

RADIO PERSONALITY'S CONTRIBUTION TO STORE PERSONALITY   The radio voice should present a personality with which listeners identify. This vocal personality should reflect the character of the store. An up-scale fashion store might use a woman's voice that reflects a cultivated person. On the other hand, a promotional store might well use a voice that talks a little faster and persuades more aggressively.

RELATIVE LOW COST   Time costs for radio are comparatively inexpensive when the size of the radio audience is considered. Furthermore, there are a wide range of time costs for the various periods of the radio day. *AA time* has the highest cost, and *C time* has the lowest. These costs can vary between stations in the same community (see Figure 10.1).

RADIO'S AUDIENCE PENETRATION   A significant advantage of radio is its ability to reach people wherever they are. Radio broadcasting has no delivery problems and can reach people no matter what they are doing.

The message can be heard by any person driving a car, working in the kitchen, working in the office, sitting at the tennis game, lying on the beach, or turning in for the evening.

CAPACITY FOR SELECTIVITY   An important advantage is radio's capacity for selectivity. Radio can reach male blue collar workers as well as female office workers. By carefully selecting the station and certain program periods advertisers can reach any age group from alert young customers to more mature men or women. It is radio's versatility in program planning that makes this possible.

"NARROW CASTING"   Radio stations in most metropolitan areas specialize in various type of programs, such as round-the-clock news programs, variety programs, talk shows, ethnic programs, and music programs that feature rock, classic, semi-classic, contemporary, or country and western. Radio's capacity for such "narrow casting" offers important promotional values to the fashion advertiser. Rather than using radio to interest a wide group composed of many cultural segments of the audience, advertisers can reach special target groups that represent the distinct variations of any store's consumer complex. A store catering to younger customers can use stations that broadcast music or entertainment that appeals to this group. Rock or country music programs are usually best for such groups. On the other hand, the more mature customer who is particularly interested in news programs or mature discussion will listen to radio stations that specialize in these types of programs.

VARIETY OF SHOWMANSHIP TECHNIQUES   Another advantage of radio is the variety of showmanship techniques, from the straight exposition of facts to a creative jingle. People remember a good jingle, and it provides an entertainment dimension that newspapers cannot. One of the best advantages of using radio is that an advertiser can create an advertising personality by the careful selection of a distinctive voice. By creative use of the voice and appropriate music to emphasize certain selling facts, the advertiser, in effect, creates a distinctive audio logo that quickly identifies the store.

VERSATILITY   Radio's versatility is another advantage. With a few exceptions, radio can be used to sell the listener almost every type of fashion merchandise. It can sell the quality characteristics of a garment, or it can emphasize the value inducements with vocal emphasis on price. In another time period the radio message can focus on the reputation of the famous brands that the retailer carries as well as emphasizing the wide assortments in the store.

Radio can be extremely versatile in terms of the variety of messages it can send to the listener. It can be used to sell merchandise aggressively through creative persuasive techniques. It can build a classification or

Figure 10.1. A typical radio station's rate card. Note the variety of time-buying plans. (Courtesy of The Radio Advertising Bureau, New York.)

TIME CLASSIFICATIONS

CLASS "A": 6:00 A.M. to 10:00 A.M. & 3:00 P.M. to 7:00 P.M., Monday through Friday.

CLASS "B": 10:00 A.M. to 3:00 P.M. & 7:00 P.M. to 8:00 P.M., Monday through Friday; Sign on to 8:00 P.M., Saturday & Sunday.

CLASS "C": 8:00 P.M. to 1:00 A.M., Daily.

ANNOUNCEMENTS
Fixed Position

No.	Class "A" Mins.	S'b'k's.	Id's.	Class "B" Mins.	S'b'k's.	Id's.	Class "C" Mins.	S'b'k's.	Id's.
1	40.00	32.00	24.00	30.00	24.00	18.00	22.00	17.60	13.20
52	39.00	31.20	23.40	29.00	23.20	17.40	21.00	16.80	12.60
156	38.00	30.40	22.80	28.00	22.40	16.80	20.00	16.00	12.00
260	37.00	29.60	22.20	27.00	21.60	16.20	19.00	15.20	11.40
312	36.00	28.80	21.60	26.00	20.80	15.60	18.00	14.40	10.80
520	34.00	27.20	20.40	24.00	19.20	14.40	16.00	12.80	9.60
624	32.00	25.60	19.20	22.00	17.60	13.20	15.00	12.00	9.00
1040	30.00	24.00	18.00	20.00	16.00	12.00	13.00	10.40	7.80

No additional discounts. May be combined with announcements in Saturation Plans to earn lower Plan rates. Stationbreaks may be 20/30 seconds; ID's, 10 seconds.

5-MINUTE NEWS, WEATHER, SPORTS

Rates per broadcast, including time, talent and production:

Per Week	Class "A"	Class "B"	Class "C"
1	$44.00	$33.00	$23.00
3	43.00	32.00	22.00
6	42.00	31.00	21.00
12	40.00	30.00	20.00
18	38.00	29.00	19.00
24	36.00	28.00	18.00

10% discount for 52 weeks' consecutive use of a minimum of 1 weekly. For ten and fifteen minute broadcasts, add 50% and 100% respectively, to above rates. Rates for other programs, on request.

HELICOPTER TRAFFIC REPORTS

Monday through Friday between 7:00-9:00 a.m. and 4:00-6:00 p.m. Rates:

No. Wkly.	Each	Total
1-2	$50.00	—
3	45.00	$135.00
6	40.00	240.00
12	38.00	456.00
18	36.00	648.00

10% CWD for 52 weeks use.

SATURATION PLANS

Figure 10.1. *(continued)*

To be scheduled on rotating basis in respective segments within 7 day period.

Rates Each:

	Minutes	20/30-Sec.	10-Sec.
CLASS "A"			
1-5 Weekly	$35.00	$28.00	$21.00
6 Weekly	34.00	27.20	20.40
12 Weekly	32.00	25.60	19.20
18 Weekly	30.00	24.00	18.00
CLASS "B"			
1-5 Weekly	$25.00	$20.00	$15.00
6 Weekly	24.00	19.20	14.40
12 Weekly	23.00	18.40	13.80
18 Weekly	22.00	17.60	13.20
24 Weekly	21.00	16.80	12.60
30 Weekly	20.00	16.00	12.00
CLASS "C"			
1-5 Weekly	$18.00	$14.40	$10.80
6 Weekly	17.00	13.60	10.20
12 Weekly	16.00	12.80	9.60
18 Weekly	15.00	12.00	9.00
24 Weekly	14.00	11.20	8.40
30 Weekly	13.00	10.40	7.80

10% discount for 52 weeks consecutive use of at least one announcement weekly. Do not earn quantity discounts for fixed position announcements. Stationbreaks may be 20/30 seconds; ID's, 10 seconds.

MAXIMUM AUDIENCE PLANS

Rates Per Week:

	60-Sec.	20/30-Sec.	10-Sec.
12 PLAN			
4A, 4B, 4C	$284.00	$226.80	$170.40
18 PLAN			
6A, 6B, 6C	402.00	321.30	241.20
24 PLAN			
8A, 8B, 8C	520.00	415.20	312.00
30 PLAN			
10A. 10B. 10C	630.00	504.00	378.00

department by focusing on the store's brand names and fashion leadership. It can build a store's character and reputation by emphasizing certain non-merchandising characteristics such as store hours, charge accounts, special in-store promotions, and fashion shows or demonstrations.

Disadvantages of Radio

LACK OF RETRIEVABILITY   The most important disadvantage of radio is that the message is not retrievable. The message has a one time 30- to 60-second life. Unless the budget can afford continual repetition of the message, many customers may not hear it. Much of the audience may not have the radio turned on, or something may be diverting the listener's attention at the time the message is on the air.

LACK OF VISUAL IMAGE   Radio cannot offer the listener a picture of the merchandise other than the verbal description. Since the message must be brief, the advertiser has little time to provide details to stimulate visualization of the apparel. Radio cannot present a new fashion silhouette or an unfamiliar style to the listener, nor can it describe a new color satisfactorily.

THE RADIO MESSAGE CAN BE IGNORED   Many listeners use the radio to provide a background sound to their normal day-to-day activities. Many in the audience listen to discussion or sports programs and intensely focus their attention on these particular subjects. To interrupt such intense attention to present an advertising message demands highly creative broadcast techniques. Without excellent showmanship, the message will fail to capture the full attention of the listener.

AUDIO CLUTTER   A distinct disadvantage of radio broadcasting is the proliferation of advertising messages. This audio clutter is because radio is so inexpensive to advertisers in terms of reaching large groups of people. When there are so many messages being broadcast over any one station, usually back-to-back, the listeners develop the ability to turn off their "listening apparatus." Even the most effective ad messages can fail to penetrate to the listeners' awareness because of audio clutter.

Best Use of Radio

Radio should be used to appeal to certain customers, such as young adults, who do not usually read newspapers. Because the tonal character of voice is important in broadcasting, a note of urgency is best expressed over the radio. An exciting message advertising the last few days of an event is not as effective in print as is the continual persuasion of an aggressive radio voice.

Selection of Stations

To select a station the advertiser should start by defining the store's typical customers in order to be aware of the lifestyle of that customer group. With this information the advertiser can now select the stations that cater to these special groups. Advertisers can request listener demographic profiles from the stations in the market. In making program selection decisions, stores use this data as a basis for decisions about the times when special listener segments are an important part of the audience (see Figure 10.2).

Such planning guides the advertiser in selecting the best time of the day or night for the message to reach target customers. Radio stations can easily provide many kinds of demographic information that will be useful in helping advertisers select the station and the best time segments. Further help in this area can be supplied by the Radio Advertising Bureau or the management of the various stations.

Radio stations usually will provide services to help create advertising copy text, music, and jingles. To help in selecting the voice to be used, audition tapes are usually available.

Television[1]

Television has brought big changes in the lives of the public by offering a major source of entertainment and information. Television is no longer radio with pictures. This dynamic graphic medium has its own techniques of delivering messages to the audience and its own disciplines in creative values.

Because television is a combination of pictures and a persuading voice, this medium offers the fashion retailer opportunities to attain several significant objectives such as (1) increasing store or departmental traffic through special promotions, (2) selling specific fashion merchandise, (3) building a distinctive store image or personality, (4) developing an image for certain categories of goods such as youthful fashions, active sportswear, or quality accessories, and (5) introducing new lines or services. The advertiser can achieve these and other objectives when the selling message is based on television's strengths in delivering entertainment and information in visual form. The human voice of radio advertising must be the articulate servant of the pictures on the screen.

[1]   This section was guided by the research and writings of Howard P. Abrahams, formerly vice president of the Television Bureau of Advertising, New York, NY.

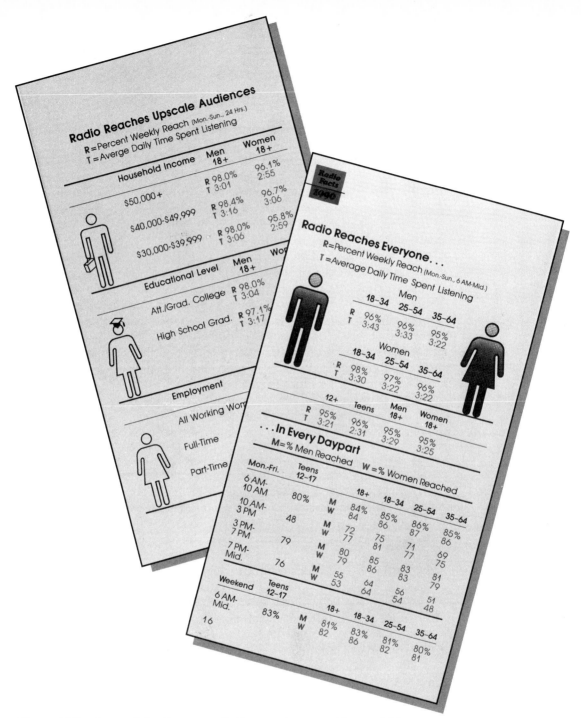

Radio Reaches Upscale Audiences
R=Percent Weekly Reach (Mon.-Sun., 24 Hrs.)
T=Averge Daily Time Spent Listening

Household Income		Men 18+	Women 18+
$50,000+	R	98.0%	96.1%
	T	3:01	2:55
$40,000-$49,999	R	98.4%	96.7%
	T	3:16	3:06
$30,000-$39,999	R	98.0%	95.8%
	T	3:06	2:59

Educational Level		Men 18+	Wo
Att./Grad. College	R	98.0%	
	T	3:04	
High School Grad.	R	97.1%	
	T	3:17	

Employment		
All Working Wom		
Full-Time		
Part-Time		

Radio Reaches Everyone...
R=Percent Weekly Reach (Mon.-Sun., 6 AM-Mid.)
T=Average Daily Time Spent Listening

		Men		
		18-34	25-54	35-64
R		96%	96%	95%
T		3:43	3:33	3:22

		Women		
		18-34	25-54	35-64
R		98%	97%	96%
T		3:30	3:22	3:22

	12+	Teens	Men 18+	Women 18+
R	95%	96%	95%	95%
T	3:21	2:31	3:29	3:25

...In Every Daypart
M=% Men Reached   W=% Women Reached

Mon.-Fri.	Teens 12-17		18+	18-34	25-54	35-64
6 AM-10 AM	80%	M	84%	85%	86%	85%
		W	84	86	87	86
10 AM-3 PM	48	M	72	75	71	69
		W	77	81	77	75
3 PM-7 PM	79	M	80	85	83	81
		W	79	86	83	79
7 PM-Mid.	76	M	55	64	56	51
		W	53	64	54	48

Weekend	Teens 12-17		18+	18-34	25-54	35-64
6 AM-Mid.	83%	M	81%	83%	81%	80%
16		W	82	86	82	81

Figure 10.2. Some of the data on radio listener demographics useful in making time-buying decisions. Most radio stations can supply similar data about their own particular audiences. (Courtesy of The Radio Advertising Bureau, New York.)

Advantages of Television

VISUAL IMAGE, SOUND, AND MOTION   The most important advantage of television, because it uses pictures, is that it can demonstrate merchandise in action. Such action emphasizes the important qualities of the fashions involved. Through photographic techniques it can enhance the personality of the fashions and demonstrate the special qualities of a garment.

According to Phillips, Bloom, and Matinly[2], television establishes a believability; it carries authority; and viewers perceive products advertised on television as having greater acceptability. Television provides an opportunity to demonstrate the function of a product within a commercial format. Camera position makes it possible to show close up details of the item's special feature.

For example, the retail advertiser can use active pictures to persuade a viewer to shop for a raincoat with a removable lining by showing how the wearer removes the liner easily and quickly. A new fashion silhouette, such as a wide, swinging pleated skirt, can be shown on TV by using the graceful movement of the model simulating a dance step. The various moods expressed by a fashion can be dramatized with special lighting effects and camera techniques. For example, a casual outdoor costume when shown in action in a setting that is appropriate to the merchandise creates a persuasive impression. Dramatic camera work highlighting a silhouette will quickly emphasize the look and line of a garment much more effectively than words can. Music can help to accent the mood further. Skillful use of fashion in motion combined with sounds of a persuasive voice and appropriate music should provide the entertainment and information ingredients necessary for an effective advertising message.

VERSATILITY OF CAMERA   The television camera has the ability to move from distant "long shot" photography to demonstrate silhouette and then move rapidly to the close-up for texture demonstration all within less than one or two seconds. The camera can establish an appropriate setting as it shows fashions in action. It can also show the interaction of people in a typical social situation. Camera movement can demonstrate the total look from head to toe, back and front and side.

Another advantage is that television's graphic techniques can not only show pictures, but can supply visible words on the same screen through various electronic editing techniques. Advertisers can superimpose

---

[2]   P.M. Phillips, E. Bloom, and J.D. Matinly, *Fashion Sales Promotion: The Selling Behind the Selling*. (John Wiley and Sons, 1985), p. 142.

prices on top of the photography or have a printed message move across the screen at the same time the merchandise is being shown. By choosing an appropriate setting, television can establish subtle impressions of the lifestyles relevant to the fashions. For example, a luxury coat, when shown in a proper setting such as an elegant stairway, has an aura of quality. Television, through imaginative editing techniques, can show a large fashion assortment within a brief time period. Eight to ten garments can be shown, in action, within a 30-second unit. Since television uses cinematic editing technology, the audience, conditioned by theatrical motion pictures, can accept these "quick cuts" that permit fashion advertisers to show a wide selection of merchandise.

MODELS DEPICT TARGET CUSTOMER   A significant advantage is that a model with specific personality characteristics can be selected to represent a certain type of customer. Thus, the advertiser can relate to the target audience more accurately than with other media. With such a selection of models, television can establish a closer relationship between the retailer and the audience segment to which the message is directed.

A SALESPERSON IN EVERY HOME   Television has the effect of putting a store's salesperson in every viewer's home. Since the audience both sees and hears the message at the same time, it is more difficult not to pay attention. When the picture has motion that commands attention, the viewer will usually listen to the verbal message. Research has shown that the more the audio and visual senses are involved, the more effective the response.

TELEVISION'S LONG REACH   Like radio, television has the ability to reach many more people than the print media. Many television stations can reach bigger audiences than the radio stations in the same market. Television stations are usually more powerful and can sell merchandise in the city, suburbs, even the neighboring counties at the same time. To cover the same geographical area that television reaches, advertisers might have to run ads on several radio stations or in several newspapers in the region. Television reaches 98% of households, almost complete saturation, in every market in the country.

CONVEYS PRESTIGE ON THE STORE   Television can add to the prestige of a small retailer. Because the best national advertisers use the same medium in approximately the same time period that the small retailer does, the small retailer gains prestige by association.

FLEXIBILITY   Because television is essentially a combination of picture and voice, there are techniques for developing advertising in which the picture remains the same but the audio is used for several varied messages. For example, a store can be advertising a coat sale with a TV picture of models walking across the screen. During the week prior to this event, this scene can appear with a voice statement: "coming next week, *store name's* big coat sale." During the following week, the advertiser will use the same picture but, the voice will emphasize: "Now, get the big savings in *store name's* big coat sale." Toward the end of the event, the voice text will change to promote the last days of the sale by saying "Last three days to get the big savings in *store name's* big coat sale." The picture will remain the same.

Disadvantage of Television

HIGH COST OF AIR TIME AND PRODUCTION   The most important limitation in television advertising is the cost. Television is more expensive than any other medium. Not only are there costly time charges, but production expenses are usually high, much higher than production expenses involved in other media. The usual production expenses for TV advertisers can run from 20% to 50% of the total budget allocated for television. The reason for this is that the retail advertiser usually presents this advertising during the time periods adjacent to those of the biggest national advertisers. The retailer must make sure the store's TV advertising can compete in production values with the highly creative skills available to the leading national advertisers.

LIMITED TIME AVAILABLE   An important disadvantage is the limitation of time availability. There are only twenty four hours in a day. The prime times for viewing are the late afternoon and evening. These four to six hours are the very best and it's difficult, as well as expensive, to get scheduled into this period. Only a few of these periods are open for local advertisers at a reasonable cost. Some of these time slots are pre-bought and are not available to local retailers. They are so expensive they almost preclude a small store from using premium time. The demand for prime time results in a self-defeating action for the advertiser. To accommodate all applicants for this time period, most stations may run between four to six commercials back-to-back. This causes audio-visual clutter in which viewers often leave to get a drink of water or just switch to another station.

TELEVISION SKILLED PERSONNEL COSTS   There are more people available for creating good print media advertising than for TV advertising. Skilled experts who can create quality TV advertising for retailers are hard to find except in the larger markets. The cost of talent to prepare

TV advertising and to appear on the screen can be prohibitive. Other technicians and photographers are equally expensive.

PREPARATION TIME IS LONG   Preparation time is usually much longer than the time needed to prepare for all other media. Fashion advertising on TV involves several time consuming phases before the message can be broadcast. These phases involve careful merchandise selection and choice of models who will be fitted for the garments. Fittings are a time consuming process. Make-up and hair styling sessions prior to appearance before the camera take more time. After the photography is finished, time is needed for editing and matching the video segments with appropriate voice and music. To achieve the highest quality production values, experienced fashion advertisers usually plan for three or four weeks production time before the product is ready for broadcasting.

LACK OF RETRIEVABILITY   Like radio, each TV message has a one-time life. If the viewer is looking at the television set at the time the message is on the screen, the message may attract and impress the viewer. Often, the viewer at first may ignore the message and not be persuaded by it. Unless the budget permits continual repetition of such advertising, the message is lost. Furthermore, many prospective customers may not be viewing TV at the time the store's message is on the screen.

UNCERTAIN AUDIENCE SIZE   It is difficult to get an accurate measurement of the size of the television audience at the time the advertisement appears. Unlike newspaper advertising or direct mail, which both have circulation figures that can be pinpointed with reasonable accuracy, broadcast media are not able to establish the exact number of people who heard or saw the advertising when it appeared. Audience measurement figures are available but only on a general basis.

Best Uses of Television

Viewers of television depend on its excellent capacity to present (1) news, (2) demonstration of products, and (3) entertainment. Retailers should plan their advertising on TV to fit into these categories. Under the heading of news would be advertising for special events such as storewide sales, store or department openings, and departmental or classification promotion events. The introduction of a new brand is news worthy for television advertising.

Retailers who take pride in their in-store fashion shows can use TV to extend their fashion showmanship to a larger audience. Such TV activity, as entertainment, can further strengthen a retailer's fashion reputation.

Basic Principles for Time Selection

It is most important for the fashion advertiser to know when to reach prospective customers. This requires constant awareness of the viewing patterns of the various segments of the public that are the targets of the store's advertising. Thoughtful scheduling of the advertising according to the optimum audience and their viewing times is necessary. The usual categories that guide advertisers in selecting time segments are:

Housewives: Adult women who are at home

Men: Young men and adult men

Young women (teens): Usually high school or college age

Family: Predominantly adult women and men with young women and young men

Children: Up to 12 years

Table 10.1 is used by many retailers to guide them in scheduling time segments. This information applies to weekday viewing only. Because of more available leisure time on weekends, viewers may spend more time in front of the TV set when programming is dominated by sports. This particular audience is probably not interested in fashion promotion. An important consideration when buying TV time segments is the daily amount of time the television audience spends in front of the TV screen.

Table 10.1. Television Time Periods.

Time	Eastern	Central	Mountain	Pacific	Audience
Daytime	10 AM– 5 PM	9 AM– 4 PM	9 AM– 4 PM	10 AM– 5 PM	Adult women and children Men who work on "swing shifts"
Early evening	5–7:30 PM	4–6:30 PM	4–5:30 PM	5–7:30 PM	Adult women, teens, children. Men during the latter parts.
Prime	7:30– 11 PM	6:30– 10 PM	5:30– 9 PM	7:30– 11 PM	All groups except young children. Teens (gradually increase in later hours.)
Late evening	11 PM– Sign off	10 PM– Sign off	9 PM– Sign off	11 PM– Sign off	Adult men and women

Families as a household group—345 minutes a day

Adults—131 minutes a day

Young adults, 18 to 24—136 minutes a day

This information suggests that selecting TV time segments to spread over the lengthy daily time available to reach the fashion aware adult and young adult customer can demand daily frequency scheduling. One message per day may not be enough for acceptable results.

Length of TV Messages

Television time segments are purchased in these specific lengths: 10 seconds, 20 seconds, 30 seconds, and 60 seconds. The 10-second segment is usually part of the station identification segment (I.D.'s). This special I.D. segment limits the ad message to just eight seconds to allow for two seconds to say "This is station WWXX, Channel 4."

The 20-second segment can be bought throughout any part of most stations' programming—during daytime, early evening time, prime time, and late evenings time schedules.

The 30-second segment is the most popular length and is available at every station during the entire broadcasting day. Because of their popularity, the 30-second messages are often run back-to-back with several other advertisers, thus creating advertising clutter that reduces the impact of the message.

The 60-second segment is usually available at most stations. However, some stations may not have 60-second availabilities during prime time periods due to previous bookings by national advertisers.

Economic Time-Buying Guide

Frugal budgets have no place in planning television schedules. To accomplish the objectives of television advertising strategies, the budget must provide for enough television segment frequency to insure reaching the most members of the target audience. Just one TV time segment during a prime time program will not be effective.

A few ad messages on more than one station may not be worth more than a small size newspaper ad. Experienced retailers who want to get the most for their money usually plan to take advantage of the following discounts.

FREQUENCY DISCOUNTS   When the advertiser plans to use TV segments during a continuous 52-, 26-, or 13-week period, many stations give a discount for the frequency of advertising. This is similar to the frequency arrangement offered by most newspapers.

PACKAGE PLANS   Most stations offer a lower cost per segment when the advertisers can schedule a certain number of segments per week.

ANNUAL BULK PLANS   If an advertiser can contract for a large number of ad segments per year, some stations will offer special rate discounts. This permits the retailer to schedule heavily during seasonal peaks and save money when fewer ads are needed. This type of plan permits the advertiser to maintain continuity of impression.

RUN-OF-STATION RATES   The advertiser who is not seeking immediate results may find it advantageous to buy time segments on a Run-of-Station (ROS) basis. This is useful for certain TV ads, for service messages, or for store hour changes. This category is scheduled throughout the broadcast day at *non-specific* times determined by station management. ROS costs are usually less than the costs of fixed-time scheduling.

ADJACENCY RATES   A time segment next to, or close to, a prime time show is called an adjacency. This time period can be almost as effective as advertising inside the prime time broadcast. Such adjacency availabilities do not cost as much as premium prime time. Since there is great demand for this choice period it is best to make the adjacency segment part of the total long-term schedules.

   Many television stations offer variations of the above discount plans, and retailers usually can negotiate advantageous TV rates in the same way they negotiate with their fashion resources.

In-Store Video

Customers in the store are still part of the total TV audience even when they are shopping. They continue to respond to attractive visual messages that are skillfully produced. This public can react in the same manner when they view video screens located throughout the store. Because of increased technological improvements in video cassette equipment, in-store video has become an important advertising medium.

   The video message should be extremely simple with no visual complications or distracting editing cuts because it must be remembered that in-store videos should stop people on their way somewhere. If the video portion is jumpy, incoherent, or lacks simplicity, the viewer will quickly move away. Another important consideration to achieve effective in-store video is the quality of the picture. Since the video apparatus may be placed in areas that are badly lit or in areas where there are distracting lights, the quality of the video picture must be able to compete with these visual challenges.

The in-store video apparatus requires special positioning and mounting in the store. To increase color intensity that will compete with the variations of light in the rest of the area, stores often place a large black framing around the video screen to increase the color intensity of the picture. A bank of multiple monitors can create a "video wall" that will serve to increase the advertising impact of the message.

Advantage of In-Store Video

ATTENTION GETTING   An important method of attracting the interest of the viewer is to arrange for a bank of 3 to 12 units in one area, showing the same subject material to give the maximum impact to the in-store video message. Such massing of video screens will attract many more viewers and each one will be able to see the multiple screens simultaneously.

MOOD SETTING/CREATING   Another benefit of the in-store video is to help create the mood of the department. For example, in Junior fashions, a store can have a high-action video featuring appropriate fashions and energetic music to help set the youthful ambience for that particular department. The qualities that make a television broadcasting commercial highly attractive to a junior customer are equally useful for in-store videos.

USE IN PERSONNEL TRAINING   Any in-store video programming can be used for personnel sales training. When they are provided by fashion manufacturers, management can develop an effective sales training program. Many in-store video programs have been useful in sales training, especially when the program trains salespeople to be effective in persuading customers to buy the merchandise.

Disadvantages of In-Store Video

NOISE FACTOR   The in-store video's sound should be turned down periodically to reduce its distracting effect on the customer. Sales personnel usually welcome such a reduction in noise. Thoughtful management should frequently check on the noise levels of all in-store video as well as the piped-in music that is everywhere.

USES UP SHOPPING TIME   The selling message of the in-store video often may be construed as mere entertainment with no attempt to focus on the qualities implicit in the fashion merchandise. The "show" may be so good that the customer may miss the sales message and may think of the video strictly as entertainment. The customers can get too interested in the entertainment qualities and limit or delay their shopping. Many of these video tapes seem endless because they are showing an entire line of fashions. The time allotted to in-store video, in any location, should be carefully considered because long video sequences can take too much of the customer's time for actual shopping.

Best Uses of In-Store Video

Video is very good for showing up-scale designer merchandise, such as that designed by Ralph Lauren or Anne Klein, in the setting of a fashion show. Intimate apparel fashions, accessories, and cosmetics are excellent candidates for videos because these categories need to be seen on a person. Children's apparel is ideally suited for in-store video. The agile action and the happy faces attract parents and at the same time attract the children who may be visiting the store. Videos for men's apparel usually attract a large audience, especially when active sportswear for men shows attractive male models in sports activity. Not only do men stop to see the action, but women find such videos equally attractive since women influence many purchase decisions made by men.

Video Use in Small Stores

Smaller stores that want to use in-store video presentations may be able to secure appropriate video cassettes from their manufacturers who offer these at a low rental cost. Video monitors can be rented from local specialists in such equipment. A video monitor that is used for in-store video resembles the typical home television unit except that it lacks many of the dials that would be used at home.

When a store prepares its own in-store video programming or secures video material from a manufacturer, it should make sure the tape is in loop form so that it can be continuously repeated. Retailers, large or small, wishing to prepare their own in-store video programming will usually find facilities available for a fee at local television stations. In larger communities, there are television production studios that can produce quality in-store videos.

Warning

When the larger stores are using banks of many types of TV sets to sell in their departments as well as showing banks of multiple monitors in fashion departments, one unit alone is not impressive. An exception might be in the scarf department where the various ways of trying a scarf are being demonstrated to the customer. In this case, multiple monitors may only confuse the customer. A single monitor should be mounted so that it becomes a part of the department fixturing and does not look like a home TV sitting on a television cart. Furthermore, one monitor might not be adequate if there are a number of customers gathered around it. Take into consideration the number expected for the audience and have enough monitors to accommodate all of the audience so they can view the message at the same time.

Summary

Radio and television are the most-used components of the broadcast media. Less important categories include in-store announcements over public address equipment, and in-store video presentations. The principle advantage of radio is that it offers advertisers a wider audience than print media. Because the live human voice is an important ingredient, the listener can be more easily persuaded to decide to shop the retailer. Television has the effect of having a store's salesperson in every viewer's home. This is especially valid because television can reach a bigger audience than any other medium. It is best used for presenting promotion news, product demonstrations, and entertainment relevant to fashion goods.

CHAPTER 11

Mechanics of Building an Ad: Broadcast Media

Radio

Introduction

The main purpose of retailer advertising on radio is to persuade listeners to take action to visit the store and make a purchase decision. Such advertising is essentially an interruption of the programming of news, sports, music, entertainment, and discussion. Such interruptions are often considered annoying by people listening to an interesting program. Unless the ad message is equally interesting, the listeners can easily "tune-out" the advertising message without turning a dial. Consequently, a formidable task faces the retailer who wishes to use radio media to attract customers. Within the limits of the time allocated, the advertiser has to arrest the attention of the audience and deliver a persuasive message.

To accomplish this, effective radio commercials draw upon the creative skills of the copywriter. This individual understands the special nature of radio communication, the verbal qualities of the human voice, and the effects of the images generated by the music and sound effects that may supplement the human voice.

The Spoken Word

In many ways, the advertising messages on radio employ creative principles similar to those used in print media. (See Chapter 8.) However, producing a vocal advertising message requires making creative decisions based on an understanding of how the ad copy will sound when it is spoken by a human voice.

Since the prime vehicle for persuading the customer is the voice, speaking or singing to musical accompaniment, the copy style should show familiarity with "*people talk.*" Current popular vernacular is an important ingredient for arresting the listener's attention.

QUALITIES OF GOOD RADIO COPY

Simplicity;   Because most radio commercials are 30 seconds or less, the listener must understand the message within that time limit. This requires simple statements in people talk, so that listeners can grasp the message in a short time.

Clarity;   The message should clearly express the benefits of the merchandise in easy-to-understand terms. Complicated or long phrases that slow listeners' comprehension should be avoided.

Familiar Verbalization;   The copywriter should choose easy-to-understand words that are part of the everyday vocabulary of customers. Using formal phrases, trade language, and verbal fads can impede the listeners' attention and reduce the effect of the copy.

Ease of Pronunciation;   Words and phrases that are difficult to pronounce should be avoided. Terms, such as foreign expressions, that are unfamiliar to the listener can reduce the impact of a commercial and should be omitted.

Repetition;   A well-written commercial should repeat a significant benefit or important fact. This permits added emphasis in the short time allowed. The store name requires repetition at least three times, at the begining, in the middle, and, most important, at the end.

TYPES OF APPEALS   As in print advertising, effective radio and copy should be based on important emotional and rational appeals, because customer behavior is motivated by skillful messages that focus on these appeals. Several kinds of emotional appeals are especially useful in radio advertising.

Surprise;   This quality depends on an unusual sound effect, a special musical arrangement, or a unique sound from instruments such as trumpets or drums. A special voice quality can also supply the element of surprise. For example, a husky female or male voice, or voices with unique foreign or regional American accents.

Curiosity;   Beginning a commercial with a provocative question that makes the listener wait for the answer is one of the most common ways to stimulate curiosity.

Assurance;   The average radio listener has often been skeptical of radio commercials as many of these use tired words such as "sensational," "the greatest," "incredible," "the finest," or "unbelievable." Such expletives are easily ignored. The listener needs assurance that the goods advertised are backed up by the reputation of the store. The ad copy should emphasize, when appropriate, the brand name of the resource. Warranties and guarantees should be emphasized when possible.

RATIONAL APPEALS IN THE MESSAGE   The rational appeals that can motivate the listener are very much the same as those discussed in the chapter on print advertising copy. Among these appeals are the need to be comfortable, the need to be cool or warm, the need for ease of action, and the need to save money.

Although these appeals to the customer seemingly are the same as for print, there are differences in the creative styles that are used in writing the copy for radio. These are (1) the *factual* message, (2) the *narrative* message, and (3) the *"You"-directed* message. These categories should serve as guides for planning radio commercials.

The Factual Message;   This style uses a *direct* approach to sell the customer. This is often called *hard sell,* and is used mainly by aggressive retailers. The success of the factual message depends on emphasizing the salient facts that will persuade the listener to take action. Creative use of sound effects and voice characterization can increase the effectiveness of the message.

The Narrative Message;   This style presents a story that focuses on human interest. Various story-telling techniques are used, from the monologue to multiple voices. Imaginative use of humor, drama, or song to articulate the message can make effective commercials. Entertainment is a prime requirement in such radio advertising.

The "You"-Directed Message;   This style is essentially a one-on-one relationship between the radio voice and the listener. The voice explains the benefits of the merchandise directly to you, the customer. The word "you" is an important ingredient in the message. Phrases like "you asked for bright fashion tones for Spring" would replace "Spring fashions highlight bright tones." (For an example see Figure 11.1.)

Variations in Verbal Presentation

MONOLOGUE   The monologue is the most commonly used form of commercial. It is popular among advertisers because it requires the skill of only one person and is less costly than other methods. When the monologue message is enhanced by music or a special sound effect, it can be very effective. A disadvantage of a monologue is that, unless it is done very well with a distinctive voice and sound effects, it quickly loses the listeners' attention if it is frequently repeated.

DIALOGUE   An advantage of this method is that two different tones of voice stimulate increased interest in the listener. Creatively, the narrative style of copy is often best expressed in dialogue situations. Dialogue is one of the best ways to deliver a factual message without boring the listener.

A distinct disadvantage of the dialogue style is its higher cost of production. In addition to the cost of two voices there can be the cost of directing the proper use of the voices. Also, there is a need for more theatrical direction to dramatize the advertising story. Story-telling techniques to present the ad message effectively require more skills than the monologue style.

MULTIPLE VOICES   This technique is most often used in the "jingle" commercial. Because of the extra talent costs, multiple voices are rarely used for delivering verbal messages. The need for uniquely creative ad copy and special directorial skills can add to production cost. Furthermore, the ad message may lack necessary simplicity and clarity as a result of vocal confusion.

Variations in Types of Ad Copy

REASON WHY   This type of ad copy depends on factual presentation. The significant fact or facts are the basis for this category. The advertiser can employ any of the three creative approaches discussed earlier as long as the writer understands the listeners' need to be entertained while they are assimilating the facts. Humor or drama can help to underscore factual details.

"YOU"-DIRECTED COPY   Since this category represents a one-on-one relationship between the voice and the listener, this type of radio copy

```
PROFITT'S RADIO

SUBJ:          Profitt's For Her grand opening
LENGTH:        :30
RUN DATES:     3/6-3/11
WRITER:        Pete

MUSIC:         Uptempo, bright, and happy. Up then under for copy.
```

ANNCR
FEMALE: We're putting on the ritz, rolling out the red carpet,

and throwing a party in style, all to celebrate the

grand opening of Proffit's For Her at Northgate Mall!

Come join us and discover an exciting new store filled

with the latest fashions, accessories, cosmetics, and

much more, all from your favorite makers. While you're

there, register for fabulous merchandise giveaways and

enjoy exciting special events. Plus, you could win one

of the many instant winner prizes we're giving away.

It's all happening now through March nineteenth during

the grand opening celebration at Profitt's For Her at

Northgate Mall. The store that's just your style!

ANNCR
MALE: No purchase necessary to win prizes. You need not be

present to win.

Figure 11.1. A radio script for a 30-second commercial using "You"-directed
copy. Note the music cues and that two voices will be used. (Courtesy of
Proffitt's, Alcoa, Tenn.)

depends on frequent use of the word "you." The writer must make sure that all facts are presented *to the listener* in terms that he or she is familiar with. In effect, the best copy implies "We Know What You Want" as the creative concept for persuading the listener. Since the copy is in the spirit of direct selling to the customer, monologue techniques are most appropriate.

INTERROGATORY   One of the basic emotional appeals used by copy writers is *surprise;* therefore, the provocative question asked by the radio voice should surprise the listener enough for him or her to heed the rest of the message. This form of copy can easily provide the beneficial facts in the answer to the question. The facts part of the message should focus on the rational appeals in the text. For example, "Got enough sweaters for the cold days ahead?" This opening line of a commercial should offer attentive listeners with informative answers that promote the retailer's sweater stocks. The interrogatory format is creatively a simple style that can use monologue or dialogue equally well.

NEWSCASTING   As this variation in presentation suggests, the advertising message emulates the urgency of a newscast. This treatment also can make good use of the emotional appeal of *surprise.* The copy uses the factual message style to dramatize the significant benefits of the merchandise. Important to this category of copy styles is the *interrupting shock* of the opening statement. To achieve successful arresting of listener attention, many copywriters resort to theatrical exaggeration. For example, to advertise a promotion for Winter outerwear the opening of the commercial can shout, "Cold War Victory!" and go on to emphasize the benefits and savings in the outerwear event. Important to the success of a newscast-style advertisement is the characteristic urgent voice. This should resemble the style of the typical newscaster who breaks into any daily radio programming.

Importance of Voice and Sound

Radio is the only advertising medium that appeals to just one of the senses to deliver a message. Whether the advertiser uses words, music, sound effects, or all three, the listener's ears are the sole receivers of the message. Therefore, to achieve effective radio advertising, all the qualities of the voice and sound should be considered. These two elements are, in effect, the "illustrations" in radio advertising. Creative use of voice and sound should be directed to enhance the verbal message. When this combination is well planned the advertiser can achieve significant advertising distinction. Often unique sound and music, in combination or individually, can establish valuable identity for the advertiser. Just as often, the voice that speaks the message can add further to the identity of the store. Consequently, knowledgeability about voices and sound effects is an important qualification for a creative producer of radio advertising.

THE PURPOSE OF VOICE   The purpose of the voice is not only to enunciate the written text but also to dramatize it to arrest and hold the listener's attention. The voice should use various shadings and tones to add a personality character to the message. By relating to the image of the store and the target customer, the character of voice can act as the store's audio logo.

TYPES OF VOICE   There are many types of voices: cajoling voices, strongly persuasive voices, and musical voices that can sing the text. Also available are voices that represent various ages, from the child to the authoritative senior citizen. Some stores use feminine voices that reflect enthusiasm. Male voices can be argumentative, cajoling, or persuasive. Usually retailers will use a man's voice to advertise men's clothing and sportswear. However, some upscale men's stores seeking distinction might well use a woman's voice with a slightly foreign accent to cajole and to persuade a man that he will look especially attractive in certain apparel. The voice would say "Love, you should take a look at this jacket. It would do more for you than that old jacket hanging in your closet." Men's voices can sometimes be used to sell women's fashions, and women's voices can be used to persuade men to shop a men's store.

Whatever type of voice is used, it is most important that the ad message is delivered with genuine enthusiasm to be able to convince the audience. Breathless enthusiasm is characteristic of young people, whereas positive persuasion copy is effective with the more mature voice.

Although a variety of voice choices are available, it is best that the advertiser select one type of voice to establish a vocal identity that represents the store. Too many different voices on a store's radio schedule will create listener confusion. Radio advertisers should avoid colorless voices that lack definite personality. At all times, advertisers should avoid voices that are easily identified with any other local radio advertisers.

MUSIC AND SOUND EFFECTS   Music and sound effects are usually used as background for the verbal selling message. Such background sound can be used most effectively when it becomes a part of the message. Using a musical effect or a sound effect such as a locomotive whistle can hold the listener's attention. Certain musical rhythms such as Latin music can establish dramatic atmosphere for a fashion event. Dixieland rhythm or a contemporary jazz rhythm can be used in developing the musical background for the verbal phases of an announcement of a promotional event.

Certain sound effects, such as those from a trumpet, a bugle, or a fire engine siren, can replace a verbal statement that was intended to arrest the listeners' attention. Music can be important when the rhythm of the verbal text is related to the rhythm of the music. Such music and sound effects are not difficult to obtain during preparation for a commercial. Music and sound effects can be used in creating an audio logo to identify a store.

Most radio stations have sound libraries that are collections of various sounds, from the sound of a rooster crowing to the opening bars of a Sousa march. These libraries also contain variations of musical phrases, waltzes, fox trots, or march music, and are usually available, at no cost, to help advertisers create their own advertising message.

When used properly, music and sound effects can strengthen a retailer's radio advertising. They can be used to underscore an important point in the text or to create a distinctive mood that enhances the ad message.

THE JINGLE, PRO AND CON   Sometimes, an effective selling message can become the lyrics of a simple song, commonly called *a jingle*. Many ad experts believe that messages with a music background are retained more easily than nonmusical text. Because of this belief, the jingle has proliferated so that there is now a jungle of jingles out there in radioland. Sometimes, a person listening will hear one that is so pleasant that she cannot get the jingle out of her mind. The more familiar the music is, the easier it is for listeners to accept and remember it.

Often, it is difficult to understand the words, particularly when they are sung by a small choir or a few voices. Advertisers who prefer jingles should have the lyrics sung by one voice accompanied by a simple tune. Frequently, the music is so wild and noisy that the audience rejects the jingle and the ad message.

Some noisy jingles may be effective, but good-selling ad copy with a gentler music background is more acceptable in the jingle jungle. David Ogilvy, one of America's leading advertising creators, states in his biography *Confessions of An Advertising Man* (Athenium, 1965):

> Candor compels me to admit that I have no conclusive research to support my view that jingles are less persuasive than the spoken word. It is based on the difficulty I always experience in hearing the words in jingles, and on my experience as a door-to-door salesman: I never sang to my prospects. The advertisers who believe in the selling power of jingles have never had to sell anything.

There are several creative services that produce jingles, on order, for various retailer advertisers as well as national advertisers. These jingles are usually in 30-second segments. The music has a familiar ring to it, yet it is original composition. These services will create various messages whether they are announcing sales, clearances, store hours, or parking facilities. When the music background is reminiscent of another song and is constantly repeated, the retention value of the total message is greatly increased.

According to Anderson and Rubin, "The ear takes in information 22% faster than the eye. Auditory stimuli are retained 4 to 5 times as long as visual ones. 'Pepsi Cola hits the spot' commercials, originated in 1950, are still remembered today."[1]

PAUSES   The silent pause has its place in a radio commercial. It should be considered as the equivalent of white space in print advertising. A 30-second commercial should not start on the first second and it should not end on the last second. The first second and the last two or three seconds provide enough silence to keep the commercial from overlapping the ending of the previous commercial and at the same time overlapping with the commercial that follows. It does not take more than one to three second in each period to create a little anticipation that can further help to arrest the attention of the listener. Carefully chosen pauses in the commercial should be used to punctuate the various important points in the text. Silence in pauses can be as provocative as a long verbal statement.

Broadcast/ Television

Introduction

As in all forms of advertising, the television commercial's prime objective is to sell a product, or an idea about the product, or an idea about the store. Essentially, the same principles that determine "A" advertising, "B" advertising, or "C" advertising in print media should apply to the preparation of television commercials.

Although the elementary principles of "A," "B," and "C" advertising are the same, the basic techniques for creating effective television should focus on the principle that television requires a one-on-one relationship

---

[1]   Patricia M. Anderson and Leonard G. Rubin, *Marketing Communication*, (Englewood Cliffs, New Jersey: Prentice-Hall, 1986) p. 225.

between the advertiser and the viewer. Because television is live and moving, it has a realistic quality that none of the other media has. To that extent, there is an intimacy that comes across in television ads that does not occur in any other medium.

THE IMPORTANCE OF A SINGLE STORY LINE   A TV commercial is essentially a limited theatrical production presented in a 30-second or 60-second interruption of an entertainment being enjoyed by the audience. Therefore, the significant selling information should be assembled for one strong message, since the TV commercial depends on one story to hold viewers' attention. Other relevant selling points may support the principal message but should never interfere with the message. When the story line is resolved, the presentation concept can be developed.

THE SIGNIFICANCE OF THE CONCEPT   Because TV is a visual medium, what appears in front of the TV camera is of prime importance. Creating effective TV advertising requires that everyone concerned think "pictures" first. For example, if the story line is to focus on a seasonal fashion theme such as Citrus Colors, the TV concept should concentrate on apparel with citrus colorations such as bright yellows, hot orange tones, and variations of lemon or lime shades. To generate further visual images that emphasize the concept, display-like backgrounds such as giant-sized oranges and huge glasses of orangeade can serve as props in a fashion show. The setting is now ready for the "actors", the fashion models, to play their parts. When the visual concept is established, the next production step is the storyboard.

Storyboard

DEFINITION   The storyboard acts as a blueprint for the TV advertising message. It is a series of pictures in sequence showing what the advertisement will look like when it appears on television. The visual changes are shown in frames that each represent one-thirtieth of a second of the ad. Adjacent to each frame is the section of the audio that relates to the picture. There are two kinds of storyboards. One uses sketches to portray the action. The other employs a polaroid camera to establish the action sequences by photographing models or merchandise. These photos then become the various elements of the storyboard.

PURPOSE OF THE STORYBOARD   The storyboard acts as a blueprint to show the advertiser how the commercial will look when it appears on television. The storyboard also acts as a guide for the production staff, directing them as they create a connected sequence of situations that will finally make up the commercial.

When a storyboard is well planned, expense can be effectively controlled. Estimates of production costs can be based on the number of sequences indicated in the storyboard. The pacing and the sequencing of the verbal message is controlled to tell the complete visual and verbal story. The storyboard also establishes the nature and positioning of the store's logo. The best storyboards are developed so that there is little opportunity for error or for omissions of the various elements needed to promote the merchandise and the store.

Ordinarily, the storyboard for a 30-second spot consists of 10 to 16 frames. It takes at least that many to tell enough of a story to sustain the viewers' attention. Storyboards with fewer frames can limit the camera positioning and slow down the action.

Creative people, when preparing storyboards, should think in terms of the cinema. This is essentially thinking in terms of actions that sequence into other actions. One of the sins committed in television commercials is letting the camera linger too long on one subject or situation.

Message Text

SCRIPT   The script is essentially the spoken text for the commercial. It is written in such a way as to relate each element of this message to each pictorial unit of the storyboard. Everyone concerned with production should know what is being said while the picture is on the screen. Another essential part of the script is the cues for the camera and for various music or sound effects.

Although it has been said that television is merely radio with pictures, it is useful to keep in mind that the audio sections of the script should deal with the mood of the merchandise as well as express the benefits that are not shown in the video sections. One important advantage of television is its ability to combine pictures with actual words that are superimposed on the image. This is a useful graphic device for emphasizing certain words in the script.

WRITING TV COPY   Since the television advertising message is a spoken message in which the store talks directly to the viewer, most print copy does not easily convert to television copy. The advertising philosophy or concept that is the spirit of print copy can be maintained, but usually only the headline can be easily adapted for television.

As in radio, television copy should use words that are conversational more than commentary. Since this is a one-on-one relationship between the advertiser and the audience, the language for such text should be "people talk", that is, vernacular or slang.

Furthermore, because people talk is the basis for the text, it is important that the character of the voice selected reflect a friendly relaxed personality compatible with the advertising concept of the message. The audio message can lose credibility if the voice fails to reflect the image and character of the store and its fashion merchandise. The casting of the voice or voices is critical to the success of the audio message.

In writing the copy message for the audio section of the script, the advertiser should keep in mind that the text *supplements* what is seen on the screen. The copy should not describe details that are obviously visible. Instead, the writer should choose words that have emotional appeal relevant to the images. Words that describe details not evident in the video sections of the script are useful.

The copy should be short and simple. Again, as in print or radio copy, tired overworked terms like terrific, fantastic, sensational, incredible, or amazing do not belong in good TV messages.

A useful tactic in the development of the storyboard is planning for the video to appear on the screen first and run for one or two seconds without any audio. As in radio advertising, the resulting silent pause increases audience anticipation for the message from the advertiser. This action helps to dramatize the opening statements of the copy. This pause is a fine opportunity to create an attention-getting message at the start. The end of the commercial can be equally emphatic when the copy invites the customer to "come in and select," etc. Asking for a purchase decision is always appropriate at the end of a radio or television message.

The timing and the length of copy depend on the length of the individual images on the screen. Experienced TV copywriters usually time their copy by reading it aloud in the manner it will be voiced when it is on the air. A stopwatch is a necessary tool for creating TV advertising.

THE IMPORTANCE OF THE LOGO   Since the prime objective of all television commercials is to sell a product or an idea, advertisers should consider the store logo as a product or an idea. It is not an inanimate element of graphic art used in print media. It is, like any other important product, a statement of the store's personality, and it should be given equal creative attention.

The logo can be enhanced with use of color and animated effects. Computerized graphics can cause it to "zoom" larger on the screen for an impressive close-up. Often such animation of the logo is accompanied by musical rhythms.

A good rule to follow to make sure the commercial identifies the store is to repeat the store name in the audio at the same time the logo is visible on the screen. Many stores prefer the dramatization of the logo at the begining, middle, and end of a commercial. Tacking on the logo just at the end often leaves the viewer the challenge of trying to relate the entire message with the advertiser. Some advertisers use a special video effect that emphasizes the logo when it appears at the end of the commercial. The logo appears in a superimposition over the picture on the screen very near the end, then the picture quickly fades, allowing approximately one or two seconds for the logo to remain on the black screen. This visual isolation helps to dramatize the logo and any other information.

Many manufacturers who use TV for their co-op advertising programs allow the store to tack on the logo at the end or in a superimposition near the end of the commercial. Advertisers who use the photographic material provided by the resource can gain a stronger identity by animating the logo instead of merely placing it at the end of the commercial. In this way, the lively logo becomes part of the visual action that takes place on the screen and does not have the second-rate look typical of much cooperative fashion advertising on TV.

Video Styles

The video portion of the message can be presented in three basic styles: (1) live action that uses people in motion; (2) animated cartoons similar to the animated films in the theater; (3) static pictures that show movement on the screen by using the various computerized editing equipment available to the television producers. These effects can be in various styles of quick cuts in which one picture appears after the previous picture in rapid succession, at the time the voice describes what is being seen. Another style shows each picture dissolving into the next picture by using cinematic fade-in fade-out techniques.

LIVE ACTION   Live action is the technique that is most natural and most familiar to the viewer, particularly when it reflects the cinema. It has the ability, especially important for fashion, to exhibit the qualities of a garment demonstrated by graceful motion or vigorous sports activity. However, these effects can be costly as they take more time to produce.

ANIMATED CARTOONS   One of the advantages of the animated cartoon is that it is effective for attracting the eyes of children as well as parents. It may contain an amusing sequence with worthwhile entertainment value. Another advantage is that it is an ideal way to create considerable visual excitement for a special event. The disadvantage of the cartoon is its high cost because it takes time and talented animators to produce quality films.

STILL-LIFE PICTURES   This is the most economical category and takes the least time to produce. Manufacturers often will provide stores with excellent still photographs so that they can have top-quality pictures for low-cost commercials. However, these static pictures lack the reality that is so valuable in live-action commercials. Quick-cut video techniques can add a more dynamic quality to the message.

Voice and Sound

With one exception, the use of voice and sound in television is very similar to their use in radio. The one exception is that the audio should not distract the audience from watching the video. On the other hand, because of the attraction of the video phases much of the verbal message can be missed by the viewer. The audio message should rarely be the dominant element of the commercial. Many commercials may show a few seconds of the picture before the voice starts.

"Generic" Commercials

Retailers who have limited budgets for producing television commercials can make use of several services that provide stock videotapes that can be incorporated into a store's TV programming. For example, there are generic types of commercials that are based on attractive pictures of fashionable women in seasonal settings such as a garden or country scene. These usually run from 20 to 30 seconds. This permits the store to record its own voice-over, a generalized selling statement about the merchandise, and then add its video logo. Such tapes are a form of institutional advertising since no specific merchandise is identified. Other similar tapes devoted to sales events use excellent animated graphics or montage sequences of fashion images. Another offered to stores is usually described in broadcasting terms, as "the doughnut." The outside of the doughnut can be the beginning and the end of a generic videotape. The tape starts with a spring scene and ends with a spring scene. In the "hole" of the doughnut the store inserts its own video section. This can be either live action or the quick cuts of still photographs. The store's logo can be superimposed in the middle or at the end of the commercial.

These generic tape producers supply very attractive and persuasive tapes that can be used to fill out a retailer's television plan. Stores can get information on such generic services from their local stations, especially those in the larger markets.

Several important retailers operate their own TV production studios. However, their production work often becomes limited in imagination and variety of techniques. Such captive studios have also proved to be costly. Most retailers prefer to employ outside production resources so that each television campaign has a different style or creative touch. Also, there are times when major retailers may be simultaneously producing commercials for several departments or classifications. The advantage of having outside resources is that this work can be done by different producers with each having a different style. This variety gives the advertiser a more distinctive TV image.

Vendor Cooperation for TV Ads

Among the many resources that supply television programming for retailers are the various cosmetic companies. Much of these vendor's cooperation money is allocated for this television expense. These firms supply attractive and persuasive tapes that enhance a retailer's television image.

Summary

Since radio is the only ad medium that appeals to only one of the senses, the advertiser must understand the importance of the voice, music, and sound effects.

Ad copy for radio should contain these qualities (a) simplicity, (b) clarity, (c) familiar verbalization, (d) easy pronunciation, and (e) repetition. Voices should be able to cajole, persuade, explain enthusiastically, and at the same time reflect the store's image. Music and sound effects are more effective when they are an integral part of the message. Good use of sound can develop into a distinctive radio style.

Television shares the same objectives as print advertising. However, because it is live and moving, it has a realistic quality that no other medium has. It is a limited theatrical production that depends on one story line to hold the viewer's attention. With one exception, the use of voice and sound is similar to radio. The exception is that too much audio can distract the viewer's attention from the video. The picture should be the dominant element.

CHAPTER 12

Publicity and Special Events

Introduction

An important part of a fashion retailer's operation is the store's public relations activity. Public relations involves everything the store does to influence favorable public opinion. This includes quality of sales personnel, store housekeeping, variety of services offered, style of advertising, and assortment and quality of merchandise.

The public relations process is directed to meeting these objectives:

1. Attracting attention to the store
2. Establishing the credibility of the store
3. Convincing the public to adopt favorable impressions regarding the store and its merchandise
4. Emphasizing the store's fashion image
5. Creating long-term goodwill for the store

One of the principle methods employed to help retailers to attain these objectives is called *publicity*.

Definition of Publicity

Publicity is news or information about a product, service, or idea that is published on behalf of a sponsor but is not paid for by the sponsor. Such publicity, to be acceptable by all media, print or broadcast, must be truly newsworthy and credible. Without these qualities, the publicity message descends to puffery that can injure the public's perception of the retailer. Media acceptance of valid publicity provides an effective form of free advertising, thus limiting the costs of paid advertising. For an example of publicity in a newspaper, see Figure 12.1.

Consultant says retailers boost sales when they put products on

DISPLAY

From staff and wire reports

The 65 to 75 displays of outfits in Janice Spoone's West Knoxville shop, Rickie's Petites, are no accident.

Spoone intentionally uses bright, eye-catching colors and color combinations, adds belts and jewelry to the outfits, then sometimes drapes them over a few props like antique furniture and trunks. The clothes, most of natural fibers, then are accented with bouquets of fresh flowers.

For Spoone and many other small and large retailers, displays (or visual merchandising, as it's called in the business) can help sales.

"If something is not selling, I deliberately try to put it together in a different way," said Spoone.

Deanna Harpham, a Colorado-based merchandising consultant who travels the country helping retailers, said 80 percent of the people who enter a retail store have yet to decide what they want to buy. But she says many retailers don't understand that, and do little to excite a customer's senses.

In most stores, Harpham sees merchandise stacked on shelves or jammed on display racks. She contends such displays do nothing to attract buyers.

"Retailers don't do enough presentation," she said. "That's what gets those add-on and impulse sales."

Changing and coming up with imaginative displays also help salespeople, said Spoone, by keeping the merchandise from getting stale, so "it looks fresh and new to them."

As a major in textiles and clothing in college, Spoone took many art courses, and she applies those art priniples, like balance and proportion, today in her shop.

Mary Frances Drake, professor of textiles and apparel at University of Tennessee, said color is the first element customers see in a display.

"Bright colors are the best to attract the eye, but if the fashion is not bright, an interesting color combination or interesting use of colors," said Drake.

Interesting materials, such as metallics and fur, also call attention to a display.

"The whole basis was to develop affordable displays for small business retailers," Harpham says. "You don't have to be a huge concern or have a lot of money to develop good displays."

Harpham has a whole list of advice for retailers who want to perk up their visuals:

■ Mannequins aren't required. Everyday materials such as fiberboard, crepe paper, ribbon, paint, stencils and cardboard carpet tubes give a splash of color and can attract attention.

■ Make a realistic display schedule and stick to it.

■ Think more creatively than just seasonal or event-related displays.

■ Hold brainstorming sessions with employees to find out what customers are talking about and what is or isn't attracting attention.

JACK ROSE/The Journal staff

Janice Spoone, owner of Rickie's Petites in Homberg Place, arranges a jewelry display in her store window.

Figure 12.1.   A publicity item in the newspaper that brings the customer's attention to the store is more positively received than is an advertisement. (courtesy of *The Knoxville Journal*, Knoxville, Tenn.)

Purpose of Publicity

Image

The prime objective of publicity is to create a favorable public image for retailers. This includes news about the store itself, the personality of the store, and the various types of merchandise that the store sells. Such publicity takes many forms. It can be news articles in the printed media, it can be part of the news reporting on radio, and it can also appear on the television screen as a news feature. Consequently, its essential ingredients must be newsworthy and credible. Such qualities take on the added dimension of word-of-mouth advertising in which the general public often discusses the favorable impressions regarding the retailer.

The Value of Goodwill

Publicity has a special and important task in the public relations function of a store. It should create a store image that strengthens goodwill toward the store. In addition to publicizing the various internal qualities such as fashion leadership, credibility, and customer services, publicity should also be used to emphasize the store's relationship and service to the community.

Such activities include highly visible participation in community projects such as The United Fund, the Arts Council, the museum, and other similar programs. Taking part in various public activities that focus on health care is another worthwhile effort that can build customer goodwill. Many stores plan for special discount days for senior citizens to build favor in a growing segment of the market (see Figure 12.2). Participating in community functions such as citywide celebrations or parades are also effective ways to earn public goodwill. Probably the outstanding star of community involvement publicity programs is the famed Macy's Thanksgiving Day Parade, which has created excellent goodwill for this New York retailing giant. The publicity for this holiday event has given Macy's an international reputation.

What Is Newsworthy?

In planning a publicity program, the publicist must think in journalistic terms as an experienced reporter would. This requires an understanding

Figure 12.2. Examples of building goodwill by having discount days for senior citizens. Note how one store offers a variety of discounts, depending on the ages of the customers. (Courtesy of Globman's, Martinsville, Va., and Proffitt's, Alcoa, Tenn.)

Proffitt's
SENIOR CLASS
SC CLUB

FOR MEN & WOMEN AGES 55 AND OVER

RECEIVE A SPECIAL DISCOUNT ON YOUR CASH AND CHARGE PURCHASES*

10% · **15%** · **20%**

DISCOUNT **DISCOUNT** **DISCOUNT**
FOR AGES 55-59   FOR AGES 60-69   FOR AGES 70 PLUS

*All Claiborne merchandise, Cosmetics, Gucci and Fine Jewelry Watches, Designer Furs, Hartmann Luggage, Lalique, Gift Certificates and Layaways excluded.

At Proffitt's we believe in seniors! "Class" is what you're all about... Living your life to the fullest, and doing it in style! So we've created a special club that will help you get even more out of life. On designated "Senior Class" Tuesdays (4 times a year plus your birthday), club members can take advantage of special savings and an array of complimentary services, including:

- FREE alterations on purchases made on Senior Class Tuesday
- FREE gift wrap (up to $1.50) on purchases made on Senior Class Tuesday
- FREE postage & mailing on purchases made on Senior Class Tuesday
- FREE mini health checks
- FREE refreshments all day
- FREE cosmetic makeovers

- **"INVESTING FOR INCOME" SEMINAR, TUES., 12 NOON AT WEST TOWN**
  Don't miss this informative 30-minute presentation, hosted by Mr. Joe Woodruff of Morgan Keegan and Company, Inc. Seminar will be held in Proffitt's auditorium.

HEALTH SCREENING FOR SENIOR CLASS CLUB MEMBERS TUESDAY, APRIL 10

WEST TOWN: 9AM-12 NOON
HCA Park West Medical Center will offer free blood pressure checks. Cholesterol screening will also be available for a $4 fee.

HCA Park West Medical Centers

EAST TOWNE: 9AM-12 NOON
St. Mary's Medical Center will offer free height and weight checks, hemoccult testing and health education information.

SM ST. MARY'S MEDICAL CENTER

SENIOR TOURS
"The Travel Club for Senior Adults"

SENIOR CLASS CLUB MEMBERS, REGISTER TO WIN A TRIP TO THE OZARK MOUNTAINS
You could be the lucky winner of six days and five nights of sightseeing and fun by motorcoach tour, compliments of Senior Tours. Highlights include Eureka Springs, Christ of the Ozarks, Shepherd of the Hills and some of the most spectacular mountain scenery in America. One winner will be selected from all entries at our West Town, East Towne, Foothills, Oak Ridge and Athens stores. Winner will be notified by phone. No purchase necessary; you need not be present to win. Proffitt's associates and their immediate families not eligible.

If you haven't already joined our Senior Class Club, you can sign up at any time at any Proffitt's store. There's no charge or obligation to join: just ask any sales associate for an enrollment card, show proof of age, and receive your membership card with appropriate discount. Sign up today and be part of the club where seniority really counts!

Figure 12.2. *(continued)*

of the nature of news, what makes a story interesting, and what is of value to the fashion aware public. Such stories usually fall into these major groups:

1. **Human Interest News** focuses on fashion personalities or subjects that relate to the lifestyle of the customer.
2. **Hard News** concentrates on an important event or a situation within the store. Personnel changes or staff promotions are typical of such publicity. The opening of a new store or department would fit into this group.
3. **Feature News** is made up of stories that take more space to cover unusual situations or a significant trend in merchandising. Feature news offers opportunities to be more imaginative in order to hold the public's attention.

The various subjects that are candidates for effective publicity usually are developed from these categories.

A special event could be the opening of a new store or a 50- or 100-year anniversary of a store opening. Along with these can be typical, less eventful, but equally newsworthy situations, such as the arrival of new fashions or a special visit from a well-known designer. The relocation of departments can make a publicity story if there is special news. A revision of store policy on shopping hours will produce a small news item. A special event that is newsworthy must be something that is not part of the normal pattern of events in the store. It must have qualities of showmanship or drama that make it special to the store and to the community. Such events can be the personal appearance of the designer of a soon-to-be-introduced line of fashions. Another special event can be the personal appearance of a well-known popular sports figure in the men's sportswear department. A popular competition such as a beauty contest or the selection of a high school queen is another example of a special event. Publicity can be created for almost any activity in the store, from the introduction of a new way to microwave all the way to a comprehensive fashion show of back-to-school apparel. Each situation should have news content that is of interest to the public.

Charitable activities help to create newsworthy publicity. For example, at Christmas time, donating toys to the children's ward at the hospital can help create favorable impressions of the store and can build goodwill not only with the recipients of the toys but with the general public as well. A dinner for a group of retiring employees can be publicized to embellish the reputation of the store further. Giving a benefit fashion show with the symphony to make the arts more available to all income levels would be a newsworthy event that would add to the image of the store and would help to establish goodwill between the store and potential customers.

Creative Publicity

A retailer wishing to capitalize on public interest must start the creative process by developing a truly newsworthy idea or situation. This situation must have hard news qualities or elements of human interest. Furthermore it must be interesting to a large group of people, not just a limited number. And finally, it must have qualities of originality and innovation. Just doing something that has been done before by others is not enough. Although the media people may ferret out some stories, it is up to the retailer to furnish the newsworthy information or tempt the reporter into investigating that particular retailer's story. The retailer who seeks publicity must usually initiate the effort to be publicized. Such an effect is rarely generated by the media. Unfortunately, only bad news is discovered by the media. The good news, which is the objective of all retailers, must come from the retailer.

Newsworthy Ideas

New Item or Process

New items, new processes make news. The essential ingredient of any publicity of a new item or process must first present what the process or item has replaced, and secondly it must focus on the most important benefits of the new item.

New Fashion Trends

New fashion trends, to be worthy of publicity, should demonstrate innovation and suggest how previous versions of such merchandise are outdated. When innovative fashion relates to new developments in the lifestyle of the public, these innovative qualities should be emphasized.

Celebrity Visit

A celebrity visit offers exceptional opportunities for publicity. Whether it is a champion boxer or a very popular actor or actress, the visit does not necessarily have to possess any relationship to merchandise in the store. However, when a boxer appears in the men's sportswear department, this makes him more newsworthy than if he appeared in the men's clothing department. On the other hand, the famous actor can appear in almost any department, even in children's wear, and be newsworthy.

The personality and charm of the actor is the big news. Also, such personalities can visit a section of the store where they can perform. Popular daytime television stars can appear anywhere in the store, but it is best if they appear in the fashion departments because more women will be in these areas.

New Collection

The introduction of a new collection of merchandise, such as in the cosmetics section of the store, is often worthy of publicity. This is especially important when the name of the product reflects beauty, fame, and distinction. An example of such a collection would be the Elizabeth Taylor line or new line of spring fashions by a clothing designer who is already well known.

Major Change or Development

A major change or an unusual new development in the retail store is an opportunity for valuable publicity. Since most retailers are part of the lifestyle of their community, whatever happens to any leading store, whether it expands or unfortunately closes its doors, is meaningful not only to the employees but to their families and to the people who have shopped in that store. A store that opens an entirely new area, such as a specialty boutique, is news to the community because the store is offering added service to its customers.

Management changes are of particular interest to the business community. Providing photos of the people involved will draw additional attention to the article. These types of changes are "hard" news.

Unusual Event

Anything the store does that is very unusual is sure to gain appreciable publicity as news. An interesting example of this took place several years ago in a New England community. The leading store in town, which occupied almost a square block and was six stories high, was celebrating its 100th anniversary. The town's newspaper did not consider this a newsworthy story. However, the store decided it would erect a giant "100" on the front facade of the building. The number ran from street level all the way up to the roof. To hang the structure on the front of the building, a three hundred–foot derrick had to be brought in from another community. This was a newsworthy event, and the newspaper photographed the giant "100" for a front-page story on the tallest derrick ever to come to the region. And so the New England community discovered that its favorite store was having its 100th anniversary. Management of the store had previously visited the offices of the newspaper to discuss the possibility of obtaining publicity for its 100-year celebration and the newspaper said that it would do its duty but in a limited way. However, when the store created a major newsworthy event, it had the reward of having its 100th birthday dramatically publicized.

Finding Outlets for Publicity

The best publicity outlets are the leading print media (newspaper or magazine) or broadcast media in the area. The store should consider the use of various other lesser media such as local college or high school papers to build a publicity personality. Publicity with various religious groups that have bulletins is useful when the store is mentioned as a contributor or when a special fashion show is held for the benefit of the group.

It is the retailers' top management's responsibility to meet with the management of the various media to develop publicity channels. Once this has been done, a special events or publicity manager can be appointed to work with the editors of the newspapers or the news editors of the broadcast media.

Newsworthy events do not have to be announced to the general public only. Many of these events can be publicized in trade journals to inform the market resources. The opening of a new department or a new store or a major change in management is important news in trade journals. When a new buyer for a children's or sportswear department is introduced to the community, it is also good practice to notify the various trade journals that cover children's wear or sportswear.

The Press Kit

To gain a maximum amount of publicity, particularly for a major special event, experienced public relations people prepare full information packages. These are usually called press kits and are distributed to all media either prior to the event or on the opening day. Many retailers may hold a press preview party when the event is extremely newsworthy. Most press kits contain the following items of information:

1. *Fact Sheet*—This contains short sentences or phrases listing the basic details of the project.

2. *Clipping Sheet*—This is a reproduction of clips from other media that provide additional background information regarding the event or story.

3. *Photos with Descriptive Backings*—Photos are usually 5 × 7 or 8 × 10 and should be in black and white for print media. Typed information is usually placed on the back of the photo.

4. *Biographies*—If the event features celebrities, a short biographical text for each person is helpful to the media.

5. *Publicity Schedule*—This is very useful when a series of related events may occur at various times or locations. In effect, this is a timetable with a limited descriptive text.

6. *The News Story Release*—This is a well-written news story of the event. It should be in typical newspaper style complete with headline, sub-heading, and the significant facts in the first paragraph. The story should not take more than two sheets of paper. Most reporters prefer typewritten text to be double spaced.

7. *Contact List*—Media people frequently lack sufficient time for thorough interviews with those involved with the event. A listing of names, addresses, and phone numbers of those who can answer questions is a welcome item in a press kit.

Some manufacturers and retailers prepare elaborate, colorful press kits. However, a manila envelope with the data discussed above will be satisfactory (see Figure 12.3).

Special Events

Definition

The activity or group of activities that attracts the public and also generates publicity is usually referred to as a special event. It is an occasion that is not typical in the usual retail scene from day to day or week to week. An important ingredient in a successful special event is showmanship. To attract the public and hold its attention, show business techniques often are most effective.

Objectives of Special Events

CREATE STORE TRAFFIC   A principal objective of the special event is to attract more customers to the store or to a department. By doing

Figure 12.3. A comprehensive press kit full of fashion information, photographs, and sketches coordinated with fabric swatches. (Courtesy of Maria Rodriguez, Chicago, Ill.)

this, the retailer can expose the merchandise to a larger number of prospective customers. For example, one store publicized a special Children's Day just before Mothers Day. The store invited girls and boys to the store where they were entertained by clowns, magicians, and musicians. The store had simple gifts for the youngsters. While they were in the store, the boys and girls could shop for gifts for Mother (and grandmother) that were sold at prices that they could afford. Prior to the happening, the media had run a news story announcing the event. After Mother's Day there was a human interest picture story showing the in-store entertainment. Local television covered the various activities in which the youngsters participated. The added traffic was gratifying because each child was accompanied by at least one adult who also purchased gifts and merchandise.

CREATE CUSTOMER INTEREST   The special event is an ideal way to stimulate customer interest in a particular phase of the store's merchandising. By drawing attention to a special merchandising effort by way of the showmanship of a special event, the retailer can effectively impress the customer with the unique character of the merchandise.

For example, a fashion specialty operation known for quality sportswear planned to develop its growing market for distinctive ski wear and winter wear. To accomplish this, the management scheduled a special event to introduce a new line from Finland. A "Finnish Breakfast" Fashion Show was planned for a Saturday morning from 10:00 A.M. to 11:30 A.M. The manufacturers from Finland provided Finnish skiing celebrities as well as some items for a Finnish breakfast menu. The publicity the store received was exceptional, and pre-event stories were abundant. The actual fashion show received news coverage, and the celebrities were interviewed on radio and TV. Even the food sections of the local papers gave space to the breakfast. The special event resulted in the store's successful development of a new category of sportswear.

ENHANCE STORE IMAGE   Although most special events are directed toward generating traffic or focusing on a particular department or category of merchandise, many retailers plan special events in which they use showmanship to project a "fun-to-shop" image. Customers often prefer to shop in a store that is known to be interesting since so many stores are more or less boring. Theatrical staging effects are important to such special events. These events must take place regularly during a sequence of several years to enhance a retailer's image as an entertaining and interesting place to shop. Bloomingdale's, in New York, is an outstanding example of how a retailer can enhance an upscale image by using showmanship in special events. They have built a store image with their international roster of special events covering goods from China, India, the Far East, Ireland, France, and other countries. Each of these events has displayed super-showmanship qualities in visual presentation. Using superb display techniques to present fashions and home goods from the various regions, this store has created a unique image and identity.

Budgeting for Publicity and Special Events

Budgeting in this area can be accomplished in a similar manner to budgeting for other promotional activities. Breakdown methods or build up methods can be used. However, the build up process is usually favored by experienced professionals in this field. According to Robert Ross[1] "Specific objectives lend themselves to making specific plans. These plans may then be priced out. Budgets based on priced out plans will be closer to actual costs than those developed in other ways. By having specific task oriented projects, one may make budgeting a logical process rather than only a manipulation of some figures to appeal to the financial end of the business on an occasional basis." When management plans a budget without knowing the specific realities of the project, often they must reduce the scope of important events or sometimes omit them from the schedule.

When management plans the total sales promotion budget, it should allocate money for special events. This budget, usually planned on a six-month basis, can influence the breadth of the publicity event or special showmanship event that is being considered. For example, for the back-to-school season, retailers who feature this type of merchandise will decide on the budget for newspaper advertising, broadcast advertising, direct mail advertising, and so on. Along with this, there should be a budget for any special events during the back-to-school period such as a fashion show for children. Such an event may involve music, refreshments for the audience, and a special entertainer to hold the attention of the youngsters and their parents. A store in a southern city usually launches its back-to-school period with a Circus Day in which children come in and have their faces painted so they look like clowns. A photographer is available to take pictures of them. Often strolling musicians will move around the various departments to attract the customers and children. Simple gifts such as balloons and inexpensive school bags are distributed. Events as extensive as this are carefully planned and budgeted.

Planning Special Events

Successful special events are the result of thorough planning, not much different than the planning that goes into a successful military operation. Smoothly run events are usually the products of meetings in which every phase is discussed and responsibilities are defined and assigned.

To insure a painless special event, a planning agenda should cover the following:

1. The objectives of the event
2. The idea or concept
3. The audience or customer segments
4. The merchandise to be featured
5. Dates and times for the event
6. The physical properties in the event
7. Store personnel to be used in the event
8. The departments to be involved
9. Unusual or special items to be required
10. The need for special talent
11. The amount of paid media advertising
12. Newsworthy publicity material
13. The probable costs

The planning session usually includes management representatives from merchandising (buyers, supervisors, etc.), store operations, advertising, and visual merchandising (display). Larger stores usually have a special events executive who may preside at a planning meeting. Central to the success of the event is the assignment of responsibilities for every detail discussed and accepted at the planning session. Failure to do this can cause problems later.

Since special events rarely happen instantly, every eventuality must be anticipated. The planning should consider every phase of the operation of the store. The store operations office or manager, should be involved in the selection of the area for the event and also provide for the security of the merchandise. Attracting a large audience can increase the likelihood of an unfortunate accident for which the store may liable, so the store's insurance should be reviewed. The location of the event must be carefully planned so that traffic to other departments is not impeded.

Most large stores print a planned calendar of special events that is distributed to everyone involved in advertising or in the event. This helps with the tremendous amount of coordination that is required for such events. Table 12.1 is from the planned calendar for one month in a department store with 10 branches involved in an extensive special events program.

Measure of Success

One obvious measure of success is increased sales; however, that is not the only criterion. Increased traffic in the store with customers enjoying the event is another gauge of success. The amount of coverage the event receives in broadcast or print media is also very important. Special events can generate word-of-mouth advertising for the store that is difficult to measure, but very desirable to have.

The Function of a Special Events Director

The special events director works closely with top management to provide insights for opportunities in gaining frequent publicity for the store. Because of the need to gain sufficient coverage for the store's activities, a special events director keeps in close touch with the store's advertising department as well as the various media at both the advertising and the editorial level. Furthermore, the special events director should have a keen awareness of display opportunities, both in-store and out-of-store. For example, when a promotion is jointly planned with the store and a local art gallery, it is expected that some paintings or art objects will be moved into the store to enhance fashion displays for the mutual benefit of both participants. In many major cities, when fine art has been released for display purposes, there often has been distribution of related posters, photographs, and reproductions shared by leading museums and important retailers. The store executive who is involved with such arrangements is usually the special events director. Working with advertising and display associates as well as selected buyers, this person coordinates the dramatic presentations, which can often be integrated into merchandise areas of the store. These mini-events enhance a store's image by making the store an integral part of a community event. Customers usually respond to the promotion of such events by visiting the store to participate in the excitement and staying to shop.

Many events can be culturally relevant, and, just as often, they can tie into current television programs, newspaper columns, or "how to" activities that have a contemporary point of view. By exploiting the latter category, stores have built reputations as being the sites of cooking

Table 12.1. A section of a calendar of Planned Special Events.

Date	Event	Store	Ad Date	Time	Location
Wednesday, March 1	Ribbon-cutting ceremony	Northgate		9:10 A.M.	Mall entrance
Thursday, March 2	Charm/beauty course	West Town		4:00–7:45 P.M.	Proffitt's auditorium
Thursday, March 2	Sunbeam Mixmaster demo	Hamilton Place		12:00 noon	Housewares
Friday, March 3	Microwave cooking class	Oak Ridge		12:00 noon	Housewares
Friday, March 3	Microwave cooking class	Downtown		11:00 A.M.	Housewares
Saturday, March 4	Children's Easter fashion show	East Towne	2/19	12:00 noon	Mall entrance—upper level
Saturday, March 4	Children's Easter fashion show	Hamilton Place		1:00 P.M.	Children's department
Saturday, March 4	Microwave cooking class complete meal	Athens		12:00 noon	Housewares
Saturday, March 4	Microwave cooking class	Highland Plaza		12:00 noon	Housewares
Sunday, March 5	Northgate grand opening	Northgate	3/5	1:00–6:00 P.M.	Throughout store
Monday, March 6	Mexican fiesta—Oster cooking class	Foothills		11:30 A.M.	Housewares
Tuesday, March 7	Mexican fiesta—Oster cooking class	West Town		6:30 P.M.	Ann's Place
Tuesday, March 7	Cuisinart—fruit desserts	Hamilton Place		12:00 noon	Housewares
Tuesday, March 7	Cuisinart—fruit desserts	West Town		12:00 noon	Ann's Place
Wednesday, March 8	Oster demo	West Town		11:30 A.M.	Ann's Place
Wednesday, March 8	Krups demo	East Towne		10:30–2:30 P.M.	Housewares
Thursday, March 9	Cuisinart—hot cross buns	West Town		12:00 noon	Ann's Place
Thursday, March 9	Panasonic bread maker	Hamilton Place		12:00 noon	Housewares
Friday, March 10	Petite fashion show	West Town		12:00 noon	Petite department
Friday, March 10	Petite fashion show	East Towne		3:00 P.M.	Mall entrance
Friday, March 10	Cuisinart—hot cross buns	East Towne		12:00 noon	Housewares
Friday, March 10	Krups demo	West Town		10:30–2:30 P.M.	Housewares
Friday, March 10	Mexican fiesta—Oster cooking class	East Towne		6:30 P.M.	Housewares
Friday, March 10	Cuisinart—hot cross buns	Dalton		12:00 noon	Housewares
Friday, March 10	Krups demo	Hamilton Place		10:30–2:30 P.M.	Housewares
Friday, March 10	Petite fashion show	Hamilton Place		12:00 noon	Upper level
Saturday, March 11	Petite fashion show	Northgate		3:00 P.M.	Petite department

SOURCE: Proffitt's Department Store, Alcoa, Tenn.

schools, beauty schools, and health centers. Sometimes special events tie in with fashion adjunct departments such as gourmet foods, cosmetics, beauty salons, sporting goods, and book departments. An alert fashion executive who keeps close contact with the special events operation can usually discern where an appropriate tie-in can be developed to the benefit of the merchandise in the department.

Summary

Publicity is important to every store regardless of its size. An article by a reporter creates an added degree of status or believability that cannot be provided by an ad created and paid for by the store. The cost of publicity is usually little more than the time involved unless a special event is planned. An ad in the same newspaper section as the publicity gives added reinforcement for the store.

Special events can cost large amounts of money but may be a very effective way to enhance an image, produce traffic, and create customer interest. A special event requires extensive planning and coordination. Obtaining publicity for these events is the goal of a special events coordinator.

CHAPTER 13

The Fashion Show

A fashion show as defined in Chapter 1 is the presentation of merchandise on a living, moving form to tell a fashion story. It is the only promotional activity that presents the merchandise on a real person and, therefore, gives a true presentation of the goods as they look when worn. A display can show apparel completely accessorized on a true dimensional form; however, the display mannequin cannot show the garment in motion on a live form with personality. Also, the fashion show has music, action, and an elevating mood not possible in a display.

A good fashion show is a dramatic, entertaining story about how to look and how to wear the newest styles the market has to offer. It tells the viewer what to wear and when to wear it, and it demonstrates correct accessorization. At its best the fashion show embellishes the dream that the viewer can look as attractive as the models and have as much personality. It animates the apparel. Nothing can bring apparel to life like a fashion show.

A fashion show is the promotional vehicle par excellence for better goods and the newest fashion ideas. Because new fashions are a type of innovation, they require that the person proceed through the various stages of the innovation process as discussed in Chapter 2. Shows are excellent tools to use for persuasion, the second stage of the innovation process, because they can involve all the viewer's senses in a mood-setting event.

Why Give a Show?

The primary objective of any fashion show is to sell merchandise. In addition, the show should build prestige for the store by developing the viewer's confidence in the store as a fashion leader in the community as well as educating the customer in the current fashion trends featured by the store. Successful shows will help build a steady sales growth in fashion departments. When the show is given for a specific audience, such as large-size women, immediate sales results can be measured. By seeing new fashions correctly worn and accessorized on attractive models, the viewer can see how they will look. The customer gains self-confidence because the knowledgeable commentator speaks with authority.

Shows are expensive and very time-consuming to produce. A show given outside of the store may cost at least $1,000 or more in a medium-size town. Since the time involved in producing a show takes some of the staff away from productive selling on the floor, management should make sure that the show will produce added sales and build the store's fashion reputation as well.

Determining the customer audience for the show is one of the most important steps in planning the event. Most department stores and specialty stores feature ready-to-wear and accessories because these fashions will appeal to a large segment of the population. A large group of women could include varied ages and occupations ranging from students to professionals. It is important to determine the specific group to target for the show, and to develop the profile of this group so that the show will appeal to their particular fashion wants and needs. Flashy merchandise purchased only for the show may not meet the needs of the target audience and will create a false impression of the store's fashion statement. A skillfully produced fashion show with merchandise at moderate and better prices can appeal to a wide range of customers.

Men can be bored with a show that is well received by women. When men are part of the target audience, the addition of more entertainment should be considered—dancing, familiar music (not singing), or a particularly exciting set design. Theatrically glamorous fashions will add the spark needed to hold the attention of guests not typically interested in current styles. Successful fashion shows educate with emphasis on the newness, entertain with fashions for fun, and upgrade with choice, high-quality garments.

Planning the Fashion Show

The character of the show will depend on the target audience's fashion interests, age, and income level. The store image and the time of year are also important considerations in planning. Refer to Chapter 2 to determine the fashion levels of the audience. In deciding whether the store should give a fashion show, it is important to ask about the size of the group and how many members will attend the show. Management should determine if the group is seriously interested in fashions, what their income level is, what their ages and occupations are, and where they live in relation to the store, since most customers shop within a few miles of their home. A show should never be given just to be cooperative with a community group.

Trends in Show Themes

Fashion shows have trends in production style. Current Broadway shows such as *Cats* and familiar revivals like *Putting-on-the-Ritz* are often used as idea sources for a fashion show. Musical themes, such as "New York, New York," are easy to work with. A few years ago one of the fashion show trends was an emphasis on the beat of the music. In one show the models, in groups of three, walked to military marches. In another show, models moved to a rap music beat.

A famed designer or a leading manufacturer is often the basis for a show theme in large and small stores. These shows can be presented within or near the department involved. Anne Klein II, Liz Claiborne, and Catalina are makers that bring success when staged in this type of show. These firms often offer a representative who will assist in the show. Satisfactory sales result from these shows because the representative speaks with authority and enthusiasm for the product and often assists in selling the company's fashions after the show. Customers like to attend shows where the commentator is considered an authority.

A show should always have a theme to ensure continuity. The emphasis should be on the clothes regardless of other variables. After the theme has been selected, the number of scenes and merchandise to be shown in each scene will be decided. A general guide for selection is to show current merchandise the store believes in and stocks sufficiently.

The order of the scenes showing various fashion looks should be carefully planned to build excitement for the finale. For example, furs would not be featured in the opening scene if traditional suits are in the final scene. Rather suits, dresses, and sportswear could build to a dramatic finale that shows furs worn with glamorous fashions.

Variety in the show can be achieved by using clothes of one color or look in a scene. For example, an all red or a black and white scene can be very striking. A summer scene of shorts modeled in all available lengths will create an impression of the importance of this category. Strapless dresses, cropped pants, bathing suits, double breasted jackets—using a single type of clothing in a scene is memorable in a fashion show. It can be inserted anywhere in the show for impact.

Working Out the Theme

The fashion show director must be highly imaginative and creative to conceptualize a theme that is fashion exciting and current, one that will stimulate the staff to help create a great show. She or he can develop further creativity by being active in the community and constantly watching people and their habits. A director benefits from being involved in music, museums, travel, theater, radio, and television. The New York Metropolitan Museum's exhibits of clothing are a "must visit" for fashion directors as well as buyers. Fashion magazines also stimulate ideas that should be filed by the season for later use. Such experiences will guide the director to a feasible and exciting show theme that fits the audience, the clothing to be shown, and the budget.

Department stores often feature back-to-school shows. The director's task is to create a new, exciting back-to-school idea to stimulate everyone on the staff. For example, *Seventeen* magazine's back-to-school show ideas create excitement and are versatile enough to be used by many stores across the nation. Some past themes have been "Pick Hits," "Passport to Fall," and "A Class Act."

A travel theme is easy to execute because it allows the store to show all types of clothing. An example would be "Road to Morocco," starting at the airport. Some years the clothing and accessories come in animal prints and Moroccan desert colors that fit into the theme easily. A summer show titled "Summer Sizzle" does not limit the merchandise shown but says something about what the customer can expect to see.

Every show can include some bridge merchandise such as Anne Klein II, Ellen Tracy, and Adrienne Vittadini and designer merchandise such as Anne Klein, Adele Simpson, and Bill Blass to increase the fashion awareness of the customers and to move them to a higher level of fashionability the next time they are shopping. Shows should educate the customer in the store's latest fashion trends and in how to coordinate clothing for these looks.

Length of the Show

The maximum length of a show should be about 45 minutes so that the entire event, including introductions and closing remarks, is no more than 50 to 60 minutes. A show of this length would be very large and prestigious. Usually a show is 20 to 30 minutes including the welcome. This amount of time is appropriate for in-store and small room shows.

The Fashion Director's Budget

The fashion director must plan a six-month budget to include scheduled shows based on the previous year's expenses, on new commitments by management, and on creative ideas that develop later. Table 3.2

on page 52 is an example of a fashion director's six-month budget. The six-month budget is an estimate prepared as far as twelve months in advance of the shows. More exact expense estimates are necessary when a specific show is being planned. A checklist of expense items is helpful in establishing a realistic budget to avoid omitting any potential expenses. An accurate record of each show's expenses is necessary for future planning. Table 13.1 provides a chart for planning and recording typical fashion show expenses.

Considering all these expenses, it is apparent that a small, simple in-store show could easily cost at least $500 not including the value of store personnel who help with the show. Any show away from the store will cost a minimum of $1,000, and a large show could cost $8,000 to $20,000. Analysis of the expense categories of a fashion show budget indicates that shows can be expensive. Advance planning and skillful coordination can aid in budget control.

Music and models are the largest expense categories for shows. The size of the show determines other expenses such as dancers, photographers, and advertising. When printed programs, tickets, food, and table decorations are needed, the outside group benefiting from the show often shares in the expenses. Groups that sponsor these events may also be able to obtain a lower fee for the auditorium use when the show is for charity.

Choosing the Location

The fashion show can be in the store or out of the store. There are advantages to both locations and each one presents special problems.

In-Store Shows

The fashion show held in the store has the advantage of getting the customer closer to the merchandise. It brings customers in to see and touch the fashions, thus making it easy to fulfill their desire for the merchandise. The customers can shop immediately after the show with the show merchandise being available to them very easily and quickly. The department or the shop may need to add salespeople on the show day to handle the expected customers. Customers who are aware of the show, but cannot attend, will often come to the store during the day to examine the merchandise.

In a department store, the show may be held in an adjoining area to allow the department sponsoring the fashion show to remain in selling order. A show can be so disruptive that if this is not done, selling

Table 13.1.   A sample form for listing typical expenses for a fashion show.

FASHION SHOW EXPENDITURES		
Name of show_____ Date of show_____		
Location_____		
Audience_____ _____ _____		
open to public or special group	planned attendance	actual attendance
	BUDGET	ACTUAL
1. Fashion Office		
Preparation time		
fitting models	_____	_____
selecting clothes and accessories	_____	_____
writing up models' charts	_____	_____
removing tags and pressing	_____	_____
Models for fitting	_____	_____
rehearsal	_____	_____
show	_____	_____
Backstage assistance—cue person	_____	_____
dressers	_____	_____
Choreography and dancers	_____	_____
Music—tapes or musicians	_____	_____
Supplies (as dress shields, hosiery)	_____	_____
Alterations—pressing, damages	_____	_____
2. Show expense		
Room rental for show	_____	_____
for rehearsal	_____	_____
Mileage and travel	_____	_____
Microphones	_____	_____
Food and beverages	_____	_____
Transporting of clothes and props	_____	_____
Taping of show	_____	_____
Favors, gift certificates	_____	_____
Set up and clean up	_____	_____
3. Decoration		
Display: runway backdrop	_____	_____
stage	_____	_____
set-up	_____	_____
supplies	_____	_____
Props	_____	_____
Lighting	_____	_____
Flowers, decorations	_____	_____
4. Advertising		
Store advertising	_____	_____
Publicity	_____	_____
Invitations	_____	_____
Programs	_____	_____
Tickets	_____	_____
Posters	_____	_____
Photographer, photos	_____	_____
Entertainment of press	_____	_____
5. Miscellaneous	_____	_____

efforts could be hindered for the day of the show. Pushing away racks of clothes and the crowding of garments can make customer shopping quite difficult. Paradoxically, a smaller group can result in more sales than an overflow audience because salespeople can concentrate on interested customers and complete more sales. Regardless of the size of the audience or store, a show creates excitement for customers, and sales usually increase for several days after the event.

Tearoom or restaurant space in larger stores can be useful at times when it is not normally occupied. The setting can be pleasant and not disrupt the regular selling departments. However, tearoom modeling during regular restaurant hours can be the weakest way to show fashion if the models are not fashion knowledgeable. Tearoom modeling can be disruptive and irritating to some diners; therefore, the model should know when to speak to patrons having lunch or tea and when to just smile and move to the next table. The model must know the name of the manufacturer of the garments. He or she should be familiar with the fabrication, the fiber content, and especially the price as well as with additional ways to use accessories. An evening show can be advantageous for a specialty store because it does not interrupt the day's sales, and the time is convenient for customers who are employed during the day.

Out-of-Store Shows

For out of store shows, a coordinated effort with an important organization in the area that acts as a fund raiser for charities will supply the optimum audience. Shows for large groups can be in hotel ballrooms, theaters, country clubs, school auditoriums, or other public areas. The size of the place determines the size of the audience the store can expect, and will also influence whether the show will be on a platform, runway, or stage. Building or renting runways can be expensive and time consuming but may be necessary in order for the viewers to see the fashions easily. The location should be chosen carefully.

It is important to attract customers into the store after the show, otherwise the excitement from the show may not be translated into sales. To accomplish this, many stores use a gift offer for the fashion aware customer; a typical gift could be from the cosmetic department.

The facilities for dressing models will frequently be poor in out-of-store locations. There can be inadequate lighting, very few mirrors, and dirty floors and ledges. Working space can be so minimal that easy movement is limited. All of this can be very damaging to the garments. An alert and caring fashion director will be aware of these flaws and make sure the models and assistants are advised to be careful. The distance between the dressing area and the stage will have an effect on the number of models needed because of the extra time required to walk to the stage and then return to the dressing area. Such walking time is costly because it results in the need for more models.

How to Decide to Give an Out-of-Store Show

Every store, large or small, will be asked by groups to give fashion shows. In a larger store, one person should have the responsibility of deciding whether to do the show; the owner usually decides in a smaller store. The executive who makes the decision in a major store could be the president, the general merchandise manager of ready-to-wear, or the vice president of promotion. The special events coordinator or the fashion director participates in such decisions.

Some stores will decide not to give out-of-store shows because of the expense and staff time required and the apparent advantages of in-store shows. Others may decide on one or two large shows per year and will choose the sponsoring groups and time of year very carefully to build the store's fashion image and prospective customer base. There are stores that will work with several groups to reach as many potential customers as possible. Such actions are often advantageous for a store that is new to the community or a store planning to change its fashion image.

Because stores receive show requests continually, a policy must be established to never decide immediately or yield to pressure. Mistakes in judgement can be made, and the store's image may be damaged. If a proposed show date does not give the fashion director enough time to organize properly, most stores do not hesitate to say no.

It is important to ask the group requesting the show what kind of audience will attend and how many can be guaranteed to be present. Further questions will determine if the audience will represent the store's typical customer. Because there is tremendous time and much expense involved, it is important to be very careful in audience selection. There are other ways to acquire new customers that could be less costly in time, energies, and money.

Timing of the Fashion Show

Timing is just as important to merchandising a show as location is to the store. It has been said that the three most important factors in retailing are *location! location! location!* Success in getting good attendance may be because of timing! timing! timing! The time of year, the day of the week, and the time of day should be planned thoughtfully for all fashion shows. Records should be kept of good and poor attendance results, and these should be discussed with others who have experience in fashion shows.

Choosing the Best Time of Year

Merchandise must be shown ahead of the consumer need and the timing must correspond with the receipt of goods in the store. The date of the show will be determined by arrival of new inventory and the needs of the group sponsoring the show. Timing around major events in the region that require fashion apparel can result in measurable sales. Sizable events where people dress up are occasions to consider for timing a fashion show. Such events can include the opening of the symphony and opera seasons, Mardi Gras, and the Kentucky Derby. The show should be scheduled far enough in advance to attract customers before they make their fashion purchases elsewhere. If these shows are timed too close to the event, it can be too late for the best sales results.

Fall is an excellent time for fashion shows involving women, because new, creative designs abound each fall and cooler weather permits the use of many fabrics including heavier wools. Customers are ready for newness and fresh colors at this time of year. August and September are good times to feature fall shows. Back-to-school shows appealing to high school and college students must be timed within a three-week period prior to the starting date of most classes. High school shows can be given three weeks ahead; a college show appealing to students moving onto a local campus could be given during orientation week. Also remember that many purchases will have been made before students arrive for the fall college term. Campuses with sororities and fraternities often hold rush periods before classes begin, thus bringing a percentage of freshmen onto campus earlier than usual. It is important to remember that opening dates for local school systems vary greatly and colleges vary opening dates as much as six weeks. Planners should consider sports event dates and the dates of home games for shows involving school age groups and their parents.

If careful planning is done, festive in-store holiday shows can be very successful in November. A show using teenagers from a model's makeup class was very successful at Proffitt's in Knoxville, Tennessee. Parents and friends came to watch the teens use their newly acquired skills while it was time to buy fashions for holiday parties. The attendance was excellent and appreciable interest was created, resulting in added sales for the store. The November date was good because it was not too close to Christmas and New Year's. Shows too near the holidays can be disruptive to the store's selling staff, already busy at this time due to heavy store traffic.

Merchandising for spring is based on Easter time, which varies from year to year. A spring show should be planned four to six weeks prior to Easter. Because customers nowadays buy fashions nearer the occasion, a four-week interval may be more suitable than the six-week interval of past years. If the date of Easter is later than usual, it is a good idea to have the show earlier than four weeks before the holiday because customers begin to buy when the weather becomes warmer. The National Retail Federation calendar gives a spread of four years of the changing dates of holidays that is important to use in planning. Table 3.4 on page 56 shows the changing dates of holidays for 1989 through 1993.

Summer shows are often held in late April or early May. A show in this season can be difficult, but it is of special interest because customers want to know how to keep cool and fresh looking in the summer. Transitional looks in darker colors and cooler fabrications should also be shown.

A difficult time for a good merchandise presentation is the first week in January. Much of the stock is limited to clearances, spring merchandise is in broken sizes because of holiday gift buying, and the percentage of new and fresh merchandise is low. The best type of presentation at this time would be a talk on fashions for midwinter vacations, using one or two models.

Choosing the Best Day

To determine the best day of the week for a fashion show, the show director should observe the people's habits in the locality. Tuesday can be good for a big-audience fashion show because of its situation between weekends. In some college towns, weekend shows would not be practical because students are not present. Saturday can be a poor choice, because mothers of children are not free, and working women may not want to attend an event on their day off. It is worthwhile to check the store's records for the size of previous audiences and obtain information from others in fashion retailing.

Choosing the Best Time of Day

To decide what time of day to give a fashion show, planners should ask the question, "For whom is the show being given?" For mothers who do not work outside the home, a morning or early afternoon show will allow shopping time before they leave the store to pick up schoolchildren. This type of show needs to end by 2:00 P.M. or earlier.

For women who work outside the home, a show immediately after work or later in the evening can be successful. The timing for designer or upscale fashion shows is not rigid; the customer is more accommodating because she may not work or is an executive with a flexible schedule. A designer show can be held in the late morning (for example, 11:00) or mid-afternoon if it ends by 4:00. A luncheon at 12:00 and a show at 1:00 makes efficient use of scheduling. The starting time and length of the show are important because most women are busy, and many have appointments or other plans for the afternoon. A very special evening show can begin at 8:00.

In summary, the time of year, month, day, and hour for a fashion show depend on community events, locality, and weather. The show director should consult the people involved when working with a group, and consult store personnel and customers. Timing, when well planned, can be most important in delivering the maximum audience and satisfactory sales.

The Fashion Director's Selection of Models

A fashion director should have modeling experience or training because the director will do much of the training of the models. She or he must be involved in the arts available in the community and should have the benefit of extensive cultural experiences. Attending every fashion show possible when in the garment market is a must. The director looks for newness and trends in such attributes as postures and stances. It is also helpful to study walking character, hand placement, posture attitudes, and hair styles. The New York International Films for Models produces a film of runway shows that can be purchased to help update the looks and postures of the store's models.

Where to Find Models

Schools and colleges can be sources of models. Friends, customers, and job applicants can also be considered. Models previously used by the store may suggest others. Dance schools for younger people often can provide candidates. Suitable employees could be held in reserve and used when other models are unavailable. Since these employees have other responsibilities in the store, fashion directors should not take advantage of their time.

Advertising for a specific type of model, such as large-size women, can bring hundreds of applicants. Ten of the applicants could be selected for a special training session in order for the store to have a professional-looking large-size show. They will need training in makeup and hair styling as well as in modeling techniques. These ten trained models can fill a significant need in the fashion department for several years.

How to Select Models

When the potential model arrives for the interview, the fashion director observes how she walks. This will indicate if the individual possesses the poise required for the runway. She must have self-confidence in order to show clothes to the best advantage. Does she have a pleasant, friendly expression? Is her complexion clear and attractive? If the feeling is positive, the director should look at how the person shows his or her clothes and at what can be done with the hair styling to update the model's look.

A model's hair must be relatively easy to manage and well cared for. If the female model's hair is long, how can it be brought up off of the neck? It is important to remember that the store is planning to sell clothes, not hair styling. A good test of the model's attitude could be the answer to "What are you going to do to bring the hair up?" Modeling is important to the retailer, and models must be willing to do whatever is asked of them so that they are most attractive in front of an audience.

The model must be able to wear clothes from store stocks and to wear more than one size. For example, a short size 2 model can present problems since she is limited to wearing only size 2 garments and is too short for pants unless there are some alterations. A taller, size 8 model should be able to wear 6s and 10s.

The fashion director should observe the neatness and cleanliness of the prospecting model. It is very important that clothes are always carefully protected so that damages will not result in expensive repairs. Models must be constantly aware of this and of any damages or soil from makeup left on the clothes. A professional model takes care of the store's clothes.

Types of Models

A store should develop a group of models who can perform professionally, a group who know what to do. They should promptly follow directions, know how to accessorize, know how to take care of the store's clothes, know how to appear on the runway, and be able to assist with less experienced models. Good models assist at fittings, provide their makeup, and style their hair appropriately. Some of them can become part-time assistants when extra help is needed to produce a show.

A department store fashion director will want to build a list of professional models to include the following types:

Several models sizes 4, 6, and 8 in the 23 to 45 age group. Most will be 25 to 35 years old. A 23-year-old must look mature enough to wear designer clothes. The size of the shows given will determine the number of models needed. If large shows are given, a list of 20 to 30 models will be needed.

Two size 10 and 12 women ages 25 to 45.

A size 14 or 16 woman who has a good clothes figure. Many in the audience will relate to her. A plus-size model who relates well to an audience can "steal" the show.

One grey- or white-haired woman, age 55 to 60, with a young appearance.

Several Junior models ages 15 to 19. Six to eight models will take care of most shows. An important show such as the *Seventeen* show will require a larger selection of models.

One petite model—5'4" inches or under.

One group of dancers to use in more elaborate shows. These can also be used as Junior models.

In addition to age and size, models must vary in "look" or personality. A store's pool of models needs to include, at a minimum, the following looks:

One ingenue or "girl-next-door" look.

Two high-fashion or couture looks.

One bright-eyed, energetic look with her own personal style.

No model will be available at all times, so the director should continually look for additional models. The type or theme of a show can also eliminate several models who do not have the right look or age.

Just like the department stores, a small store giving shows requiring five to six models will need a list consisting of ten to twelve models varying in size and age. Stores should use models who can wear two or more sizes and who are the store's customer type. If the show is for working women, it should not use teenage models who might never shop in the store.

The Master List

A list of the models available and employed in shows should be kept up to date. The following information should be registered:

Name

Address

Telephone numbers

Measurements and sizes

Hair and complexion shades

Age

Fashion look
Shows modeled in previously

Audience Identification

The audience should identify with the models appearing in the show in order for them to see themselves in the clothing. For example, stores select teen models for a junior audience, middle-age and older models for an audience of older women, petite models for petite show customers, large-size models for a large-size show, and sophisticated, chic models for a designer show. These portraits are essential for a successful production.

For in-store shows, the models should establish eye contact with individual customers in the audience. This gives the customer the perception that the show is just for her and that there is no one else in the audience. Eye contact is a good way to involve the men in the audience. This may be difficult to teach, but it is imperative for the success of a small show. A good show model will help to make the audience very responsive by using this technique. Models will develop their own personal style after a few years of runway experience. Individual style cannot be taught; the models must figure this out for themselves.

Using Amateur Models

Many requests will be received to give a show using the sponsoring group's members as models. The presence of family and friends of the models often guarantees that there will be a good audience, and the members will be excited about the event. The models will become familiar with the store personnel and will develop a feeling of goodwill toward the store, and thus influence others in a positive way about the store. Group members will often purchase the fashions modeled and develop a habit of shopping in the store. The fashion director can also discover other potential models for future shows. Using sponsoring group members as models has more advantages for the small show than a large one and, perhaps, for the specialty shop more than the department store.

The disadvantages of using amateur models are that they seldom have experience and poise in modeling, and they lack the self-confidence necessary to show the clothes in the most appealing manner. They are not disciplined to arrive on time or to take care of the clothes. Extra assistants will be needed to tie bows and scarves, place hats correctly, and take care of the other details of preparation for the runway. Amateur models' opinions about what to wear will often differ from those of the fashion director, thus creating a time challenge in selecting and fitting garments for the show. Being diplomatic and explaining the store's philosophy takes time. Volunteer models are also slower when changing garments during fittings and the show, and backstage activities become more like social occasions than work situations.

Selecting Merchandise for the Fashion Show

The smart fashion director confers often with the store's buyers and merchandise managers about the merchandise purchased for the store. She has worked with the buyers previously during market trips, gaining a feeling of the new trends that they believe will be saleable. When the director is working on show ideas, she can often receive good suggestions from sales personnel and department managers and can solicit ideas casually when she is surveying the merchandise available.

The merchandise should be checked at least three weeks before the show for missing looks and fashion items previously discussed with the buyers. The buyers should then inform the fashion director if the merchandise is on order and confirm the estimated delivery so necessary adjustments can be made if deliveries are unreliable.

The fashion director should make a list of the newest designs, fabrics, textures, and colors she wants to show. The kinds of merchandise shown will depend on the type of show and the audience. All appropriate departments of clothing should be represented in the show except areas such as coats and swimsuits when they are out of season. One of the scenes should be trendy merchandise, with classics and traditional looks included in other scenes in the show. Most of the merchandise shown will be the most exciting fashion pieces available that will appeal to the show audience. The price points of clothes and accessories should be comparable. For example, the customer will not accept a $100 belt on a $60 dress.

Garments should be selected that do not need alterations, because the alteration department will be busy enough with the minor problems and pressing the clothes. Because models must wear stock sizes, care should be taken to select the best possible garments for each model. Many shows use dancers, who wear clothing from the store while dancing. This treatment is another way that a fashion director can be creative in presenting the store's fashion leadership.

The fashion director who disturbs the floor as little as possible will receive lots of cooperation and enthusiasm for what she or he is doing. Buyers and department sales associates should attend as many shows as possible. When they attend a show, they will be more knowledgeable and helpful to the customers who shop in their departments. Many store personnel forget this simple yet logical idea.

Table 13.2 is a fashion show worksheet that is easy to use and gives the director information for completing the accessory selections and finalizing the lineup. This method provides guidance for writing the commentary and aids in compiling the security data required by most department stores when merchandise is away from the department or the store. This data is also given to each department involved so that the sales personnel know which garments and accessories are in the show. Sizes are also included in the salespersons' information for when customers inquire about merchandise that appeared in the show.

The worksheet eventually becomes the information sheet for the models to use during the show. When the models arrive, they check to see

Table 13.2. A fashion show worksheet reduced to one-fourth original size. Developed by Jan Penner while Fashion Director for Proffitt's Department Store.

FASHION SHOW WORKSHEET

Show   Date ___ / ___ / ___   Dress Size _____   Model _____
                                        Shoe Size _____

LINEUP NUMBER	COSTUME	MANUFACTURER	PRICE	HOSE	SHOES	OTHER ACCESSORIES, JEWELRY & PROPS

that all clothing and accessory items are present and that they understand any changes made since the fitting. Each model's position in the lineup is also verified. Using the same sequence of models makes it easier for them to know their places in the show lineup. The person responsible for cuing the models will also be aware of the lineup, and this prevents confusion during the show. For example, if there are ten models and Suzy is number one, she will also be number eleven, number twenty-one, and number thirty-one in the lineup, always following the model who is number ten. If there is a change from this pattern, the fashion director will make this evident to her during the preshow preparation.

Selecting the Set Design

Set design becomes part of the theme and should be related to the show, especially in the first and last scenes. The director should work with the display department for the best set design that is within the budget and the time limitations of the employees. Most shows use the same set design throughout the show. Complicated changes may be creative but may not be worth the time and expense involved.

For in-store and small shows, a simple folding screen is appropriate. Live plants and blooming flowers are colorful, enlivening, and chic. The flowers can reflect the colors of the season or repeat accent colors used in the store. There should be enough flowers to make a strong statement. This is especially attractive for smaller stores' shows. When there is a natural setting for a show, a constructed backdrop may not be necessary.

Selecting the Music

Ideas for music that support the show's theme will also come from involvement in the fashion market. Selecting music is difficult: it must be upbeat but not interfere with the concentration of the audience or distract attention from the models and the merchandise. The music should be somewhat familiar so that the customers will identify with the sounds and thereby feel part of the event. There are various popular sounds and rhythms that can be used. A mix of soothing and upbeat sounds is best; the models need a fairly strong beat in order to walk smoothly. For example, a denim show held in a mall used an album of country and western music played by a leading symphony orchestra. The music moved from song to song without disrupting the flow of the show, and the sounds of instruments and familiar tunes appealed to everyone.

Live music is not often used because it is too difficult to obtain the sounds needed. Special music can be taped from selections made by the fashion coordinator. This is very time consuming and costly and requires the fashion coordinator to be multitalented. She or he can pay an audio specialist to make the tape; however, the fashion coordinator is the director and still must select the music to be used. Tapes for some shows can be purchased, such as the tapes used for the *Seventeen* shows. Manufacturers such as Anne Klein II offer show tapes prepared for each fashion season.

Preparing the Commentary

For the fashion show commentary, the writer should begin with a list of points to include about the clothes so that nothing will be omitted or repeated too often. The introduction serves several purposes; the first is to welcome the audience and create a relaxed, friendly atmosphere. The introduction should include the theme of the show and generate a sense of expectation and excitement, and it must establish the store's authoritative position as a fashion leader in the community. All of this introductory material should be brief so that the curtain rises in approximately two minutes. When describing each costume, the commentary should relate it to the theme of the scene and skillfully point out fashion features of the clothes and, when important, the accessories. Using a written script instead of improvising will guarantee that the same features will not be repeated.

As each model appears, the commentator highlights the fashion points of the garment. He or she should not comment while the model walks the runway. No one will notice comments made at that time because the audience is interested in the model. The accessories can be described as the model returns. It helps to point out the most important fashion feature as the model finishes. It is not necessary to talk all the time that the models are walking. When showing prestige merchandise, keep comments to a minimum. Merely give the designer or label name of each garment. Allow the visual impact of the model to enhance the fashion statement.

Between scenes, it is a good idea to discuss new fashion thoughts or ideas the store would like to promote, such as the new wardrobe consultant service now available. Fill-in commentary is necessary if there are scenery changes or to give models time to change.

The fashion coordinator should take notes continually during fittings. Changes should be made at rehearsal to allow time to rewrite, polish, and rehearse the commentary. It is important for the commentator to feel confident and at ease. If an adjustment is necessary during the show (for example, a model accidentally appears out of order in the lineup), the commentator can adjust more easily if she or he is prepared for such mishaps.

The fashion coordinator should deliver the commentary because she created the show and will know the fashion story. An inexperienced coordinator should consider taking a public speaking course. Practice with a tape recorder can improve the commentator's performance. A good commentator speaks distinctly and slowly with a variety of vocal tones and does not rush. The voice should express enthusiasm about the merchandise. A little of the personality of the commentator should be evident in various phrases so that the comments sound impromptu.

If an outside commentator, such as a celebrity, is used, it is important to remember that he or she often will know very little about fashion. In this situation a script prepared by the fashion office is required. It is beneficial to brief this person and to give him or her a rehearsal. Even if the commentator is from the fashion world, it is best to plan a written commentary and to rehearse if possible.

The commentator needs to have a microphone for comments to be heard over music, even when there is only a small audience. Because sound is different when the room is full, the director should station people in various parts of the room to let the commentator know if everyone can hear the commentary over the music. The microphone and music need to be tested during rehearsal and again before the audience arrives. Even with prior testings the director can expect problems in large rooms and should choose someone to be in charge of adjusting the sound during the show.

The Fashion Show Rehearsal

It is very important to have a rehearsal for big fashion shows with fifty or more garments. Small shows using four to eight models usually do not require a rehearsal. These shows are more relaxed in feeling, and trained models can perform well with simple directions.

Most rehearsals take $2\frac{1}{2}$ to 3 hours for a 50-minute show. The entire cast should run through the show in the planned sequence with all clothes and accessories. The models are required to bring dress shields and all hosiery required as determined during fittings. They should arrive fully made up with their hair in the styles chosen for the show. All of this is important so that the fashion coordinator can make suggestions, revisions, and improvements prior to the show.

During the rehearsal, the models should concentrate on the proper way to walk for each scene, and they should become accustomed to the music tempo. The placement of the models onstage and their movement according to their positions in the lineup will be finalized. Each participant in the show needs to be as alert during the rehearsal as during the show. Models are paid a lesser fee for the rehearsal than for the main show.

Coordinating the Fashion Show with Other Events

The most important consideration in coordinating store events is the total number of events in the store and the size of staff. Holding too many events that require the assistance of many employees of the store will overload the staff and thus achieve poor results. The attitudes of those involved will be more enthusiastic if enough time and space are allowed to carry out each event properly. For example, if the Easter Bunny is employed to talk to small children, an in-store fashion show should not be given in that immediate floor area. It is best to consult with the special events coordinator before setting dates and always to inform him or her once a date has been confirmed. This action can avoid conflicts.

Buyers should be informed that they are welcome at all shows. Introducing them at small shows and in-store shows can be a pleasing gesture, and the customers can identify with another authoritative staff member.

Promoting the Fashion Show

The fashion coordinator must plan carefully to ensure that customers know about the show and to control the cost involved in the advertising and promotion of the show. The objective is to fill the seats of the facility selected for the show. The coordinator is responsible for turning in informative copy and advertising ideas to the advertising department and for generating creative enthusiasm for the presentation.

Advertising for the show can be through the use of newspapers, radio, television, posters, printed invitations, publicity, and interviews on radio and television. Newspaper, radio, and television ads should begin one to two weeks prior to the fashion show, depending on the community. This could begin with small invitation-like ads in the store's larger newspaper ads or with a tag-on to a radio or television commercial for the store. These efforts cost little and continually repeat the time, place, and location of ticket sales. Posters or show cards should be exhibited three weeks in advance of the show.

When invitations are used and an R.S.V.P. is required, the invitations should be sent two to three weeks in advance because food and seating arrangements must be confirmed at least one week before the show. Everyone involved feels better if they know well in advance of the show the number expected to attend. Invitations are most often used for luncheon, cocktail, tea, and designer shows. Some of these may not require an R.S.V.P.

Publicity often brings the greatest response from the public. The fashion coordinator should contact fashion editors of the local newspapers with a newsworthy item relevant to the show. This could be about the group benefiting from the ticket sales, or a new and provocative fashion idea, a dramatic show idea, or the fame of the guest commentator. This information should always be typed and should include a photo of the guest commentator. Many newspapers will send their photographer to take pictures for a publicity story. If so, the coordinator should suggest an interesting location for the photo. For example, if the show is a takeoff on the musical *Cats,* the photo could be in an appropriate alley with the fashion models and the alley cat dancers from the show. The coordinator should locate possible sites for the photographs. The easier it is for the newspaper staff to function, the more publicity the store can receive, not only for the show but for other events during the year.

The guest personality can often be interviewed for the newspaper, radio, or a local television talk show. If the show benefits a group, the sponsors should aid in obtaining publicity. In many cities this is one of the best ways to acquire much-needed publicity for the show. Advance publicity for the show will often lead to a follow-up photo and coverage. Using as many cost-free ways as possible to promote the show will increase the numbers in the audience.

Returning the Clothes after the Show

All clothes should be returned to the department as quickly as possible. This is imperative for selling an activity and creating good will with customers, store employees, and the buying staff. One effective idea is to place the clothes in shipping buggies or rolling racks on the selling floor. The clothes can be arranged, by scene, with accessories and props laid on top of the buggy. This alone creates further customer interest.

Clothes should always be returned in prime condition. Makeup stains must be removed and repairs made. Price tickets should be in the proper place on the garments. Returning the clothes, shoes, and accessories in good condition is the mark of good show management.

Evaluating the Show

The success of the show can be determined by many factors: the number of guests, the audience enthusiasm for the show, reaction per scene by the viewers, and the audience's response to specific garments. Sometimes a model will create a special rapport with the audience; frequently a song can be the spark of excitement. The amount of traffic in the store after the show and the volume of added sales are excellent measures of the success of the show. The simple fact that the store is creating an event can produce added sales the week of the show. For instance, Rickie's Petites, a small specialty store, had limited attendance at its spring show, but sales for the week were excellent. The following year sales dropped during the same week, possibly because no special event was held in the store.

The fashion show can be used specifically to create a position of fashion leadership. This type of image building requires special shows with imaginative theming and careful planning over many years. Therefore, success in this area cannot be measured immediately after a specific show.

The Small Store Fashion Show

The owner of the small store will often be the fashion coordinator for a fashion show. An owner who is also the buyer should be involved in selecting the theme of the show, the fashion trends to be presented, and the clothes to be shown. Many of the other responsibilities can be performed by a staff employee. A very capable employee may perform many of the duties described in this chapter. All employees can be involved in such tasks as assisting in the fittings, selecting accessories, borrowing shoes from a nearby shoe store, pressing clothes, and removing tags. Other functions include assisting models in dressing for the show and returning the clothes to stock. The owner will assign these tasks to various employees with appropriate capabilities and direct them so that the tasks are completed in the proper sequence.

For a small fashion store, the commentary usually should be written and given by the owner unless someone else is much more experienced in this function. Customers like to see the proprietor as much as possible in order to perceive more of management's involvement in the show. A guest commentator can be used, such as a local celebrity or a designer's representative. Manufacturers' representatives frequently give shows in stores, and they include smaller stores with good reputations when they offer strong dollar support of the manufacturer's line. The store setting should have a current and fresh appearance so that the representatives will be impressed and report favorably to the management of their company. This will aid the store in obtaining more of these shows in the future. Manufacturers often assume the cost of their representatives' expenses. This style of show generates enthusiasm among the employees and customers as well as providing a source for publicity.

If the store is located in a shopping area, often a neighboring store will aid in providing such assistance as makeup or shoes for the models or refreshments for the show. Such cooperation should be generously acknowledged during the show. It is a good practice to promote and support other stores in the immediate area so that customers will develop a habit of shopping for their needs in the locality.

Several stores of various sizes can participate in a large fashion show. The number of garments shown per store could be from six to twelve. This could be an excellent opportunity for a small store if the planned audience includes the store's type of customer. However, a small store should not become overly persuaded by the feeling of prestige from being in this type of show. It may be too costly in dollars and time if the store will not benefit sufficiently from sales and will not acquire an increased fashion leadership character in the community.

Summary

Timing and planning are the ingredients of a successful fashion show. The goals should be to entertain, to create goodwill, to build a positive fashion image, and to produce sales. The amount of money and time required for a show to be a quality presentation is sizable, so the potential results should be weighed carefully before deciding to stage a show. The producer of the show must be involved in the fashion business, the world of art, and the community in order to create exciting shows.

The following case studies demonstrate the details of two successful fashion shows. Note the information regarding the fashions to be shown. Also note the music and lighting cues for each scene in Case Study B. Such detailed planning resulted in a top-quality show.

Case Study A

Name of show—"Putting on the Ritz."

Inspiration of show—A popular song and movie revived in 1983.

Audience—Better customer, the elite and best-dressed living in a small community.

Club of 125 members of civic-minded women volunteers who want to make their county a better place to live.

Number in attendance—250.

Show place—Two large meeting rooms in a hotel using two commentators. Show produced and directed by Jan Penner, Fashion Director of Proffitt's Department Stores, Alcoa, Tennessee.

Scene 1	"Putting on the Ritz." Merchandise: Very dressy; sophisticated chic scene. For example: a silk charmuese blouse with wool trousers and hats.
Scene 2	"She Works Hard for Her Money." (From a popular song and the recent lifestyle trend of the working woman.) Merchandise: Suitings and dressings for work.
Scene 3	"At Ease." Merchandise: Casual, leisure wear, sophisticated fabrics.
Scene 4	"The Sophisticated Lady." Merchandise: Designer, higher-fashion clothes and accessories.
Scene 5	Finale "Putting on the Ritz." Merchandise: Furs, short furs shown with only fashion hosiery and leotards under the furs. A glamorous ending.

Case Study B

Name of show—"Cats," from successful Broadway show *Cats*.

Audience—Better customer. Sponsored by The Symphony League of Knoxville. Luncheon and show for 750.

Setting—Large ballroom of hotel. Show produced and directed by Jan Penner, Fashion Coordinator of Proffitt's Department Stores, Alcoa, Tennessee.

Preshow—Dancing Cats walk among tables to music of "Naming the Cats."

Two minutes.

Scene 1	"Ladies' Man." Merchandise: Pants, suits, shirtwaist dresses, cardigan sweater looks. Models called Fashion Cats (not alley cats)

Music: "Pink Panther." 7 minutes
Lights: Blue and amber alley.
Choreography: All six cats.
Scene 2   Weekend Wear.
Merchandise: Weekend wear, swimwear, colorful jeans, pants, jumpsuits.
Music: "Beat It." 7 minutes
Lights: Street scene in blue alley.
Choreography: Six cats.
Scene 3   Japanese and Geometries.
Merchandise: Japanese influence, geometries in black and white, color blocks.
Music: "Siamese Cat Song." 7 minutes
Lights: Street alley in black and white.
Choreography: Black and white Siamese cats.
Scene 4   The 50s.
Merchandise: Junior looks, misses designer, mixed 50s looks.
Music: Cat Sounds, "Rock Around the Clock," "Stroll Down the Avenue," "At the Hop." 5 minutes
Lights: Red and blue in trashy alley.
Choreography: All six cats.
Scene 5   Pink and Grey
Merchandise: All designer silhouettes with emphasis on pink and grey color trends
Music: "Stray Cat Strut." 7 minutes
Lights: Rose alley.
Choreography: Pink and grey cat, then four more cats.
Scene 6   Furs
Merchandise: Furs worn over designer clothing.
Music: "Jellicle Ball." 8 minutes
Lights: Amber street alley.
Choreography: All cats with top hats and canes.
Scene 7   Finale
Merchandise: All models in designer clothes and furs with cats
Music: "Memory," "Jellicle Song for Jellicle Cat." 2 minutes
Lights: Street.
Choreography: Balloons and confetti streamers tossed into audience.

CHAPTER 14

Personal Selling

Definition of Personal Selling

In Chapter 1 personal selling was defined as a dialogue between a salesperson and the potential customer for the purpose of selling merchandise and thus satisfying the customer's needs. Selling is the final step toward which all previous promotional efforts have been directed. Because the ultimate goal of promotion is to increase sales, the dollars spent for promotion are unfortunately wasted if the sale is not made. Sales promotion is designed to bring the customer into the store and to the point of sale, already predisposed to buying the goods. When the fashion customer arrives at the point of sale, the salesperson's role begins. The salesperson's task is to help the customer make a purchase decision. Sometimes this means clarifying customers' thoughts as well as determining their wants and wishes.

Personal selling is extremely important in merchandising fashion goods, as pointed out in Chapters 1 and 2. Fashion reflects the way of life at a particular time and changes as that way of life changes. With a general perception of current fashion trends, the customer seeks out merchandise that expresses his or her lifestyle. Because of continual change, customers redefine themselves in terms of each season's offerings. There is a social risk in being out of fashion and lacking a personal fashion style. A skilled salesperson can lead the customer through the maze of goods to ferret out the items that create the best fashion statement for that individual. The salesperson guides the customer through the sometimes difficult task of interpreting general fashion trends and choosing specific items appropriate for that individual customer. This can decrease shopping time as well as increase customer satisfaction. Personal selling is especially helpful for persons with little shopping time. For those who have a limited sense of style and want an updated look, personal selling is a necessity.

Customers may have less money than before to spend on fashion, and they certainly have less time to spend for shopping. These days more women who are fashion-minded are in the work force, and traditionally, most men have seldom been known to enjoy a lengthy shopping experience. Thus, any effort to decrease shopping time can increase customer satisfaction. Truly fashion-oriented stores do not depend on self-service, but rather depend on personal selling to tell the fashion story and complete the sale.

Interpersonal Communication

Advertising and other promotion techniques are one-way forms of mass communication, whereas personal selling is a two-way communication process that usually takes place when the communicators are face to face. This interaction provides information to both the salesperson and customer. It is this flow of information that enables the salesperson to help customers locate the goods that will satisfy their needs. When the customer has a question about the goods, the salesperson has an opportunity to provide useful information. If the customer has objections to the merchandise, the skillful salesperson can draw these out and overcome the objections or suggest other goods that do not provoke the same objections. Personal selling is the flow of information designed to locate for customers specific merchandise that will meet their needs.

Personal Selling Cost

Personal selling cost is not included in the promotional expense of the store but rather is part of the retailer's operation budget. In fashion departments, especially for higher-price merchandise, personal selling is the most effective activity for promoting the sale of goods. The newer the fashion and the higher the price, the more essential the contact character of personal selling becomes. Specialty stores and designer departments cannot survive without well-trained, fashion-wise sales personnel. Unskilled salespersons and a customer self-service approach are doomed to fail in a quality fashion store because the upscale customer demands individual attention in meeting his or her fashion needs.

Personal selling can be the most expensive promotional activity due to salary cost; however, good salespeople generate enough business to offset their higher compensation. Table 14.1 is a guide to use in evaluating sale effectiveness in terms of cost.[1]

[1] Retail Merchandising Service Automation, Inc., *Retail Reporter* 2, 8 (September 1986), 3.

Table 14.1.

Selling costs: Wages vs. Sales Production

Hourly Wage	Monthly Wage	Annual Wage	Annual Sales 40,000 / Monthly 3,333 / Daily 150 % to sales	50,000 / 4,167 / 200 % to sales	60,000 / 5,000 / 240 % to sales	70,000 / 5,833 / 280 % to sales	80,000 / 6,667 / 320 % to sales	90,000 / 7,500 / 360 % to sales	100,000 / 8,333 / 400 % to sales	110,000 / 9,167 / 400 % to sales	120,000 / 10,000 / 480 % to sales	130,000 / 10,833 / 520 % to sales	140,000 / 11,667 / 560 % to sales	150,000 / 12,500 / 600 % to sales	175,000 / 14,583 / 700 % to sales	200,000 / 16,667 / 800 % to sales	250,000 / 20,833 / 1,000 % to sales
$ 3.35	$ 558.33	$ 6,700.00	16.75%	13.40%	11.17%	9.57%	8.38%	7.44%	6.70%	6.09%	5.58%	5.15%	4.79%	4.47%	3.83%	3.35%	2.68%
3.50	583.33	7,000.00	17.50	14.00	11.67	10.00	8.75	7.78	7.00	6.36	5.83	5.38	5.00	4.67	4.00	3.50	2.80
3.75	625.00	7,500.00	18.75	15.00	12.50	10.71	9.38	8.33	7.50	6.82	6.25	5.77	5.36	5.00	4.29	3.75	3.00
4.00	666.67	8,000.00	20.00	16.00	13.33	11.43	10.00	8.89	8.00	7.27	6.67	6.15	5.71	5.33	4.57	4.00	3.20
4.25	708.33	8,500.00	21.25	17.00	14.17	12.14	10.63	9.44	8.50	7.73	7.08	6.54	6.07	5.67	4.86	4.25	3.40
4.50	750.00	9,000.00	22.50	18.00	15.00	12.86	11.25	10.00	9.00	8.18	7.50	6.92	6.43	6.00	5.14	4.50	3.60
4.75	791.67	9,500.00	23.75	19.00	15.83	13.57	11.88	10.56	9.50	8.64	7.92	7.31	6.79	6.33	5.43	4.75	3.80
5.00	833.33	10,000.00	25.00	20.00	16.67	14.29	12.50	11.11	10.00	9.09	8.33	7.69	7.14	6.67	5.71	5.00	4.00
5.25	875.00	10,500.00	26.25	21.00	17.50	15.00	13.13	11.67	10.50	9.55	8.75	8.08	7.50	7.00	6.00	5.25	4.20
5.50	916.67	11,000.00	27.50	22.00	18.33	15.71	13.75	12.22	11.00	10.00	9.17	8.46	7.86	7.33	6.29	5.50	4.40
5.75	958.33	11,500.00	28.75	23.00	19.17	16.43	14.38	12.78	11.50	10.45	9.58	8.85	8.21	7.67	6.57	5.75	4.60
6.00	1,000.00	12,000.00	30.00	24.00	20.00	17.14	15.00	13.33	12.00	10.91	10.00	9.23	8.57	8.00	6.86	6.00	4.80
6.25	1,041.67	12,500.00	31.25	25.00	20.83	17.86	15.63	13.89	12.50	11.35	10.42	9.62	8.93	8.33	7.14	6.25	5.00
6.50	1,083.33	13,000.00	32.50	26.00	21.67	18.57	16.25	14.44	13.00	11.82	10.83	10.00	9.29	8.67	7.43	6.50	5.20
6.75	1,125.00	13,500.00	33.75	27.00	22.50	19.29	16.88	15.00	13.50	12.27	11.25	10.38	9.64	9.00	7.71	6.75	5.40
7.00	1,166.67	14,000.00	35.00	28.00	23.33	20.00	17.50	15.56	14.00	12.73	11.67	10.77	10.00	9.33	8.00	7.00	5.60
7.25	1,208.33	14,500.00	36.25	29.00	24.17	20.71	18.13	16.11	14.50	13.18	12.08	11.15	10.36	9.67	8.29	7.25	5.80
7.50	1,250.00	15,000.00	37.50	30.00	25.00	21.43	18.75	16.67	15.00	13.64	12.50	11.54	10.71	10.00	8.57	7.50	6.00
7.75	1,291.67	15,500.00	38.75	31.00	25.83	22.14	19.38	17.22	15.50	14.09	12.92	11.92	11.07	10.33	8.86	7.75	6.20
8.00	1,333.33	16,000.00	40.00	32.00	26.67	22.86	20.00	17.78	16.00	14.55	13.33	12.31	11.43	10.67	9.14	8.00	6.40
9.00	1,500.00	18,000.00	45.00	36.00	30.00	25.71	22.50	20.00	18.00	16.36	15.00	13.85	12.86	12.00	10.29	9.00	7.20
9.50	1,583.33	19,000.00	47.50	38.00	31.67	27.14	23.75	21.11	19.00	17.27	15.83	14.62	13.57	12.67	10.86	9.50	7.60
10.00	1,666.67	20,000.00	50.00	40.00	33.33	28.57	25.00	22.22	20.00	18.18	16.67	15.38	14.29	13.33	11.43	10.00	8.00

Courtesy of the Retail Merchandising Service Automation, Inc.

Selling cost is defined as the salespeople's compensation expressed as a percentage of their sales. Each salesperson should have a selling cost of 7.5% to 10% to be of value to the store.[2] If the selling cost is below 7%, the salesperson deserves a salary raise. The percent expected would be based on several factors including the time the store has been in business, the time the employee has been with the store, whether the employee is full-time or part-time, and the price level of merchandise.

Motivating the Salesperson

The retailer should set attainable goals and objectives for salespeople and create ways to reward good performance. Oral praise, a note of commendation, recognition on a bulletin board or in the company newsletter, time off, a bonus, a compensation increase, or a promotion to new work assignments are some suggestions. Be consistent in discipline methods with all employees and direct action toward correcting the behavior, not the person. Reinforce any positive changes by identifying improvements with rewards.

The following RMSA article reminds retailers that selling is their only business.

> Selling is an art and a profession. Why do some sellers succeed and others fail? First, the fact must be recognized that not all persons can sell. Sellers have various personal traits but do have in common the following attributes: They are intelligent, self-satisfied, and quick in judgement. They like people and are never content to be alone. They are amateur psychologists, always trying to read reactions in the customer's voice, look and attitude. A true salesperson can sell almost anything, but only if he knows his merchandise....
>
> Every store knows the few who are salespeople and the many who are order takers. The successful salesperson loves his work and each new customer is a challenge. Seldom is he satisfied to write a single item salescheck. There-in lies the difference between selling and order taking. Most salespersons, excluding the order takers, can be categorized into three classes: 1—High pressure, 2—Determined, 3—Low pressure. The first type pounces on every opportunity—he writes large books but has little personal following. The second doggedly persists until he wears the customer down—his slow method seldom produces volume sales. The third type sells customers like himself by generating enthusiasm and instilling confidence. His prime concern is that customers like and trust him. This person is a slow starter, but in the long run he will sell ever-increasing amounts as he develops a personal following.

[2] Ibid.

Dollars spent on salespeople are a better investment than pennies spent on order takers. In most cases you will find that your selling costs are less than 9% of sales produced by your best sellers. The order takers' selling costs are usually in excess of 14% of sales. The success of any retail store is directly proportional to the ability of its selling force."[3]

Basic Steps in Personal Selling

Selling may come naturally to some people, but most individuals improve with sales training. In most department stores sales training begins in the training department with the mechanics of recording the sale, making out charge tickets, and doing other routine procedures. The training department may teach the basics of selling, but practice usually occurs on the selling floor of the department. Thus, sales training is a joint effort of the training department and the department manager. However, the buyer who has contact with the salesperson will need to reinforce the steps in personal selling that relate to up-to-the-minute fashion information on the merchandise offered in the department.

Approaching the Customer

The first step in personal selling is to greet the customer with a smile and call her by name if possible. The salesperson should greet the customer promptly as she approaches and should always stop any nonselling activity. If already helping one customer when a second one appears, the salesperson should simply greet the second customer, assuring her that someone will quickly be available to assist her. To a stranger a simple "Good morning" is an appropriate greeting. "May I help you?" usually draws a negative response and should be avoided. If the salesperson knows the customer, an appropriate greeting is "It's good to see you, Mrs. Jones."

Opening the Sale

Customers who know what they want may open the sale by asking for specific merchandise. If the item is in stock, the sale can move right along. If it is not in stock, a similar substitute should be offered. The salesperson should always present an alternative, showing the style or color available in stock. If the request is for a fuchsia blouse, and none is

[3] Retail Merchandising Service Automation, Inc., *Retail Reporter* 2, 8 (September 1986), 5.

in stock, show the fuchsia sweater that might serve the same purpose. If it is the color that is out of stock, ask what colors the blouse is to go with and propose another harmonious color that is in stock. Avoid giving the customer a flat "no." It may feel like a rejection, and the customer is left with the need still unsatisfied.

For the customers who are unspecific about why they are in the store, the salesperson can invite them to browse and tell them to be sure to see the advertised special of the day or the display of the silk scarves so important this season. From such a merchandise approach the salesperson may discover that the customer is or is not interested in that style. This serves to stimulate dialogue so customers reveal something about themselves—some information the salesperson can build on.

At this stage the salesperson wants to establish that he or she has the customer's interest at heart and wants to help the customer in doing whatever the customer wants to do. Salespersons should align themselves with the customer in a helping way and avoid falling into a confrontation over the merchandise or over the customer's attitude toward the merchandise. A confrontation puts the salesperson in the role of an adversary and makes a sale almost impossible. It helps to listen to what the customer is saying.

Discovering the Customer's Needs

The salesperson should observe the customer's reactions to the merchandise and listen closely for clues to what the customer is looking for and likes. For instance, if the customer says she thinks scarves are pretty but cannot manage to tie them attractively, that is the salesperson's cue to demonstrate some of the methods of tying scarves starting with a new but simple method. On the other hand, if the customer says "My neck is too short for scarves, besides I never did like them," the salesperson is better advised to suggest something else, such as a long silver necklace to accent the suit the customer is wearing.

After having the scarf display pointed out to her, the customer may volunteer that she isn't interested in scarves, but actually needs a blouse to go with a new gray tweed business suit. The customer is giving information that can guide the sales person in meeting her needs.

Selecting Merchandise for Presentation

By observing the customer's manner, speech, clothing, and personality, the salesperson can roughly estimate the price and quality the customer may be interested in. However, do not make the mistake of eliminating higher-price merchandise. A customer could be insulted if shown only garments that are priced below the prices she expects to pay and flattered when shown higher-price garments. The customer is pleased when someone thinks she can afford more expensive clothes. Looks are very deceptive, so a skilled salesperson does not overjudge customers — they will direct the salesperson who listens. It is best not to ask a lot of questions about what the customer wants in a blouse, because this will limit what can be shown. Estimate the size, although it is acceptable to ask what size usually fits. Select from stock blouses that vary in style, color, fabric, and detail, thus allowing the customer to make the choice. In this way, the merchandise prompts the customer to respond, thereby giving the salesperson information that can be used to find the merchandise that will satisfy the customer's needs. Pointing out features and benefits stimulates more interest.

If a question must be asked, state it in such a way that it is not easy to answer with a "no." For example, more information is given if the question is "Do you prefer beige or red?" rather than if it is "Do you like this beige?" To the first question the customer may reply she prefers red, whereas to the second question she might simply say "no."

To avoid confusing the customer, never show more than three items at a time. Limiting the number of items also allows the salesperson time to observe the customer's reactions. Remove an item the customer does not care for, noting the reason. If she did not like the yellow, offer a different color that would be good with the gray suit and her coloring. Customers often do not know what they want or do not express their wants in a straightforward manner.

Stimulating the Customer's Interest

The salesperson should give the customer reasons to buy each item, keeping in mind the customer's motives for buying. With fashion goods the motivation is most often the prestige of having the newest style in quality goods, but each item has its particular benefits. As the merchandise is presented, point out the benefits of each item. One could be the new, fitted style, another is washable, and one matches her blue eyes. Since one item cannot have all the benefits, it is best to avoid contrasting the benefits and thus confusing the customer. It is good selling practice to help customers decide which benefits are most important to them.

Overcoming Objections

Many objections can be overcome, but not all. For example, if the customer is allergic to wool, all wool items must be removed, because this condition cannot be changed by the salesperson. However, most objections are actually requests for more persuasive selling, rather than true rejection of the item. A customer who says she has never worn a longer jacket needs to be shown how the longer jacket looks on her with the correct skirt. Many petite women are still convinced they can only wear short jackets because they were told this for years. Petite-proportioned jackets now available allow them to wear all styles, whereas before, they were attempting to wear regular sizes which were incorrectly proportioned for them. Reassuring and educating the customer with truthful information should begin to convince the open-minded customer who wants to make a purchase.

When the customer likes the item but objects to the price, the salesperson should point out the fit as well as the styling and proceed to state other advantages. If the customer thinks the item is too expensive, then it is seemingly expensive to her regardless of the price. Agreeing that the item costs more than the others helps to establish the salesperson's credibility, whereas disagreeing only creates an unpleasant atmosphere. The key is "yes, but" followed by the reasons it costs more as well as the benefits it offers.

Trading Up

When a price is mentioned by the customer, the salesperson should show that price, but it is good business to show the next higher price also. This is called *trading up*. The customer may like the quality or styling of the more expensive item and be willing to purchase it. On the other hand, if the customer seems to hesitate about the price, a slightly less expensive item can be offered.

Be prepared to justify the higher price without downgrading the less expensive merchandise. For instance, the more expensive blouse is made of silk, whereas the less expensive one is made of polyester. Or the more expensive one has more top stitching or novelty buttons. If the less expensive item has been downgraded but is all the customer can afford, she will leave without making a purchase.

Helping the Customer to Make the Purchase Decision

Many customers are clear in their preferences and quickly determine which items they wish to purchase. Others are undecided and need guidance from the sales person. The first task is to discover the reason for the indecision. The salesperson can help the customer think through the requirements for the item by asking questions and making suggestions, for instance, "This solid blouse will go with several skirts, if versatility is important to you," or "This is the newest look in blouses, and it will add spice to your wardrobe."

When the customer knows her requirements for the item, but is not sure which blouse if any will satisfy her requirement, the salesperson should provide relevant information. For example, if the blouse is needed for travel, the salesperson should point out which blouses resist wrinkles, wash easily, and are not bulky. If the indecision is because of price, help her justify the expense in terms of what the item will do for her. Often the attractiveness and fashionability of the item carry more weight with the customer than does ease of care. Obviously this varies with the customer and the merchandise. In the last analysis, the customer must make the purchase decision based on her individual preferences and priorities. The salesperson is well advised always to act in the customer's best interest. By doing so, trust is established that will bring the customer back to the store and to that salesperson in the future.

Closing the Sale

Customers often close the sale themselves by saying, "I'll take this one." Other customers who are less direct may ask about alterations, care procedures, or gift boxing. To this type of unspoken decision, the salesperson, after answering the spoken question, can respond, "Did you want to pay cash or charge?" For the customer who is still undecided, it is appropriate to summarize again the advantages of the items being considered. If two items appeal to the customer in different ways, indicate she can buy both, suggesting occasions when each would be appropriate. Follow this with, "How would you like to pay for this?"

Suggestion Selling

Sales can be increased by suggesting other items once the original sale is secured. Also, the store's profit is greater on multiple-item sales than on single-item sales. If two blouses are sold in the transaction instead of one, there is still only one ticket processed and one bag for the goods; therefore, there is a greater profit. The following are some possibilities for suggestion selling.

1. More of the same item. This is especially good in accessories such as hosiery. Buying two or more can save the customer a trip back to the store.
2. Related merchandise. When the sale is a strapless dress, a logical suggestion is a strapless bra. Accessories for the item purchased are also appropriate; for example, a belt to go with a skirt or jewelry to accent a dress.
3. Featured merchandise. This could be unrelated to the purchased item. It may be advertised merchandise, predominately displayed

goods, a new shipment of the latest fashion look, or even sale merchandise. From observing the customer throughout the original sale, the salesperson should be able to determine which of these is likely to interest the customer.

Other Selling Points

Cosmetics super-saleswoman Mary Kay Ash, chairman of Mary Kay Cosmetics, has some additional selling points as follows:

Sales begin with your appearance. People form an impression of you in the first ten seconds. You can't be confident with a neglected appearance.

It's the sizzle that sells the steak. What the customer wants to know is: what will it do for me? In Rome, the salesman who sold all his togas told his customers it made them look like senators. Find the 'sizzle' in your product and back it up with showmanship.

Don't ask *if*, ask *which*. Say: 'Which would you prefer?'

Wear a dazzling smile.

Watch your voice. Avoid a mechanical or monotonous tone.

Know your product and believe in what you're trying to sell. Knowledge sells . . . .

Understand your buyer's needs and wants. All successful salespeople do. Charles Revson of Revlon used to say: "I don't sell cosmetics; I sell hope."

Respect your customer. An example: During a developing campaign for coffee, the coffee people insisted what the customer wanted was a rich, dark coffee. They were ignoring what the customer really wanted, a light coffee. "Selling is not just pushing a product." "You're selling a sense of trust about a product or service."

Humanity. Realize that on the other side of the desk is a human being. Be sympathetic; be an ally.[4]

The Importance of "Thank You"

After a successful sale, the customer should be thanked, if possible by name: "Thank you Mrs. Jones, you made a good choice. You will enjoy this swimsuit all summer." This reinforces the customer's purchase decision. Also, sending the customer a note of appreciation for making the purchase is a special touch used by many stores both large and small.

[4] "Selling," *Woman Entrepreneur* (March 1987), 5.

No Sale

It is not possible to turn every customer contact into a sale, but the salesperson can make every customer contact a pleasant experience. This adds to the positive image of the store as a quality operation. A "no sale" is not a failure when the salesperson and the store have made a good impression on the customer.

If the merchandise is just temporarily out of stock, offer to special order it and send it without charge. If the store does not carry the requested item, the customer can still be thanked for shopping in the store: "Thank you for coming in. Please visit us again. I will be glad to help you any time."

The Manager's Responsibility for Sales Training

To do an effective job, the salesperson must know all about the stock. Insuring that salespeople are knowledgeable about the merchandise is primarily the responsibility of the department manager. This is especially true of such details as the location of the stock and storage, colors, sizes, prices, and care. The sales personnel should be encouraged to check stock regularly and to read the hang tags and labels on new merchandise.

The Buyer's Responsibility for Sales Training

The buyer should also share in the responsibility for educating the sales force, especially on the fashion dimension of the merchandise. The buyer has had the greatest exposure to the new fashions and has benefited from information acquired during buying trips. The buyer will have seen the styles executed by several manufacturers in many versions and will have selected from all of the possibilities specific merchandise that he or she thinks will satisfy the store's target customer. The buyer is the store's expert on the fashion look as interpreted in the store's inventory. After all, the buyer was convinced enough to choose the merchandise. The sales personnel can benefit from learning from the buyer why this particular merchandise was selected.

The Fashion Story

In essence, the buyer needs to instruct the sales personnel in the new fashion trends as they relate to incoming merchandise. Buyers can begin by teaching salespeople what fashion trends are in the market and why certain styles have been purchased for the store. The salespeople need to learn the fashion facts of each important trend. Each season there are new trends, such as a change in skirt lengths, cropped pants, and longer shorts. There are continuing trends from last year or from last season. Turtlenecks may continue to increase in importance over last year. Pants may continue to have added fullness through pleats. Strapless sundresses may be a small new trend for summer and may have been purchased in a small amount for testing the consumer. Color trends are very important for impressing the sales personnel so they will be ready to accept them when the merchandise arrives from the makers.

What Is the Look?

Specific looks are important each season. These will be selected by the buyers in varying degrees depending on the department or store. The prairie look is a good example of a recurring trend that can deliver a large percent of the fashion sales in some departments and cannot in others, such as the designer fashion department.

The buyer needs to describe the look and show illustrations of it. The following is a sample description. "The prairie look is composed of a bodice that conforms to the shape of the upper body and a gathered skirt that is at least knee length and extends considerably wider than the legs. The width and movement of the skirt give a sense of activity yet femininity much like the gaiety of a square dance dress. There is a sense of freedom in the natural lines of the bodice and the easy flow of the skirt. The look gives a feeling of wholesome femininity that is clean and uncomplicated, perhaps evoking nostalgia for a simpler time. The prairie look offers relief from the pursuit of high tech and glitz."

What Is Its Name?

The labels for all features of the new look should be given to sales personnel. A name is a handle by which one can deal with the look in its entirety. With a name, one can begin to organize thoughts about the new look, to understand it, and eventually to act on it. When the name is known, the new no longer seems as strange and different as it did at first viewing. When salespeople or customers learn the name of the new look, they have taken the first step to becoming familiar with it. For example, one interpretation of the oversized look was the shoulder tuck known as the flange shoulder. Another interpretation was the dolman sleeve. The customers feel more in control and, therefore, more assured when they know the proper identifying term for describing the new and different fashion they are seeing. The new look should be stimulating, but not threatening to customers.

Coordinating the Elements

Sales personnel must learn what goes into making the total look. How is it placed on the body? What accessories are included? For example, when the sweater lengths are long, the customer must be shown the proper length of skirt to wear with the sweater. An easy way to convince some customers of the comfort and ease of the new, longer sweater is to show it with pants. Placement of jewelry, especially long beads, can be used to show how longer lengths elongate and slenderize the body.

Fabrications

In the introduction of a new look, a limited number of fabrics are used. Ones that show the look to its greatest advantage or best convey the mood are chosen. Later, the look may be executed in a variety of fabrics. For example, the fabrications for the prairie look often include chambray, denim, and calico. If these terms are unfamiliar, they need to be defined with samples for the salespeople to see and feel.

If new fibers, fabrics, or finishes are involved in the new look, they also require explanation. For instance, the wrinkled look was a treatment of the fabric to give a prewrinkled appearance to carry out a casual feeling. Prewrinkled fabrics added to the understatement of the look. The prewrinkled fabric was not to be ironed, but simply washed and machine dried to retain the desired look. Explaining what fabric characteristics contribute to the look gives the salesperson added knowledge and confidence.

Special Care Requirements

When the merchandise requires special care by the wearer, sales personnel need to be able to give information and directions. In the case of heavy cotton sweaters that need to be hand washed and dried flat, sales personnel must understand the process and equipment well enough to make the task seem reasonably simple. Knowing the proper care can contribute to finalizing the sale. Also, it encourages customers to take proper care of the goods, which impresses them and in turn increases satisfaction and may reduce returns of damaged goods to the store.

Interpreting the Look for Special Groups

Not all customers are average; they come in all shapes and sizes. The buyer should inform the sales force of ways to make the look attractive on various customers—young and old, as well as those with typical figure types. For instance, the oversized look is a challenge for the petite customer unless she can find it in petite proportioned clothing. A small frame can quickly be overpowered with large details, multiple colors, and bulky fabrics.

If the salespeople are thoroughly trained to interpret the look for various types of customers, they will be less likely to interpret the look inappropriately. A well-trained sales force can make the new look more fun to try and more appealing to the fashion-aware customer. That customer will be more willing to try new looks if she has a pleasant experience. In the process she will have learned that her salesperson can be trusted in the future to help select a new fashion look. Few people will tolerate looking foolish or unattractive just to be the first with the new look.

Each new look or trend has its own unknown dimensions that should be explored with sales personnel. The new dimension may be a new color combination such as purple with red, or it may be the strange feeling of hip huggers after wearing tight belts at the natural waistlines for several years. By pointing out these new dimensions, salespeople can meet customers' objections before they arise, making the sales process more pleasant.

Support Advertising at Point of Sale

Buyers and managers who want productivity and results with relatively little cost must put some effort into the point of sale. Follow-through at the point of sale turns traffic into shoppers and shoppers into makers of purchase decisions. For every dollar a customer spends in a store, another dollar would be spent if the salesperson motivated the customer, communicated to the customer, moved the customer around the store, and solved some special problem for the customer. Studies indicate that almost seven out of ten buying decisions are made in the store on an impulse basis. Follow-through at the point of sale can increase sales with little additional cost.

Inform sales personnel of advertised items. Reprint the advertisement and display it wherever possible in the store. Displaying the merchandise with a copy of the ad is an easy selling aid for sales personnel. Displays, bag stuffers, mailing, sales incentives, phone calls to customers, and staff meetings are a few ideas that can increase sales.

Developing the Customer Book

Each salesperson should have a "customer book" with names, addresses, and telephone numbers. This list includes regular customers, and new, potential customers. Notes about each customer may include sizes, preferred looks, fitting problems, specific needs, past purchases, and dates contacted by phone or by note. This information aids the salesperson in helping the customer build her wardrobe.

Customer books are the lifeline of better designer departments and specialty stores. The list ultimately belongs to the store so several salespeople can have the same customer in their books. However, a specific customer usually relates to one salesperson. This relationship may develop because of a similar taste in fashion, similar ages, the salesperson's confidence in selling, or special attention given to the customer. Continual contact with the customer is a definite plus in this building process. The salesperson should add names and requests to her book daily. She also consults her book daily for customers to contact on new merchandise arrivals. Many customers are very busy and appreciate salespeople who remember them and their needs. Samples of customer book entries are given in Figure 14.1.

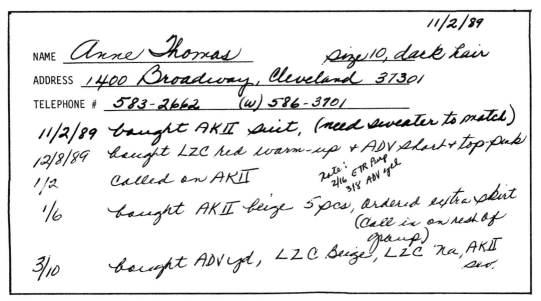

Figure 14.1. Sample of entries in a customer book.

Building a Customer Mailing List

A specialty store or specialty department should build a mailing list. Names and addresses from the customer books can form the bulk of a customer mailing list. When new customers make purchases, the salesperson can ask if they would like to be placed on the mailing list, explaining that they will receive notification of special events and sales before the general public does. Such a list is a much-valued asset as an advertising medium.

Summary

Unless there is a desperate need for an item, the desire for it can be quickly dispelled by an inept or discourteous salesperson. Management of stores must train unskilled employees in the art of persuasion. Selling begins with the greeting, continues through the presentation and closing, and includes information regarding the item's use and qualities, and reasons why the customer will benefit from purchasing any item sold in the store. To sell successfully, the seller must know the merchandise. Above all, salespeople must generate enthusiasm. Without enthusiasm, they become order takers. The most valued and most highly paid salespeople are highly skilled individuals who are never satisfied to sell only what the customer asks for. Selling can be a dignified position—not just a job.

CHAPTER 15

Synergism in Promotion

Webster's dictionary defines synergism as "The simultaneous action of separate agencies which, together, have greater total effect than the sum of their individual effects...." This is what happens when various aspects of promotion and advertising are combined in one campaign. The customer is approached in more than one media with the specific combination being selected to balance the strengths and weaknesses of the various media or promotional activities.

A promotional campaign carried out by Bloomingdale's is described in *Lorrie Eyerly's Retail Trends*. This storewide promotion used Broadway as a singular theme to create excitement and to add sales for all departments. A charity benefit, windows, interior displays, shops, ads, and special shopping bags were all included in this promotion. The following description is adapted from Lorrie Eyerly's newsletter.

One Singular Sensation: Bloomingdale's Does Broadway[1]

From the "Baubles, Bangles and Beads" (Kismet) shop in the Arcade to the Showtime Cafe on Seven, this giant event exemplified management's dedication to the concept of retailing as theater, packing in customer audiences for an eight-week run.

Opening Night—Sunday, April 8

The opening night gala, co-sponsored by American Express, was given as a fund-raiser for "Broadway Cares," the AIDS support and research

---

[1] All material in Chapter 15 adapted from *Lorrie Eyerly's Retail Trends*. (Courtesy of Lorrie Eyerly, 165 Perry Street, New York, NY 10014.

organization of the New York theatrical community. Attending the $100-a-ticket party were performers, directors, designers, and their associates along with big names in retailing, design and manufacturing. During the evening, stars of *Black and Blue, Forbidden Broadway, Grand Hotel,* and *City of Angels* entertained with songs and dances from their hit Broadway shows. "Star Cuisine" food, served on six different floors, was an exotic medley of recipes submitted by casts and crews. Proceeds of a silent auction of theatrical memorabilia, such as a signed Robert Morse Panama hat from *Tru* and Tyne Daly's autographed sweatshirt from *Gypsy,* also went to the "Broadway Cares" fund.

Interior Displays and Shops

Several props and identifying artwork were used extensively such as the following:

Al Hirschfeld personality caricatures on programs, store directories, large paper scroll displays, shopping bags, and give-away posters. These were also used for opening announcement ads in newspapers and magazines (See Figures 15.1 and 15.2.)

Playbill covers and yellow banners on store signs and programs.

Oversized replicas of the Tony award.

Life-size black silhouette of *Chorus Line* figures complete with top hats and canes in Main Floor accessories department.

Crisp black-and-white striped fabric back walls and dividers for all BROADWAY NINETY merchandise displays throughout the store.

Main Floor Ledges

The following appeared on Main Floor ledges:

Actual costumes on loan from current Broadway shows *Les Miserables, Cats, The Heidi Chronicles,* and *Black and Blue.* In the menswear area were costumes from *City of Angels, A Few Good Men, The Circle,* and *Meet Me In St. Louis.*

Gypsy robes, which are dressing gowns decorated with mementos and souvenirs from past musicals. These are sent on opening night of a new show to members of the chorus line as a good luck gesture.

Easter Parade Bonnets, which are hats created by Broadway show personnel for the Annual Easter Bonnet Competition and later sold to benefit charity.

Figure 15.1.   Cover for the program and menu at the opening night gala, "Sunday Night with the Stars." (Courtesy of Bloomingdale's, New York.)

Figure 15.2.   The Al Hirschfeld BROADWAY NINETY shopping bag. (Courtesy of Bloomingdale's, New York.)

Quilt of the American Theatre, which is a quilt of hand-crafted squares from current and past shows made by theater hands representing regional as well as New York theater.

Second Floor

"OPENING NIGHT AT SARDI'S"—JUNIOR SHOP   Sardi's, a landmark restaurant, is where the cast and principles of a Broadway show traditionally gather after the performance to wait out opening night reviews. Like the restaurant, the shop's walls were circled with framed original Hirschfeld caricatures (all on loan from Sardi's) and with mannequins holding copies of *Variety*. All of the merchandise, hot, young body-conscious dance dresses, were in black and/or white. See Figure 15.3*a* for the newspaper ad of these dresses.

Third Floor

SWEET CHARITY SHOP—SIGNATURE DRESSES   A major fashion statement in this promotion, the shop celebrates Broadway's taxi dancers with short, sexy late-day dresses. A large corner window at 60th Street echoed the shop's decor—a pink neon heart pierced by an arrow (a signature of the show) with mannequins waiting for partners behind a neon-lighted enclosure (Figure 15.3*b*).

CABARET SHOP—CONTEMPORARY SPORTSWEAR   The pattern of a featured harlequin group in black, white, shocking pink, and lime green was repeated on the shop's back walls. At the center, mannequins stood on black lacquered stairs under a marquee-lighted canopy. Lined up in front of them, silver chairs held black top hats. Color-keyed merchandise, the great majority in black and white, consisted mainly of Lycra pieces.

LITTLE ME—PETITE SPORTSWEAR   This department starred Anne Klein II and Adrienne Vittadini merchandise.

HOW TO SUCCEED IN BUSINESS—BETTER SPORTSWEAR   Soft-suited separates from Christian Dior, Diane Gilman, Evan Picone, J.H. Collectibles, and Jones N.Y. were emphasized in this department.

Fourth Floor

"THE GREAT WHITE WAY"—DESIGNER COLLECTIONS   Designer merchandise was featured in the windows, and the center aisle was backed by Tony award props.

PAJAMA GAME—SLEEPWEAR AND LOUNGEWEAR   The black-and-white theme continued with an embroidered dotted group shown in a center display. The mannequins were seated on mounds of striped and dotted pillows with mixed pattern prints suspended from an overhead clothesline. Also in black and white, lining a divider wall, was another group in a miniature fruit print with delicate black lace trim.

Fifth Floor

HOME FURNISHINGS   Home Furnishings was given the star treatment with elaborate Broadway show displays in each department. Gifts were

Figure 15.3. (*a*) Junior shop ad and for "Opening Night at Sardi's." (Courtesy of Bloomingdale's, New York.) (*b*) Signature dress department's ad for "Sweet Charity Shop." (Courtesy of Bloomingdale's. Photographer: Ruven Afanador.)

keyed to *Meet Me In St. Louis* (Victorian) in the Bath Shop, a tropical *South Pacific* and *Black and Blue* for Lamps and Rugs and*Oklahoma* (Country) in Housewares. An outstanding new astronomy pattern was highlighted in Domestics as "The Age of Aquarius" (*Hair*). These same themes appeared in the entire bank of windows on the Third Avenue side of the store.

"THE BROADWAY GRAND"—MODEL ROOMS   Set up like a series of seven celebrity guest rooms off an elegant hotel lobby, each room was designed by a well-known decorator to reflect the personality of its occupant. A sophisticated Art Deco suite for Noel Coward, 18th century French garden room for Chita Rivera, and a safari room for Christopher Plummer were three of the seven suites. All of the suites featured new furniture groups from top resources along with Bloomingdale's own imports. See Figure 15.4 for the parallel advertisement run for this department.

In addition to "The Great White Way" windows seen in Figure 15.5, Bloomingdale's had small windows that carried out the theme (Figures 15.6 and 15.7). In two smaller windows clothes are propped by oversized replicas of the Tony Award. Window merchandise, specifically created for the promotion by seven top American designers, was featured in Sunday's *New York Times* ad (see Figure 15.8).

The Bloomingdale's Does Broadway Campaign was an impressive promotional effort that will keep Bloomingdale's in the minds of customers for a long time.

Figure 15.4. A furniture advertisement in the newspaper to parallel the model rooms in the store. (Courtesy of Bloomingdale's, New York.)

Figure 15.5. On Lexington Avenue, "The Great White Way" is spelled out in eight-foot lighted letters. Fringed Roman shades and swag-back draperies edge the windows. (Courtesy of Bloomingdale's, New York.)

Figure 15.6. Mini entranceway window on Third Avenue for the "Showtime Cafe." (Courtesy of Bloomingdale's, New York.)

Figure 15.7. One of the nine Third Avenue Home Furnishing windows. This one in art Deco style of *Grand Hotel*. (Courtesy of Bloomingdale's, New York.)

THE GREAT WHITE WAY

1 DONNA KARAN 2 C.D. GREENE 3 ISAAC MIZRAHI 4 BILL BLASS 5 MARC JACOBS FOR PERRY ELLIS 6 GORDON HENDERSON 7 NORMA KAMALI 8 CAROLINA HERRERA 9 BOB MACKIE 10 CHRISTIAN FRANCIS ROTH 11 CALVIN KLEIN

CURTAIN UP ON A SPECTACULAR COLLECTION OF SHOW-STOPPING WHITE DRESSES (DESIGNED JUST FOR US BY ELEVEN LEADING AMERICAN DESIGNERS). PERFECT FOR THE TONYS* OR ANY OTHER EQUALLY GLAMOROUS AFFAIR. IT'S A STELLAR DAY FOR THE GREAT WHITE WAY, LINING BOULEVARD FOUR, NEW YORK.

BROADWAY
N I N E T Y

bloomingdale's

Figure 15.8. Under the heading, "The Great White Way," eleven dresses by leading American designers are advertised. (Courtesy of Bloomingdale's, New York. Photographer: Ruven Afanador.)

345

Index

press kits, 285–86, 287
purpose of, 279
Public relations, 277

Quad-racks, 132–34

Rabolt, Nancy, 27, 28n
Radiation, 85, 87
Radio advertising
  advantages of, 244–48
  best uses of, 248
  creative styles, 263–64
  disadvantages of, 248
  good copy, qualities of, 262–64
  importance of voice and sound,
    266–69
  jingles, 268–69
  listener demographics, 250
  music and sound effects, 267–68
  pauses, 269
  purpose of, 261
  rate card, 246–47
  sample script, 265
  selection of stations, 249, 250
  the spoken word, 261–64
  timing of, 12
  types of ad copy, variations in,
    264–66
  verbal presentation, variations in,
    264
Rational appeal, 221, 223, 263
Rearrangement (of merchandise), 144
Reference groups, 27–29
Related color schemes, 71–72
Relative advantage, 34
Repetition, 20, 82, 85
Retail Reporting Bureau, 97
Rhythm, 84–87
Rizik's, 220
Robertson, Thomas S., 30n
Robinson's, Color Plate 9
Rogers, Everett M., 30n, 31, 36n
Ross, Robert D., 289
Round racks, 135–36
Rubin, Leonard, 269

Saks Fifth Avenue, 77, 100, 105,
  141, 220, 237, Color Plate 2
Sales
  and fashion promotion, 3–5
  by region and month as a
    percentage of total annual
    sales, 54

Sales letters, 193, 194
Sales promotion
  as a controllable expense, 41
  defined, 1
  functions, 1–2, 12–13
  as an integral part of marketing, 14
Sears, 10
Seasons, 94–95
Secondary shoppers, 138
Secret sale promotion, 158, 159
Self-actualization, 17
Self-image
  components of, 17–18, 20
  and store image, 8–9
Shades, 71
Shadow box, 103
Shaffer, Harold, 212, 218n, 224
Shelves, 124–25, 140
Shim, SoYeon, 23
Shop concept, 141–43, 338–42
Shopper groups, 6–8
Shopping bags, 201, 203
Sidewalls, 123–24
Signage, 12, 110–13, 145, 201, 202
Six-way racks, 134
Space, 78–80
Special events
  budgeting for, 50, 51, 289
  director, 291
  defined, 1, 286
  measuring success of, 291
  objectives of, 286, 288–89
  planning, 290–91, 292
  role of special events director,
    291, 293
  sample planning calendar, 292
Special purchases, 144–45
Special sales, 96
Specialty stores
  budgeting for, 55, 60–63
  vs. department store planning,
    60–62
  evaluating sales promotion
    success, 63
  guidelines for, 62–63
  magazine advertising and, 186–87
  percentage of advertising expense
    by medium, 151
Split-complementary color scheme,
  72, 73
Stanford Research Institute (SRI), 24
Statement enclosures, 188, 195, 197
Store image, 8–9, 13, 288